The Native American Contest Powwow

The Native American Contest Powwow

Cultural Tethering Theory

Steven Aicinena and Sebahattin Ziyanak

LEXINGTON BOOKS
Lanham • Boulder • New York • London

Chapter 2 Parts of this chapter were previously published in *International Journal of Humanities and Social Sciences* (J-HumanSciences.com) and used with permission. Aicinena, S., & Ziyanak, S. (2019). Examining the Gathering of Nations powwow and a NCAA Division I basketball game. *Journal of Human Sciences*, 16(3), 875-884. https://doi.org/10.14687/jhs.v16i3.5742

Chapter 3 Parts of this chapter were previously published in *The Qualitative Report* and used with permission. Aicinena, J. S., & Ziyanak, S. (2021). Contest powwow: Sport and Native American culture. *The Qualitative Report*, 26(1), 27-51. https://doi.org/10.4 6743/2160-3715/2021.4517

Published by Lexington Books
An imprint of The Rowman & Littlefield Publishing Group, Inc.
4501 Forbes Boulevard, Suite 200, Lanham, Maryland 20706
www.rowman.com

6 Tinworth Street, London SE11 5AL, United Kingdom

British Library Cataloguing in Publication Information Available

Library of Congress Cataloging-in-Publication Data

Names: Aicinena, Steven, author. | Ziyanak, Sebahattin, author.
Title: The Native American contest powwow : cultural tethering theory /
    Steven Aicinena and Sebahattin Ziyanak.
Description: Lanham : Lexington, [2021] | Includes bibliographical references and index.
    | Summary: "This book examines the contest powwow to better understand what it
    means to participants and how it carries on the beauty of Native American culture.
    The authors assess how competitive dancing aligns with and differs from traditional
    sports while introducing their concept of Cultural Tethering Theory to understand its
    importance" —Provided by publisher.
Identifiers: LCCN 2021046922 (print) | LCCN 2021046923 (ebook) |
    ISBN 9781666900910 (cloth) | ISBN 9781666900934 (paperback) |
    ISBN 9781666900927 (epub)
Subjects: LCSH: Powwows. | Indian dance. | Indians of North America—
    Cultural assimilation—United States.
Classification: LCC E98.P86 A35 2021 (print) | LCC E98.P86 (ebook) |
    DDC 970.004/97—dc23
LC record available at https://lccn.loc.gov/2021046922
LC ebook record available at https://lccn.loc.gov/2021046923

Contents

List of Figures and Tables

FIGURES

TABLE

Introduction

The research firm GQR was hired by the Reclaiming Native Truth Project's administrators to determine what non-Indigenous Americans knew about Native Americans and what opinions they held toward them (Reclaiming Native Truth, 2018). GQR reported that most non-Indigenous Americans believe few Native Americans remain in the country; have never met a Native American; believe Native Americans keep to themselves and do not care to interact with those outside their cultural group; are unaware that there are hundreds of distinct sovereign Native American tribal groups with unique languages, traditions, and laws; view Native Americans as committed to preserving their culture; believe Native Americans are committed to family and family values; and that Native Americans are patriotic peoples who serve in the military.

GQR also reported that most non-Indigenous Americans believe Native Americans should assimilate into the dominant culture as have so many others who immigrated to the United States (Reclaiming Native Truth, 2018). The belief fails to recognize that Native Americans did not come to America for a better life, that they were the victims of genocide, that their ancestral lands were pilfered from them, or that concerted governmental efforts were made to rob them of their culture. Most Americans know little about their country's first peoples or their history.

In traditional Native American communities, proximity of extended family and other members of the tribal group was instrumental in the transmission of language, religion, tribal and family history, traditional educational methods, ceremonial activities, and other markers of culture. However, Native American family dynamics have changed significantly in the past 150 years. Native American youths have left reservations in droves for cities, enticed by promises of economic prosperity and a better life. As of the 2010 census, 78

1

percent of all Native Americans lived away from reservations (United States Census Bureau, 2012).

For many urban Native Americans, life in cities has led to low participation in traditional tribal culture (Straus & Valentino, 1998). Interracial marriages have resulted in lowered participation in tribal-specific culture, and an affiliated loss of cultural knowledge as generations have passed (Mihesuah, 1996). Traditional, tribal-specific Native American cultural institutions, including language, religion, family, and education, are on life support and waning with the passing of tribal elders.

Much has been written by historians, anthropologists, ethnographers, and sociologists concerning traditional forms of the powwow because of its historical primacy in the lives of Native Americans. The contest powwow, in contrast, was not well-developed or popularized as a Native American institution until the 1950s. Though researchers have described some of the differences between the two forms of the powwow, little qualitative research has focused upon how the contest powwow as an institution functions to preserve Native American traditions and values. Our ongoing research and this book are meant to partially fill this void in the academic literature. We hope this book will inform and motivate others to take a closer look at the contest powwow to better understand what it means to participants and how it, as a Pan-Indian institution, serves to carry on the beauty of Native American culture.

We sought to explore the contest powwow as thoroughly as possible in our literature reviews and the references are quite eclectic. They include works from the disciplines of sociology, anthropology, law, history, music, education, counseling, kinesiology, religion, dance, psychology, and others. This book contains over 400 references that may be explored more fully by anyone interested in further study of the contest powwow or Native American culture.

The terms used to identify Native Americans in our work include "Native American," "Indian," and "Native." In our experience, some individuals have taken offense to the use of one of the terms or another. However, each of the terms is commonly used within the literature, on contemporary Native American-published powwow websites, in newspapers, and on social media sites moderated by Native Americans. The following serve as salient examples: *Native American Times: News from the Crossroads of Indian Country, Indianz.com, Native News Online, Indian Country News, Indian Country Today,* and *Native American Report*. With apologies to anyone who might be offended, we interchangeably use the terms "Native American," "Native," and "Indian" throughout this book.

In a similar vein, we interchangeably use the terms "Pan-Indian" and "intertribal." Each term represents the values, traditions, and ceremonial activities collectively shared by various tribal groups residing in North America. Some take issue with the term Pan-Indian because the word "Indian" is used and it is considered as a derogatory term. But, as noted earlier, the term is used commonly by Native Americans, within the published academic literature, and in Native American publications.

Clarification is required concerning the use of the term "tribe." "Tribe" may represent social organization; a group or band; or residents of an area sharing common culture, ancestry, and language (Waldman, 2006). The Navajo, Comanche, and Cherokee are examples of independent tribes. Each tribe has its own history, language, values, and traditions.

In contemporary North America, many tribal groups prefer to be referred to as "Nations." The designation of nation reflects the tribe's sovereignty and independence from the American and Canadian government. For example, the Navajo tribal government prefers the Navajo Tribe be referred to as the Navajo Nation. "Tribe" is the term most authors and Native Americans we have interacted with use, and it is the term we use throughout our work.

It seemed to first author—Steven Aicinena—during the first Gathering of Nations he attended that there were many similarities between it and indoor sporting spectacles. Logically, we wondered if contest powwows such as Gathering of Nations shared promotional and staging characteristics with indoor sporting spectacles. Do contest powwow dancers believe they are competing in an athletic event? How does contest powwow dancing related to traditional Native American values? What motivates competitive powwow dancers to compete? As we sought to answer these questions, we learned more about the contest powwow, contemporary Native Americans, and what they believed the function of the contest powwow is in maintaining the traditions of their people.

There was a logical progression in the development of the research questions we used in the completion of our qualitative studies. First, we completed a literature review to determine how local, sacred, and spiritually focused powwows evolved into large, public, competitive Pan-Indian events. Second, we compared a large contest powwow with an NCAA collegiate basketball game to determine how the spectacles might differ in terms of their promotion and staging. Third, we sought to determine through interviews with competitive powwow dancers, how large intertribal contest powwows differ from traditional forms of the powwow.

Fourth, we assessed through interviews with competitive dancers how powwows have evolved during their lifetime. Fifth, we allowed participants to express, through interviews, what their goals for competing in contest powwows are. We sought to determine whether they compete in a manner consistent with individualistic goals reflected in the dominant culture or if their competitive goals and behavior aligned with traditional Native American collectivist values. We asked participants if they believed that contest powwow dancing is a sport and compared the characteristics of sport with character-istics of the contest powwow to determine if it is a sport as defined by sport sociologists and sport philosophers.

Sixth, through use of field notes, observation, and interviews with seven contest powwow committee members and organizers, we sought to determine if the contest powwow is a context within which Native American spirituality is practiced and celebrated or if it is a secular activity. Finally, we conducted extensive interviews with two contest powwow announcers and recorded their activity through the use of field notes to determine if they serve as medi-ators of Native American culture during the contest powwow. We also sought to understand how the powwow announcers we interviewed were socialized into the role of powwow announcer, how they determine what to share over the public address system, and what goes into the decision-making process. The lessons of history and the findings of our qualitative-based studies led to the development of the Cultural Tethering Theory.

Each of the research studies included in this book was approved by our Institutional Review Board (IRB). In addition, to ensure adherence to IRB principles and ethical requirements, written consent to conduct interviews was also obtained from the Gathering of Nations administration before data collection commenced. All participants signed informed consent statements and had the opportunity to withdraw from the study at any time. By signing the informed consent form, participants verified that they were at least 18 years of age. The interviews serving as the basis for the qualitative studies shared in this book were conducted at two large intertribal contest powwows: the Gathering of Nations and a second event conducted in the Northern Plain region of the United States. As the interviews taking place at the North Plains Contest Powwow (NPCP) involved the powwow's organizers and head staff, a pseudonym was used for the event and each of the study's participants to protect their anonymity. Pseudonyms were also used for participants inter-viewed at the Gathering of Nations.

The fourteen dancers interviewed at the Gathering of Nations repre-sented eighteen tribal groups including Cheyenne, Chippewa, Cochiti Tewa, Colorado River Indian Tribes, Cree, Crow, Dakota Sioux, Hidatsa, Lakota Sioux, Mandau, Navajo, Ojibwe, Potawatomi, Pueblo, Shoshone, Sioux, Tututni, and Zuni. Seven participants claimed more than one tribal affiliation. Males and females were equally represented. Participants interviewed at the NPCP included three Native Americans and four non-Natives. Interviews ranged from fifteen to ninety-eight minutes at both sites.

We analyzed all qualitative data collected via a three-step coding process (open coding, axial coding, and theme development). It was vitally impor-tant that our research be trustworthy, credible, transferable, dependable, and confirmable. Qualitative studies undertaken with these goals in mind are considered trustworthy (Shenton, 2004). In the following pages, we share how credibility, transferability, dependability, and confirmability of our study were addressed in our research with special emphasis placed upon the guidelines provided by Guba and Lincoln (1989) and Shenton (2004).

In terms of credibility, honesty was foremost in the construction and reporting of our findings. We strove to keep any preconceived notions and biases at bay during all phases of the project. Triangulation was employed as we reviewed data in conjunction with available literature on contest powwows, traditional powwows, and the responses of participants who represented twenty-one tribal groups, as well as the experiences and observations of the authors in the context of sport and Native American cultures. All dancers, powwow organizers, and announcers participating in our research were provided an opportunity to opt out at any time. This increased the likelihood that responses were honest. Reflective commentary was engaged in upon completion of each interview. Member checks were conducted during interviews when participants were asked to repeat and or to clarify portions of their responses which assisted in clarity in the process of coding and analysis. Finally, the findings reported in this study are supported by the thickness of the data collected which led to the identification of our final themes and sub-themes.

We took several steps to enhance our project's transferability. The boundaries of our research in terms of participant characteristics, setting, methods of data collection, and analysis were specified. Because our research was undertaken at contest powwows and because it involved a wide range of participants representing several Native American tribal groups, we would expect participants in other contest powwow environments to provide similar responses and insights into the social world of contest powwow dancing. Saturation was achieved in each of the studies presented within this book, and we believe our results will be confirmed in future studies. However, we acknowledge that our results and conclusions are based upon limited information and that further study of contest powwows is warranted.

In terms of dependability, we conducted data analysis over a period of seven months. The length of time taken to complete data analysis was a means to enhance the constancy and dependability of our coding and analysis by avoiding work on the project during periods of boredom and exhaustion. The methodology employed in our study did not change over time, further adding to the dependability of our findings.

In terms of confirmability, we sought objectivity in our data analysis and the writing of our findings. The use of triangulation noted earlier served to negate any potential investigator bias effects. Our findings accurately represent the responses of our research's participants.

It is important for us to explain how contest powwows became the focus of our research activity. Aicinena lived and worked on Navajo tribal lands in

New Mexico as a teacher and coach for seven years. He experienced culture shock during his first year there. Navajo traditions, values, and language were vastly different from his own. To become more effective as a teacher and coach, he worked to better understand and accept the differences through the process of acculturation. While working at Crownpoint, he attended small local powwows. In 2016, he first attended the Gathering of Nations intertribal contest powwow. The size of the event, the number of contestants, the sights, and the sounds were unlike anything he had imagined it might be. The first visit to the Gathering of Nations served as the genesis of the focused series of studies presented in this book.

Aicinena, a professor of kinesiology, has over thirty years of teaching experience at the collegiate level and has published papers focused upon sport sociology, sport pedagogy, and religion in sport. He also served his university as a collegiate volleyball coach for twenty-one years and as its athletic director for twenty-four years. The second author, Sebahattin Ziyanak, an associate professor, has published numerous qualitative studies and books focused upon culture, acculturation, and assimilation. As he was raised in Turkey, the prospect of the current study was of great interest to him, and the project falls within his primary research expertise. Since Ziyanak did not have personal experience with Native American groups, he was able to provide an additional level of objectivity for reexamining methodological and analytical research procedures. Ziyanak also served to ensure that ethical standards of research were adhered to.

ORGANIZATION OF THE BOOK

In chapter 1, "The Powwow: From Sacred Spiritual Gathering to Competitive Event," we answer four important questions concerning powwows. First, what was the origination and meaning of the term "powwow?" Second, what is a Native American powwow? Third, what types of powwows are there? Finally, what historical factors led to the development of the contemporary intertribal contest powwow? Historical factors impacting powwow cultures covered in the chapter include (1) Genocide, (2) The Reservation System, (3) Cultural Genocide, (4) The Indian Boarding School System, (5) Christian and Governmental Efforts to Eliminate Powwows and Dancing, (6) Government Restrictions on Powwows and Dance, (7) Dancing for Income and Entertainment of the Public, (8) The Marriage of Powwow Dancing and Competition, and (9) The Pan-Indian Movement.

In chapter 2, "Similarities and Differences between the Gathering of Nations Contest Powwow and a University of New Mexico Lobo Basketball Game," we determine whether the Gathering of Nations contest powwow and a University of New Mexico men's basketball game are rightly classified as spectacles. We then assess nineteen promotional and staging considerations to determine if each factor is observed in each event. We identify and describe differences observed as the promotion and staging of the spectacles are carried out.

In chapter 3, "Contest Powwow Dancing as a Competitive Sport," we explore the possibility that contest powwow dancing is a sport through the qualitative research process. We demonstrate that although the participants compete with a high degree of seriousness, they maintain traditional collectivist values and attitudes. We find that the contest powwow serves to maintain and reproduce the unique characteristics of traditional Native American culture within the competitive contest powwow environment. The participants agree that contest powwow dancing is a sport, and we find that the activity meets both sociological and philosophical definitions of sport.

In chapter 4, "The Contest Powwow Announcers: Mediators of Culture and Traditions," we review the academic work of Gelo (2005) in addition to selected published newspaper and Internet interviews with powwow announcers to ascertain the responsibilities and social functions performed by contest powwow announcers. The purpose of the current study described in this chapter is twofold. First, we seek to expand knowledge concerning the contest powwow. Second, we seek to determine if contest powwow announcers consciously serve as mediators of culture and, if so, how they accomplish the goal. Contest powwow announcers, or emcees as they are also known, are important mediators of Native American culture.

In chapter 5, "Is the Contest Powwow a Spiritual Ceremony?" we first seek to determine what individuals involved in the planning and staging of a large intertribal contest powwow believe the role of religion and Native American spirituality are in the contest powwow. Second, we seek to determine what explicitly religious and spiritual behavior is present in a large intertribal contest powwow. Historically, the relationship between religion and ceremonial activities taking place in conjunction with traditional powwows was strong. Religious worship (spiritual activity) was commonly observed during traditional powwows from the seventeenth century and into modernity. Today, many non-Natives refuse to attend contest powwows because they believe them to be Native American spiritual worship services. After completing the analysis of our field notes and interviews of NPCP's organizers and staff, we find little evidence of Christian religious or Native American spiritual practice at the contest powwow.

In chapter 6, "The Contest Powwow: A Ceremony Fostering Tradition and Social Change," we seek to determine how the contest powwow and traditional powwow differ, how the contest powwow has changed, and how the contest powwow functions to preserve Native American culture in the experience of contemporary contest powwow dancers. Our participants witnessed changes in the contest powwow during their competitive careers. They identified several factors that serve to make participation in each type of powwow enjoyable and what factors make them unenjoyable. The participants explained that "powwow drama" occurs in the contest powwow setting and described experiencing "sacred" feelings in the context of the contest powwow. Finally, they identified how contest powwows serve to maintain traditional Native American culture.

In chapter 7, "Cultural Tethering Theory," we explore the topics of culture, acculturation, and assimilation. We examine numerous factors that are precipitating change in modern Native American culture including erosion of traditional values, loss of traditional languages, changes in social organization, limited opportunity to learn culturally valued knowledge, reduced opportunity to observe culturally appropriate behavior, and technology. We then examine Native American identity and seek to determine who can legitimately claim to be a Native American. Topics addressed include blood quantum, cultural knowledge and participation, being Indian, and playing Indian. Finally, we describe the difference between being Native American and playing Indian in powwow and pseudocultural powwow environments. The chapter and our book conclude with a presentation of the *Cultural Tethering Theory*. The theory was derived from the research completed for this book and it describes how acculturation and assimilation are facilitated and restrained for individuals and groups. We believe that the contest powwow will serve as a cultural tether, grounding Native Americans to their cultural values and traditions as they continue to evolve as a people.

Chapter 1

The Powwow

From Sacred Spiritual Gathering to Competitive Event

The modern intertribal contest powwow is a commercialized spectacle in which Pan-Indian culture is celebrated and performed in a public setting. The events remove social distinction from Native American participants hailing from various tribal backgrounds while differentiating their collective identity from that of the dominant culture (Ellis, 2005; McMullen, 1996). At the same time, the contest powwow serves as a marker of Native American social identity. The contest powwow as an institution assists in the transmission and continuance of Pan-Indian culture throughout North America and the world while serving as a window into the past, present, and future of America's first people.

The popularity of contest powwows has grown in recent decades and hundreds of thousands of spectators attend the festivals annually. However, the contest powwow is a recently established social phenomenon considering the long history of Native America's distinct tribal groups. To fully understand the contest powwow and what it means within contemporary Native America, it is essential to understand how it came into being.

In the current chapter, we seek to answer four questions. First, where did the term "powwow" come from? Second, what is a Native American powwow? Third, what types of powwows are there? Finally, what historical factors led to the development of the contemporary intertribal contest powwow?

WHERE DID THE TERM "POWWOW" COME FROM?

The term "powwow" may have evolved from any of several Native American languages and spiritual traditions. Medicine men and spiritual leaders of New England's Algonquian tribe were known as the *Puau* (Cogley, 1995).

Shepard (1648) described *Pawwow* as native holy leaders and observed that *Pawwowing* encompassed the spiritual activities of their shamans. The Proto-Algonquian form of **pawe·wa* meant "he has dream-power," and *Pawa-kan* was a Cree term for "dream spirit" (Costa, 2003, p. 32). Native American Powwows were considered spiritually important gatherings and those in charge of conducting them were considered holy (Zotigh, 2007).

WHAT IS A NATIVE AMERICAN POWWOW?

Powwows are festive Native American cultural celebrations characterized by song and dance. Powwows are also known as gatherings, doings, stomps, or socials, depending upon what tribal group is hosting the event. Thousands of powwows are conducted by Native Americans throughout North America each year (Eschbach & Applbaum, 2000).

Powwows conducted throughout North America share many similarities; however, they are also impacted by local culture and history (Fowler, 2005). Seventeenth-century missionary, Paul Le Jeune (Eisen, 1978), observed:

> There are many tribes in these countries who agree in a number of things and differ in many others; so that when it is said that certain practices are common to the [Indian], it may be true of one tribe and not true of another. (p. 60)

Powwows serve to inculcate and reinforce a sense of community, identity, and pride among Native American participants (Andrews & Olney, 2007; Ellis et al., 2005; Hsiu-Yen Yeh, 2006; Lassiter, 1997, 1998). Native American Indigenous culture is maintained and reproduced through powwows (Dufrene, 1990; Kracht, 1994). Indigenous languages are often spoken at powwows, and some powwows are conducted in the Native language of the host tribe. Acts of sharing such as feasts and giveaways demonstrate the traditional value placed upon generosity. Because elders and veterans are highly valued in traditional Native communities, they are honored at powwows. Traditional foods may be shared during communal feasts and food stands often spring up on powwow grounds from which vendors might sell tribal favorites such as Bison Stew and Dried Chokeberries (LaFramboise, 2013). Native American dances and music performed at powwows may be hundreds of years old, though some music and song performed may have been composed recently. Music at traditional powwows may be played on large drums, small hand drums, or with rattles. Despite the importance of the powwow in maintenance and celebration of Native American culture, only a fraction of Native Americans attends powwows and participates in dances (Wightman, 2012).

WHAT TYPES OF POWWOWS ARE THERE?

Traditional powwows, also referred to as local powwows, are small gatherings that may involve only a couple of hundred people from the same tribal community. These local events typically celebrate and reinforce tribal-specific culture and may include sacred spiritually significant ceremonies and dances. Traditional powwows are characteristically held in small recreation centers, school gymnasiums, or within traditional gathering places such as arbors or longhouses (Andrews & Olney, 2007). People come to traditional powwows to dance and to socialize. Most do not come simply to spectate and everyone present is considered as a participant. Time schedules, if they exist, are of casual importance and are quite flexible (Deloria, 2003).

The contest powwow shares many of the traditional powwow's characteristics. However, elements of competition and the opportunity to win money and prizes are unique to the contest powwow. Often contest powwows are held in large venues, such as basketball arenas. Dancing featured at contest powwows may include intertribals (anyone can dance), competition dances in various dance styles and age groups, dance demonstrations, and dance specials which are typically held to honor an individual. Often drum and singing competitions are held in conjunction with contest powwows. Schedules at larger contest powwows are strictly adhered to.

Large contest powwows typically take place over two to three days with one or two sessions taking place each day. Most contest powwows are similar in the order of events and what events are included. We employ the schedule followed at the Gathering of Nations (2018) as an example of the events included in a contest powwow and how they are ordered.

Each session begins with a *Drum Roll Call*, which assesses the presence and readiness of each drum group participating in the powwow. The *Grand Entry* consists of the formal entry of dancers into the arena. During the grand entry, powwow officials record the participation of the dancers who will be involved in competitions throughout the powwow. A *Flag Song* is performed to honor the country and sovereign Native American nations. An *Invocation* is given in which God, Jesus, or Creator is thanked in English or a tribal language. A *Welcome Address* is given by the powwow committee's president, a prominent tribal official, or a governmental official. The powwow emcee then provides an *Introduction of the Head Staff. Competition in Singing and Competition in Dancing* occurs in various dance styles and age groups. The contests are broken up by *Giveaways, Special Presentations, Dance Demonstrations*, and *Dance Specials.* Many contest powwows sponsor powwow princess competitions that conducted outside of the contest powwow sessions. The Gathering of Nations features the pageant's song and dance competitions and includes a public *Crowning of Miss Indian World. Awards Presentations* are also conducted.

Figure 1.1   Powwow Princess Pageants. This photo was taken at the introduction of the winner and runners-up in the Gathering of Nation's Miss Indian World competition. Competitors compete in tribal knowledge, language, dress, song, dance, art, and in oration. Winners of the event and others like it represent the powwow during public events throughout the year of their reign. *Source*: Photo by Steven Aicinena

Dancers from various tribal groups compete in numerous age categories and Native American dance styles for prize money and awards. The Gathering of Nations Powwow sponsored competitions in the Fancy Shawl Dance, Jingle Dance, Traditional Northern Dance, Southern Traditional Dance, Southern Cloth Dance, Northern Cloth Dance, and Southern Buckskin Dance for females in girls, teens, women's, golden age, and elder categories. For males, competitions were offered in the Grass Dance, Fancy Dance, Southern Straight Dance, Northern Traditional Dance, Northern Fancy Dance, Southern Fancy Dance, and the Chicken Dance in boys, teens, men's, golden age, and elder categories. Boys and girls under age five competed in the tiny tots' dance events. Cash prizes and awards were issued in a total of thirty-six dance categories (Gathering of Nations, 2018).

Unlike traditional powwows, participation by members of disparate tribal groups is encouraged at contest powwows. And unlike traditional powwows, large intertribal contest powwows are reflective of professionalized commercialized American athletic events (Aicinena & Ziyanak, 2019; Albers & Medicine, 2005). Though some traditionalists view the contest powwow as being an inauthentic representation of Native American culture, it has been argued that the contest powwow functions to preserve and transmit Native American traditions.

WHAT FACTORS LED TO THE DEVELOPMENT OF THE CONTEST POWWOW?

Historical factors impacted Native Americans that resulted in alteration of their daily lives and traditional practices including their powwow cultures. In this chapter, we examine nine factors that led to the development and spread of contest powwows throughout Native America. The factors we consider in this chapter include (1) Genocide, (2) The Reservation System, (3) Cultural Genocide, (4) The Indian Boarding School System, (5) Christian and Governmental Efforts to Eliminate Powwows and Dancing, (6) Government Restrictions on Powwows and Dance, (7) Dancing for Income and Entertainment of the Public, (8) The Marriage of Powwow Dancing and Competition, and (9) The Pan-Indian Movement.

Genocide

According to Thornton (2005), when Europeans first set foot upon the North American continent, an estimated five million Indigenous people lived in the area now comprising the forty-eight contiguous United States. By 1900, the Native American population had fallen to an estimated 375,000 (Thornton, 1987). Serrato (2017) reported that as of 1910, only 250,000 Native Americans remained. Disease brought by Europeans was responsible for the death of legions of Native Americans, but so were ignorance, greed, hatred, Manifest Destiny, and murder.

Today, it is commonly accepted that Native Americans were victims of genocide (Madley, 2016; Ostler, 2015; Stannard, 1992), though some scholars argue they were the victim of ethnic cleansing (Anderson, 2016). According to the United Nations Convention on the Prevention and Punishment of the Crime of Genocide (United Nations, 1948):

In the present Convention, genocide means any of the following acts committed with intent to destroy, in whole or in part, a national, ethnical, racial or religious group, as such: (a) Killing members of the group; (b) Causing serious bodily or mental harm to members of the group; (c) Deliberately inflicting on the group conditions of life calculated to bring about its physical destruction in whole or part; imposing measures intended to prevent births within the group; (e) Forcibly transferring children of the group to another group. (para. 4)

We will demonstrate that Native Americans (1) were killed because they were Native Americans, (2) experienced mental harm because of forced assimilation efforts, (3) were subject to measures meant to reduce birthrates, and (4) had their children removed from their homes to be educated in government-run Indian boarding schools. Genocide takes place when one of the four situations occurs. Native Americans have been subjected to all four genocidal acts identified by the United Nations.

Jesus, upon whose life is Christianity based, called for all to practice reciprocity and to take the gospel to all peoples of the world (King James Bible, 2021, Matthew 22: 39, Matthew 28: 19-20). But the message of Jesus seems to have been amended by the church in the middle of the fifteenth century. In 1455, Pope Nicholas V issued the Romanus Pontifex, also known as the Doctrine of Discovery. The doctrine implored Christians to, "attack, enslave and kill the Indigenous Peoples they encountered and to acquire all of their assets" (World Council of Churches, 2012, p. 3). It was with this understanding that exploration and colonization of North America and the world began for the Spanish, French, English, and others.

In North America, there existed a widespread belief that Indians should be eliminated from the face of the earth (Addis, 2005; Jacobs, 2016). Sir Jeffery Amherst, commander of British forces in North America, callously stated in a letter written to a subordinate in 1763, "You will do well to try to inoculate the Indians by means of blankettes as well as to try every other method that can serve to extirpate this execrable race" (Gill, 2004, p. 3).

Battles with Native Americans, also known as the Indian Wars, took place between 1622's Jamestown Massacre and the massacre at Wounded Knee in 1890 (Ostler, 2015). After reviewing U.S. Army records, Utter (1993, p. 171) reported that conflict between U.S. Army personnel and Native Americans between 1866 and 1891 resulted in the death of 948 U.S. troops and 4,371 Indians. In addition, 1,058 military and 1,279 Indians were wounded. Ten thousand three hundred and eighteen Native Americans were taken captive during the conflicts. The numbers above do not include deaths related to actions of the U.S. Navy or Marines nor deaths related to state or local militias, or conflict taking place earlier or later. Regular U.S. army and militia were responsible for numerous massacres of Native Americans before, during, and after the beginning of the reservation period (Broadman, 2016; Kanon, 2017; Ostler, 2015; Worthington, 2016). Complete and accurate reports of the dead and wounded in conflicts between Native Americans and non-Natives are illusive.

It was not uncommon for U.S. military leaders to hold great animus toward Native Americans and their hatred too often led to inhumane treatment and indiscriminate slaughter of Indigenous peoples. Here, we use the words of Phil Sheridan and John Chivington to illustrate the level of hatred harbored by various military leaders during the period of the Indian Wars.

Phil Sheridan was appointed by President U.S. Grant to pacify the Indians of the plains. According to Captain Charles Nordstrom, a Comanche leader approached Sheridan and introduced himself, "Me, Toch-a-way; me good injun." Sheridan smiled sardonically as he replied, "The only good Indians I ever saw were dead" (Hutton, 1999, p. 180).

Sheridan testified before congress to oppose a law that, if enacted, would protect the buffalo (American Bison). Numerous Native American tribal groups living upon the Great Plains depended upon buffalo to supply food, clothing, and tools. During his testimony, Sheridan proposed that if the law were passed, those who broke the law and killed the buffalo should receive a medal sporting a discouraged Indian on one side and a dead buffalo on the other (Beckman, 2009).

The commander-in-charge of troops responsible for the 1864 Sand Creek Massacre John Chivington justified the extermination of Arapaho and Cheyenne women and children by stating, "Damn any man who sympathizes with Indians. Kill and scalp all, big and little; nits make lice" (Ward & Duncan, 2001, p. 12).

When it became clear to tribal leaders that their people faced extermination if they resisted the seizing of land by the American government, they agreed to sign treaties and were relocated to reservations (Ostler, 2015). By the early 1900s, armed conflict with Native American warriors had ceased. Relocation to reservations brought titanic changes to Native American cultures including traditional ceremonial and dance activity.

Genocide of Native Americans continued into the twentieth century. Few Americans know that during the 1960s and 1970s, an estimated 25–50 percent of all Native American women were subjected to involuntary sterilization by Indian Health Service (IHS) physicians (Lawrence, 2000). Native women as young as fifteen years of age went to IHS medical facilities for procedures such as appendectomies and tonsillectomies. It was only after they became aware of their infertility that they discovered they were also given tubal ligations or hysterectomies.

In justifying the sterilizations, many of the doctors working for the IHS explained that Indian women and young girls were too irresponsible to use birth control, that they were doing society a favor by performing the sterilizations, and that through sterilizations the victims and their families would be better off financially. The IHS also placed pressure upon Native American women to use birth control as a way to reduce birthrates and enhance socioeconomic standing during this same period. Forced sterilization and birth control efforts significantly reduced Native American birth rates during this very dark period in the United States and Native American relations.

The Reservation System

European pilferers and early American expansionists readily justified appropriation of Native American lands because they held a firm belief that Indians were an inferior people (Anderson, 2016). They also maintained that although Native Americans had lived in North America for thousands of years, they had no legal right to ownership of the land (Cushing, 1856; Jackson, 1817).

With the passage of The Indian Removal Act of 1830, the American government graciously granted itself authority to exchange land west of the Mississippi for desirable Indian lands within the extant United States (Cave, 2003). The "Indian Territory" was established with the passage of the Native American Intercourse Act of 1834. Indian Territory included land in the modern states of Nebraska, Kansas, Oklahoma, and a portion of Iowa (Everett, 2009). The government sought to create colonies within Indian Territory upon which relocated Indians would learn to farm and engage in domestic work, helping them to assimilate into the dominant society. The colonies later became known as "reservations" (Anderson, 2016).

Disease, raids by other Indian tribes, severe weather, and starvation were all contributing factors to the loss of life during relocation from ancestral lands to reservations (Fast, 2007). Approximately 4,000 Cherokee perished on the "Trail of Tears" from their home in modern-day Georgia to Oklahoma (Library of Congress, 2018). Nearly 2,000 Navajo died on the "Long Walk" from their homeland to the Bosque Redondo, New Mexico (Cheek, 2004). The Creek, Seminole, Choctaw, and Chickasaw tribes and others endured hardships and significant loss of life during relocation (Waldman, 2006).

Murder was also responsible for loss of life during relocation. As recorded by Goldschmidt (1951), Andrew Freeman of the Nomlaki tribe recalled, "When they took the Indians to [the Round Valley Reservation] they drove them like stock [and] shot the old people who couldn't make the trip. They would shoot children who were getting tired" (p. 313).

Indian Territory was reduced in size following the passage of the Kansas-Nebraska Act of 1854 (Everett, 2009). As the size of Indian Territory was reduced, some tribal groups that had previously relocated from their homelands in the east were forced to move again, resulting in additional privation and loss of life. The Winnebago tribe was forced to relocate three times. The first relocation of the people was from traditional lands in Northeast Iowa to Minnesota, the second from Minnesota to South Dakota, and finally, from South Dakota to Nebraska (Winnebago Tribe of Nebraska, 2021).

When Native American lands were taken, the people lost access to sacred sites, the inspiration for traditional stories and spiritual practices, and traditional food sources. Further, tribal groups lost access to materials traditionally used in creation of homes, clothing, and art that was historically important in their culture. Once on reservations, Native Americans encountered malnutrition and starvation that led too often to death (Madley, 2016). Frequently, reservation land allocated to tribal groups was described as "wasteland" by the whites (Spores, 1993).

Cultural Genocide

The concept of cultural genocide is akin to the crime of physical genocide. They both spring forth from identical ethnocentric goals (Akhavan, 2017). Cultural genocide threatens the cultural survival and identity of people groups, and it has been instrumental in the elimination of Indigenous cultures throughout the world (Maguire, 2018). Effectively, when the culture of a people disappears, the people cease to exist as a people group. Today, the United Nations Educational, Scientific and Cultural Organization (UNESCO) seeks to protect the world's various cultures and declares that doing so, "is an ethical imperative, inseparable from respect for human dignity" (UNESCO, 2001, p. 15).

As subjugated people, Native Americans experienced unceasing assaults upon their culture. According to Beyers (2017), culture consists of the practices, skills, ethics, knowledge, beliefs, and art characteristic of a social group (p. 2). Culture includes institutions central to group identity, including language, religious practices and objects, traditional practices, and forms of expression (Woolford, 2009). Cultural genocide occurs when a dominant group attempts to abolish another's language, traditional practices, religious institutions, and objects (Maguire, 2018; Nersessian, 2005). Through forced assimilation efforts, the government perpetrated cultural genocide upon Native Americans (Maguire, 2018).

Government leaders believed that forcing Indians to assimilate into the dominant society was a worthy goal. Illustratively, Indian Bureau commissioner Hiram Price (1881) provided rationale for forcing assimilation upon the Indians:

Savage and civilized life cannot live and prosper on the same ground. One of the two must die. If the Indians are to be civilized and become happy and prosperous people, which is certainly the object and intent of our government, they must learn our language and adopt our modes of life. We are fifty millions of people, and they are only one fourth of one million. The few must yield to the many. (p. IV)

The "benevolent" practice of attempting to forcibly assimilate Indians into the dominant culture was justified in the minds of those holding a Social Darwinist view (Eschbach & Applbaum, 2000). They believed that because Indian "savages" were both culturally and technologically "inferior" that they must be properly acculturated into American society to thrive (Anderson, 2016). Education is an institution used to teach children how to successfully function within a culture, and the American government saw education as vital to the assimilation of Native American children.

The Indian Boarding School System

Education was an important ally for the American government in its assimilation goals for Native Americans (Harding, 2001). Because Native children attending local day schools returned home each afternoon and spent weekends and break periods with family, educational assimilation efforts were hampered by continued exposure of the children to Indigenous culture. In response, the government created the Indian boarding school system.

Indian boarding schools were often run by Christians and Christianity was taught within the schools along with basic reading, writing, math, and vocational skills (Reyhner, 2018). The explicit goal of the Indian boarding school system was to prepare the children to farm and work in domestic trades as adults. The implicit goal of the boarding schools was to destroy the children's Native American identity and culture in the interest of assimilation. Assimilation of the Indians would take care of the government's "Indian Problem."

Richard Pratt established the Carlisle Indian School, the nation's first Indian boarding school, in 1879. Pratt clearly articulated how important it was for the government to force assimilation upon Native American children when he stated, "All the Indian there is in the race should be dead. Kill the Indian in him and save the man" (Pratt, 1892, p. 46).

In 1898, the American government passed a compulsory boarding school attendance law for Indian children (Booth, 2010). Some parents willingly sent their children to boarding schools because life was difficult on reservations where food was often scarce and living conditions were poor. Alvino Sandoval's relocation from reservation home to boarding school is illustrative. In 1947 when he was ten years old, his mother woke him up and told him he would be going someplace that had food and a warm place to sleep. He recalled, "I never went off the reservation and all of a sudden they shipped me out and I ended up here" (Bowannie, 2007).

When parents refused to send their children to boarding schools, agents were authorized to take children by force. Noncompliant children were chased down by government agents, captured, forcibly removed from their homes, and transported to Indian boarding schools.[1] The techniques used by Clyde Blair to "recruit" Navajo children to attend Albuquerque Indian School were described by Willard Beatty (1961):

> He and a Navajo policeman had started out in a buckboard drawn by two horses and went from hogan to hogan looking for children. As they got in sight of a hogan and the Indians recognized who they were and guessed at their purpose, the children could be seen darting out of the hogan and running into the brush. Whereupon the Navajo policeman stood up in the buckboard and fired a shotgun into the air to scare the children and make them stop running—if possible. Then he jumped out of the wagon and ran after the children. If he caught them (and many times he didn't), he wrestled them to the ground, tied their legs and arms, and with the help of Mr. Blair put them in the back part of the wagon, where they lay until Blair had gathered in the quota for the day. Then they returned to the Albuquerque school and enrolled the children they had captured. (p. 12)

Parents refusing to send their children to boarding schools voluntarily risked losing government-provided rations. Non-acquiescing members of the Zuni tribe were arrested and imprisoned within the notorious Alcatraz federal prison in California (Booth, 2010).

The government was quite effective in placing Native American children into boarding schools. By 1925 it ran 357 Indian boarding schools. Eighty-three percent of all Native American children of school age attended boarding schools by 1926 (The National Native American Boarding School Healing Coalition, 2019). It was not uncommon for Indian children to be in boarding schools for five years without going home to visit family (Reyhner, 2018).

To expedite assimilation of the children in the boarding schools they were prohibited from speaking their native language, wearing their hair in traditional manners, wearing traditional dress, playing culturally valued games, and participating in traditional religious activity. Frequently, the children were assigned roommates who did not share the same language. Concerted efforts were made in the boarding schools to destroy the languages, religions, traditions, educational practices, and traditional values of the children.

The Meriam Report (Meriam, 1928) exposed many problems existent within Indian boarding schools. Overcrowding, improper nutrition, ineffective medical care, beatings, and other abuses were common. The control of boarding schools was given to tribal governments shortly following issuance of the Meriam Report and many of the boarding schools were closed. One hundred and eighty-three boarding schools continue to operate in the United States (Bureau of Indian Education, 2019).

Effectively, the boarding school system served to disengage thousands of children from their traditional culture while inadequately preparing them to function effectively in the dominant society. Boarding school students experienced trauma that led to posttraumatic stress disorder, domestic violence, homicide, suicide, alcohol abuse, and mental health disorders (Warne & Lajimodiere, 2015). Objectively, boarding school students served as cultural change agents when they returned home to reservations (Adams, 1995).

Christian and Governmental Efforts to Eliminate Powwows and Dancing

Seventeenth-century North American colonialists believed they were mandated by God to Christianize the "savages" (McCoy, 2014). To North American missionaries, Christianizing the savages required putting an end to the traditional Native American religious beliefs and activities. Talbot (2006) referred to Christian efforts taken to convert Native Americans into Christians as spiritual genocide.

Christian efforts to prevent Native Americans from practicing traditional religious activities began well before the reservation period and creation of the Indian boarding school system. Seventeenth-century evangelist John Eliot concluded that powwows were the most powerful factor connecting Indians to their "pagan" ways (Cogley, 1999). In an ongoing effort to Christianize the unenlightened, "powwowing" was officially prohibited in 1646 within the Martha's Bay area of New England. In 1671, it was made illegal for Indians to, "Powwow or perform outward Worship to the Devil or other false God" within the Massachusetts Bay Colony (Brigham, 1836, p. 298).

Once Native Americans were domiciled upon reservations, missionaries from various Christian denominations intensified efforts to convert the Indians to Christianity and to eliminate all traditional forms of worship (Deloria, 2003; Spack, 2000). Destruction of traditional Native American religious activities would theoretically result in a serious disruption of established Indigenous cultures and increase the probability of successful assimilation into the dominant culture. This was both logical and reasonable, for the connection between religion and culture is profound (Beyers, 2017; Olson, 2011).

Government agencies prohibited dances associated with religious activity during the reservation period because of their importance to Indigenous culture and religious practice, (Albers & Medicine, 2005; Ridington et al., 2005). Commissioner of Indian Affairs Thomas J. Morgan established a series of criminal offenses aimed at Native American religious practices and dance in his 1892 "Rules for Indian Courts" (Morgan, 1892). He wrote:

Any Indian who shall engage in the sun dance, scalp dance, or war dance, or any similar feast, so called, shall be guilty of an offense, and upon conviction thereof shall be punished for the first offense by withholding of his rations for not exceeding ten days or by imprisonment for not exceeding ten days; for any subsequent offense under this clause he shall be punished by withholding his rations for not less than ten days nor more than thirty days, or by imprisonment for not less than ten days nor more than thirty days. Medicine men—Any Indian who shall engage in the practices of so-called medicine men, or who shall resort to any artifice or device to keep the Indians of the reservation from adopting and following civilized habits and pursuits, or shall use any arts of conjurer to prevent Indians from abandoning their barbarous rites and customs, shall be deemed guilty of an offense, and upon conviction thereof, for the first offense shall be imprisoned for not less than ten days and not more than thirty days. (p. 707)

Ghost dances involved as many as 3,000 members from various plains tribes (Serrato, 2017). Tragically, the use of military force was authorized to prevent the Lakota from conducting a Ghost Dance at Wounded Knee in 1890. Between 145 and 300 Miniconjous Lakota, many who were women and children were massacred by the Seventh Cavalry (Serrato, 2017). The Wounded Knee massacre, "is sometimes regarded as the 'last' event in the Indian wars, but more appropriately considered an instance of the violent suppression of an anti-colonial movement" (Ostler 2015, p. 39). Restrictions on Native American religious practices officially continued until 1978 when the American Indian Religious Freedom Act was enacted.

Defiance of governmental interference in worship and dance activities helped to ensure continuance of powwows and the people's dancing tradition. Despite governmental restrictions and Christian opposition to Native American dance, powwows continued to be held in secret locations outside the prevue of Indian agents as were spiritually important ceremonial activities characterized by dance (Ellis, 2003). In further efforts to continue their dancing traditions, Native leaders sought and received permission from governmental agents to conduct nonreligious dances and gatherings on holidays and special occasions such as when veterans returned from battle. In the interest of good relationships, these requests were often approved by agents. Dance was used by Native Americans to negotiate new social and cultural realities while protecting and preserving tribal values (Albers & Medicine, 2005).

Dancing for Income and Entertainment of the Public

Historically, tribal ceremonial activities involving dance and song were local affairs limited to tribal members and invited guests. Dancing and singing were not performed for consumption by the public, nor did dancers vie for prizes, or cash awards. Beginning in the second half of the nineteenth century, dances were performed for non-Native audiences to provide a source of income to the dancers (Herle, 1994).

During and following the America's westward expansion and the Indian Wars, Americans, Europeans, and South Americans harbored a great fascination with Native American culture and traditions. From the late 1800s to early in the 1900s, Wild West shows including Buffalo Bill's Wild West Show, the Miller Brothers' 101 Real Ranch Show, and others hired Native Americans to perform as they traveled the United States and the world to perform (Lottini, 2012; Moses, 1999). In 1885, over 1 million people paid to watch Wild West shows featuring Native American performers who participated in reenactment of famous battles, conducted powwows, and performed culturally valued dances (Moses, 1999). Over 500 Native Americans were paid by government entities to build Native villages, conduct powwows, perform dances, participate in reenactment of battles, and conduct traditional feasts during the World Fairs of 1898 and 1904 (Clough, 2005; Swensen, 2019).

Tribes including the Meskwaki of Iowa and the Ho-Chunk of Wisconsin began to perform for the ticket-purchasing public by the late 1800s (Warren, 2009). Many of the Nation's oldest recorded powwows are now public secular events. The Omaha tribe's annual harvest celebration is the oldest documented celebratory powwow. The gathering was first held in 1804 as a traditional spiritual *He'dewachi* harvest dance (Linck, 2004; Ridington et al., 2005). The Winnebago Tribe held its first Annual Homecoming Celebration in 1866 to honor the Ho-Chunk's last tribal war chief Little Priest (Library of Congress, n.d.; Scandale, 2018). In 1879, America's first intertribal powwow was held in Oklahoma by the Ponca Tribe (Zotigh, 2007).

The "Great American Indian National Dancing Contest" held in conjunction with Haskell Institute's 1929 homecoming was perhaps the earliest official contest powwow. Dancers from 70 tribes performed dancing demonstrations and competed in the Fancy Dance, also known as the War Dance, for a cash prize before 10,000 spectators. Based upon audience applause, the championship was awarded to Augustus "Gus" McDonald, a member of the Ponca tribe. In winning the event, the Ponca were given the right to conduct the world championship Fancy Dance competition in perpetuity (Rader, 2004).

Certainly, individuals who left their reservation communities to perform in Wild West shows broke from tradition to do so. In time, however, public performance of culture came to be accepted by Native American groups. Acceptance of public performance was vital for the contest powwow to take form and evolve into the spectacle of sights, sounds, and culture that it is today.

The Marriage of Dance and Competition

Competition does not typically take place at traditional powwows nor is it integral to their structure (DesJarlait, 1997; Herle, 1994). We believe competitive athletics in schools has been an important factor in Native American acceptance of competition at contest powwows. Within the dominant American culture, competitive athletics are believed to be an important agent of socialization and character development.

At the end of the nineteenth century, American leaders such as J. P. Morgan and President Teddy Roosevelt claimed that sports participation could, "breed a sense of hard work, discipline and the win-at-all-cost ethic of competition" (Zirin, 2005, p. 4). This belief is the primary reason that schools and colleges support extracurricular athletics throughout the United States today (Coakley, 2017; Sage et al., 2019). Public schools provide Native Americans, with interscholastic sport, intramural sport, and physical education classes to enhance health and to achieve social assimilation goals.

Native American students at the U.S. government's first Indian boarding school, Carlisle Indian School, participated in sport during physical education classes, intramural programs, and athletic competition (Bloom, 2000). Carlisle first began operations in 1879 and first sponsored football in 1893. Basketball was played by Arapaho and Eastern Shoshone boarding school students by 1910 and their schools sponsored competitive teams in 1920. In the early 1930s athletics were well-organized and meaningful events at the boarding schools (Sullivan, 2005). By 1941, athletics were widely sponsored by Indian schools and their competitive successes were used by missionaries and administrators as evidence of successful assimilation (Bloom, 1996; Sewell, 2005). Boarding school students on and off reservations considered athletic successes as a source of Pan-Indian pride (Bloom, 1996).

Native American athletes have achieved notoriety in collegiate, Olympic, and professional competition (Paraschak, 2000). Olympic competitors included Frank Pierce (marathon), Frank Mt. Pleasant (marathon), Louis Tewanima (marathon and 10,000-meter run), Billy Mills (10,000-meter champion), and Jessie Renick (basketball team). Professional sport hall of fame members includes John "Chief" Bender (Major League Baseball) and Joseph Guyon (Professional Football). Jim Thorpe, a product of the Indian Boarding school system, is considered by many to be one of the greatest athletes of all time (ESPN, 1999; Wheeler, 1979).

The Carlisle Indian School football team consisted of young men from numerous Native American tribes and is considered to have been one of the best collegiate squads in the country during the 1910 and 1911 seasons. The team's success garnered national recognition and fostered Pan-Indian identity and Native pride within team members, the student body, and Native

Americans across the country (Buford, 2012; Eschbach & Applbaum, 2000; McDonald, 1972).

Native American culture continues to adhere to collectivist values despite hundreds of years of governmental assimilation efforts (Heine, 2008; Hossain et al., 2011; Kitayama & Markus, 2000). American culture and the competitive goals associated with American sport reflect individualistic goals. Conflict caused by competing values systems of coaches and Native American athletes has been documented by Allison (1980, 1982) and Allison and Leuschen (1979). Adherence to collectivist values and behaviors, aligned with Native American traditional community values, was considered by coaches to be an impediment to competitive success and to full assimilation into mainstream society.

It appears that Native Americans athletes compete while adhering to traditional collectivist values, not those of the dominant culture. Nevertheless, Native American athletes have been successful in high school athletics and have won numerous state championships over the years (Sage et al., 2019). High school athletic contests are well attended on reservations, and gyms are packed for basketball games in New Mexico, Arizona, South Dakota, and in other states supporting Native American communities.[2]

It is likely that Native American acceptance of competition, in general, has assisted in acceptance of competition within the powwow environment. However, our research has also demonstrated that as Native Americans compete in contest powwows, their goals and attitudes toward competition align with collectivist values (Aicinena & Ziyanak, 2021).

Powwows and the Pan-Indian Movement

Dances and other components of powwow culture were shared between Native American groups long before the implementation of the reservation system (DesJarlait, 1997). For example, Ellis (2003) noted that plains tribes including the Eastern Dakota, Crow, Plains Shoshone, and Omaha warrior societies shared common values and ideals. Their kinship facilitated the sharing, adaptation, and adoption of powwow cultures between them (Kracht, 1994).

The reservation system brought tribes from various parts of North America to Indian Country resulting in the incorporation of traditional dances and ceremonial activities of plains tribes and others into their powwows (Scott, 1911). Once a tribe adopted a dance or ceremony, it was subject to changes predicated upon its unique culture. For example, the Kiowa did not allow cutting of flesh or bloodletting as a part of the Sun Dance, while the Dakota, Blackfeet, Southern Cheyenne, and Arapaho engaged in the practice.

The songs and dances of warrior societies responded to the reality of relegation to reservations. Reproduction of traditional songs, dances, and other powwow-related rituals historically assisted in maintaining traditional culture. But, because titanic upheaval was experienced by Native American tribes as they were subjugated and placed onto reservations, changes were made in powwow activities to keep them both meaningful and relevant (Ellis, 2003). Loss of the opportunity to hunt and gather in traditional ways and the inability to engage in war resulted in many traditional dances and ceremonies losing their religious significance.

As noted earlier in this chapter, Native American powwows and dance, once sacred activities, ever-increasingly were performed in public for profit. Doing so required dancers to set aside the religious meaning of the act. Ernest St. Germaine Sr. recalled that performing culture for profit in the 1950s was both a dilemma and opportunity. It was an opportunity because income could be earned and yet a dilemma because, "you had to remove yourself spiritually from what you were doing in order to do it" (Nesper, 2003, p. 447). Removing the spiritual meaning of a dance assisted in the dance's continuance; its original meaning has eroded over time.

The spiritual focus of the powwow has been deemphasized as the celebrations have become more commercialized and migrated from reservations into mainstream America (Rahimi, 2005). Contemporary powwows, particularly contest powwows are properly classified as social events or secular ceremonies (Callahan, 1993; Crawford & Kelley, 2005; Gamble, 1952; Howard, 1983; Lurie, 1971).

During Pan-Indian gatherings, such as contest powwows, that which is common to diverse tribal groups is celebrated and any focus upon differences is discounted (Howard, 1955). Pan-Indianism affords Indigenous peoples from disparate tribal affiliations the opportunity to identify as Native American (supra-tribal identity) and as member of a tribe (tribal identity) concurrently (Powers, 1980).

The Panhellenic games of the ancient Greeks, including the Olympic Games, Pythian Games, Isthmian Games, and Nemean Games united citizens from various city-states and colonies. Like Native American groups, those living in different city-states and colonies were culturally diverse, but shared commonalities in their traditions and beliefs. As Greeks came from throughout the Mediterranean to compete and to spectate, traditions and values collectively shared by the Greeks were celebrated and reinforced (Rader, 2015).

Contest powwows came to being as dancers, government leaders, tribal leaders and entrepreneurs saw that income and interest in Native American culture could be generated through public performance of culture (Clough, 2005; DesJarlait, 1997; Herle, 1994; Oxendine, 2011; Warren, 2009). Contest powwows were first conducted in Oklahoma during the mid-1800s to attract tourists and generate income (DesJarlait, 1997; Oxendine, 2011). They achieved their current structure and form between the 1930s and 1960s (DesJarlait, 1997; Ellis et al., 2005; Scales, 2007). Following the conclusion of World War II, the number and frequency of contest powwows rapidly increased (Herle, 1994). Native American activism and a reinvigorated interest in Native culture and traditions in the 1960s and 1970s accelerated the spread of contest powwows throughout North America. The amount of prize money increased during the 1970s and 1980s, resulting in greater participation in contest powwow events (Oxendine, 2011). By the end of the 1970s, contest powwows were sponsored in all regions of the United States (Arndt, 2005). Beginning in the 1980s, large contest powwows were conducted in arenas to accommodate growing crowds. In the 1990s Indian-owned casinos promoted contest powwows and provided financial support resulting in increases in the amount of prize money available, publicity, and amount of prize money awarded to champion dancers.

Additional growth in the size and number of contest powwows was experienced in the 2000s as powwow organizers were successful in securing sponsorship from major corporations. Sponsors of the 2018 Gathering of Nations Powwow, for example, included Wells Fargo, Southwest Airlines, Bank of America, Marriott, Whataburger, and Facebook (Gathering of Nations, 2018). Currently, a "powwow circuit," also known as the "powwow highway," exists and some dancers and family groups compete for cash prizes year-round.

Hobbyists are groups of non-Native Americans who gather to recreate imagined forms of Native American culture. Popular literature, movies, television shows, Wild West shows, Native American speakers, the Native American Red Power movement, and exhibitions of Native American art and traditional artifacts served to generate interest in Native American culture throughout Europe. Most hobbyists base their regalia and activities upon perceptions generated through these sources. Groups of hobbyists exist in England, Russia, Latvia, Lithuania, Estonia, the Czech Republic, Bulgaria, the Netherlands, and Germany (Matulevičius, 2013; Taylor, 1988). German Hobbyists conduct contest powwows on a regular basis that include competitors from various European hobbyist groups (Watchman, 2005). Because of the continuing interest in Native Americans and their powwow culture, millions view contest powwows via the internet annually. Questions have been raised concerning the ethics involved in the appropriation of Native American powwow culture by non-Natives (Watchman, 2005).

Participation in contest powwows is not embraced by all Native Americans or all tribal groups. Some traditionalists describe contest powwows as being inauthentic representations of Native American culture (Andrews & Olney, 2007; Dell'Angela, 2003). There are concerns within Native American communities that contest powwows can be ethically questionable and socially destructive. Such concerns are based upon the belief that tradition serves as the central and defining feature of what it means to be a Native American or a member of a specific tribal group (Scales, 2007). Proposed and observed change in the powwow causes tension within the powwow community (Browner, 2004).

Despite their commercialization and confliction with some tribal customs, Hill (1996) described contest powwows as being a positive for Native American communities and traditions:

> The powwow has now spread coast to coast, and while some see it as a Pan-Indian fabrication, I now see that it serves a vital catalyst for cultural renewal. . . No matter how we dance, how we dress, or how we live, for a few moments of the song we stand together as a people, united by tradition and connected in the certain belief that dance is essential to the expression of ourselves. (p. 8)

The modern intertribal contest powwow is the product of Native American history and the negotiation that has occurred between traditions and modernity. Contest powwows are secular events often mirroring the characteristics of modern athletic spectacles (Aicinena & Ziyanak, 2019). Contest powwows spectacles are nontraditional, public, commercialized, competitive events in which prize money is awarded. Through the contest powwow, Native Americans celebrate and transmit Pan-Indian values, behaviors, and traditions. As such, the contest powwow is a Native American cultural celebration, a source of cultural renewal, and a transmitter of culture within the current American cultural milieu.

NOTES

1. Aicinena's father-in-law was Navajo. He was not sent willingly to a boarding school as a child by his parents. When federal agents came to collect him, he tried to hide behind a suitcase and then tried to run from them. Once he was captured, he was taken to a boarding school. He and my mother-in-law who was also a member of the Navajo Nation became Christians as adults. They sent their four children, including his wife, to a Christian-run boarding school.

2. Aicinena served as a coach on the Navajo reservation for seven years. He experience conflict as his values, especially those related to competition, vastly differed from the teenagers he coached. It was common for the gym which accommodated 1,200 spectators to be filled to capacity for basketball games and volleyball playoff games.

Chapter 2

Similarities and Differences between the Gathering of Nations Contest Powwow and a University of New Mexico Lobo Basketball Game

INTRODUCTION

The current study focuses upon the Native American cultural festival known as the contest powwow.[1] Before beginning our academically focused review of literature, we provide background information salient to the development of the line of research that starts in this chapter and continues throughout the book. As is often the case, completion of this first research project led logically to those that followed.

From 1979 to 1986 Aicinena worked with Native American students at Crownpoint High School as a high school teacher and coach. Crownpoint is located within an isolated section of the checkerboard area of the Navajo Reservation. The community consisted of a 7-11, Arviso's Market, a laundry, a Kentucky Fried Chicken restaurant, a Bureau of Indian Affairs hospital, a Bureau of Indian Affairs boarding school, a public elementary school, and a public junior high/high school facility in which Aicinena worked. Single family homes and trailer houses were scattered throughout the community. His home was a house trailer located within the high school's teacherage.

The population of Crownpoint was approximately 2,500. Ninety-eight percent of the students Aicinena worked with were Native American and most were members of the Navajo tribe. Many students took long bus rides to school each day as they did not live within the community and English was a second language for a significant percentage of them. Traditional Navajo-speaking students nicknamed him Bilagaana hastiin t'óó diigis (crazy white man) of his never-ending attempts to be humorous. He is married to a member of the Navajo Tribe who worked with him while at Crownpoint.

29

During his time at Crownpoint, Aicinena attended three local powwows sponsored by the high school's Indian club. The description of the powwow below is an amalgamation of memories constructed from the events. Aicinena grew up in a different culture and at the time was trying to make cultural sense of what was witnessed. Information Aicinena gained since his time in Crownpoint is not included in the description of the powwow.

The powwow was a small one-day affair advertised by word of mouth and flyers. Social media did not yet exist. Perhaps 150 community members were present when attendance peaked about 7:00 p.m. A charge of $3 was required for admission to the powwow as it was a fundraiser. Those who brought canned foods received a discount of $1. Children and senior citizens were charged $2 for entry. The bounty of canned goods collected was given to a church that supported a community feeding program. Income was used to pay for the powwow's expenses and the remainder was used to help get Indian club members to a powwow in Durango later in the fall.

The powwow's activities were loosely scheduled: a recommended starting time of 4:00 p.m. was proposed as was the 10:00 p.m. end. As people dribbled into the school's auxiliary gym starting at 3:00 p.m., they claimed seating spaces by placing blankets on the bleachers, benches or by setting down folding chairs behind the benches.

The emcee ran late for the powwow and excused his tardiness by confessing that he functioned on "Navajo Time." The participants who were overwhelmingly Navajo, laughed because they understood. It was non-Natives who had issues with tardiness. A Christian prayer was offered in Navajo at the start of the event by a local minister, but no other religious activity took place that evening.

Most of the older women at the powwow wore skirts, blouses, and shawls that were draped across their shoulders. Some of the younger women wore pants, a blouse, and a shawl. Ribbon shirts, Wrangler jeans, and cowboy boots comprised the regalia of most of the men present.

A feast of Navajo tacos, mutton stew, yeast rolls, and Frito pie was provided at no charge. There was an abundance of food and plenty of pop to go around. Dessert consisted of Loretta brand apple pies. Fry bread made with Bluebird brand flower was sold throughout the event on a made to order basis. Honey or powdered sugar was available for those wishing to sweeten it.

The powwow circle was formed by a series of benches typically employed for basketball and volleyball games and a set of bleachers running along the east wall of the gym. One drum group consisting of six singers provided the music and song. Most of the dances were intertribal and anyone who wished to dance was welcome to. The dancers moved in a counterclockwise direction. A head man and head lady dancer led the way for each dance and the people danced as the spirit moved them. No competitions were held during the event.

The cheeks of the young children glowed red from running around the facility throughout the evening. Many of the kids pretended to shoot basketballs at the goals on the north and south ends of the gym. The emcee reminded parents that they should keep their children from running through the circle.

Committee members busied themselves selling tickets for a raffle and cakewalk for much of the event but socialized frequently as they did. Handshakes were conducted with a light grasping of hands. It was not the Navajo way to grip another's hand firmly, for doing so is to commit a disrespectful act. In the soft grasping of hands, mutual respect was conveyed.

During a break between sets of songs, a blanket was placed near the drum in the powwow circle. As a song was performed, a collection was taken for the drum. When the song ceased and the collection had concluded, the emcee placed the money upon the drum and thanked the singers for participating in the powwow. Later in the evening, a collection was taken in the same manner for a family whose home had burned down.

Most people passed time at the powwow reacquainting themselves with extended family and friends. Many conversations occurring between adults took place in Navajo. Few of the elders spoke English. Fluency in English seemed to correlate with socioeconomic standing and age. There were multitudes of smiles and spontaneous choruses of laughter throughout the event.

The powwow committee conducted giveaways at different times. Pendleton blankets with stunning designs, intricate star quilts, food baskets, and other items were gifted to elders and those who assisted in making the powwow a reality. Short speeches were made by the emcee and members of the powwow committee to extend gratitude even further. The value placed upon generosity and sharing was prominent.

The powwow ended at no specific time. People left before the last dance. Many hung around long after the drum became silent and had been lovingly carried to the truck for its ride home. Who knew when they would be together again?

When traveling to Albuquerque during the time Aicinena worked at Crownpoint, he often observed a billboard located on the western side of the city along Interstate 40 advertising the Gathering of Nations (GON) Powwow. He read that it was North America's largest powwow. The prospect of seeing the largest or grandest of anything interested him. Like most Americans, Aicinena believed bigger is better. But he never made it to the event during his time at Crownpoint. Aicinena was always coaching at track meets when the event took place in April.

In the spring of 2016, Aicinena decided he would travel from his home in Texas to Albuquerque and attend the GON Powwow. He anticipated that it would be a grand event, but the size of the affair, the sights, and the sounds far exceeded any preconceptions he harbored. At times he was emotionally overcome with what he saw and heard. On several occasions, tears streamed down his face.

To get to the parking lot for the GON, a traffic jam had to be negotiated. Aicinena noted that it was like getting to a University of New Mexico Lobo basketball game. Going through security reminded him of getting into a Lobo basketball game. The more that Aicinena observed at the GON, the more similar the environment and peripheral activities seemed to resemble those of a Lobo basketball game.

In the current study we first sought to determine if the GON contest pow-wow and a University of New Mexico Lobo basketball game could be classified as spectacles. Our second goal was to determine how the promotion and staging of the two festivals were similar and how they might differ.

REVIEW OF LITERATURE

In this review of literature, we discuss the cultural functions of festivals and demonstrate that powwows and athletic events such as collegiate basketball games are cultural festival. We then explain that both contest powwows and intercollegiate basketball games are commercialized events that depend upon income for their continuation. Finally, we describe the characteristics of spectacles.

Festivals

Festivals are events at which people join with one another to celebrate cultural values and traditions. Festivals are built around green chili, art, music, sports, cars, tulips, rattlesnakes, scorpions, and about anything else a cultural group values and might wish to celebrate. Falassi (1987) noted that festivals are social activities observed in cultures throughout the world. Festivals are defined as, "regular events of a festive character, taking place over one or more days and providing a set of performances, exhibitions and entertainment portals focused on a given genre" (Maurin & Watson, 2019, p. 171).

According to Crespi-Vallbona and Richards (2007), "Cultural festivals seem to be ubiquitous in modern societies" (p. 103). The number conducted annually has steadily increased in countries from Kenya (Akoth, 2017) to the islands of the Caribbean in recent decades (Maurin & Watson, 2019). Iyengar and Durham (2009) reported that within the United States, 1,413 outdoor cultural and arts festivals were conducted in 2008. Over 100 million people attended them. In France, 10,000 cultural programs and festivals took place in

2015 (Pellerin, 2015) and in Catalunya, over 4,000 festivals are held annually (Crespi-Vallbona & Richards, 2007).

Social Functions of Festivals

Festivals are important pathways for expression of social identity and otherness (Maurin & Watson, 2019; Ohri, 2016). Through festivals, cultural groups celebrate oneness as they demonstrate and garner collective pride (Beth, 2005; Crespi-Vakkbona & Richards, 2007). Social activities such as festivals are necessary because communities cannot exist if they fail to join and act in common (Durkheim, 1915).

According to Ohri (2016), festivals are unrivaled platforms upon which culture is performed. The gatherings also provide opportunity for culture to be consumed (Waterman, 1998). To members identifying with the culture, festivals are celebrations of their culture (Ohri, 2016). To cultural outsiders and youths, festivals are often viewed as opportunities to meet others and to have fun.

Through performances at festivals, values are enacted, and meanings are embodied (Ohri, 2016). Traditional performance of community rituals used to be considered doing work for the gods. At festivals, performances of culture are now a product of heritage worthy of maintaining (Ohri, 2016). Traditional forms of dance and music are important aspects of cultural identity that are maintained through performances within festivals (Folkestad, 2002).

Participation in festivals provides members of cultural groups living in urban environments a sense of belonging (Popescu & Corbos, 2012). The need for urban residents to maintain cultural ties has motivated The Native American Indian Association of Tennessee to conduct an annual contest powwow for the past 39 years even though there are no reservations in the state (NAIA, 2021). Events off reservations are important cultural events as they allow those identifying as Native American and living within a city access to their traditional culture.

Cultural festivals have been devalued by critics worldwide because at public festivals, "traditional culture" is being replaced with "popular" culture (Chang & Hsieh, 2017; Crespi-Vallbona & Richards, 2007). Often, activities included in festivals deviate from those of tradition (Chang & Hsieh, 2017). Most traditionalists agree that festivals should be held because of their importance in maintenance of culture, but they disagree with modernists concerning event content and aims. Traditionalists view festival promoters as social outsiders, and they see it is their duty to express displeasure with public festivals in the name of cultural preservation (Ohri, 2016). An example of refusal to allow tribal festival traditions to change in style or form and refusal to allow them to become commercialized is provided by the Iroquois "socials."

The Iroquois social or *guyno,so, ohn anndwadek, note,gawdoe* is a group of 20 songs used in public for social entertainment that have no contemporary religious significance (Logan, 1993). The Rochester, New York, Native American Community conducts four Iroquois socials a year (Krouse, 2001). Most are small events involving a few hundred people. Unlike plains style powwows, large drums are not used, instead water drums and cow horn rattles are used as is Iroquois tradition. The social's dances include the Fish Dance, Duck Dance, and Smoke Dance. Dances used in plains style powwows are not included in the socials. However, the feasting, giveaways, raffles, and socializing common to the socials would feel quite familiar to aficionados of plains style powwows.

The sponsors of the Rochester Iroquois socials face continual pressure to include aspects of plains powwows in the events. This is in part due to involvement of Natives from multiple tribes. On one occasion, a powwow drum and singers were invited to perform at a social. Several Iroquois objected at the use of the foreign drum because it was averse to tradition. The large drum was disinvited in the name of preserving Iroquois tradition. The organizing committee refused to allow the Pan-Indianizing of the event. It also has committed to prevent the socials from becoming commercialized and no vendors are permitted to sell items. The prohibitions of foreign instruments, dances, and commercial activity will help the socials remain traditional for the next generation of Iroquois.

Festivals have not always been used in positive ways. The 1904 St. Louis World's Fair was a festival at which Native Americans and their culture were featured, but the event was also used by organizers to demonstrate the superiority of American culture and American Imperialism to the world (Swensen, 2019). Recreated villages in the fair's "Congress of Nations" provided housing for over 500 representatives from twenty-nine Indigenous people groups from around the world. A cliff-dwelling structure was crafted in which Hopi and Zuni tribal members lived and sold baskets and pots. Visitors could walk through the villages, see traditional homes, and watch the people go about their daily activities. By putting Native Americans and Indigenous people from around the world on display, it was presumed that visitors would understand that Social Darwinism was real, and that social evolutionary superiority was to be found in American culture. The collection of Indigenous peoples was referred to as the "The Human Zoo" (Dyreson, 1993).

Cultural festivals are also sites in which cultures are made visible to others. The visibility provided through festivals affords cultural groups the opportunity to challenge the dominant culture's view of them as a people (Crespi-Vallbona & Richards, 2007; Henry, 2010; Ohri, 2016). Powwows as festivals provide Native Americans' visibility and a voice. Through the powwow festival, Native Americans express to all, "We're still here!"

Contest Powwows as Festivals

Native Americans have been described as a dancing people (Ellis, 2003). We use the term "powwow" to refer to Native American cultural festivals based upon song and dance. According to Jackson (2005), music and dance are prominent and embedded within the Native American powwow festival complex. During powwows, feasting, camping, gift giving, singing, and dancing take place along with other culturally significant activities. There were over 1,000 powwows listed by Hutchens (2006) in the publication *Powwow Calendar 2007*. Powwows may be single or multiple-day events.

The term "powwow" is not used by all tribal groups to refer to their song and dance festivals. "Wacipi," meaning dance in Dakota and Lakota, is often used in place of the term "powwow" (Black Hills and Badlands, n.d.). Other tribal groups throughout North America may call their culturally specific song- and dance-centric festivals as gatherings, doings, stomps, or socials. The term powwow has no meaning to some Native Americans as they never use the term nor hear it spoken in their communities.

The Omaha tribe's annual harvest celebration is the oldest documented powwow. The event started out as a traditional spiritual He'dewachi harvest dance (Ridington et al., 2005). The Omaha people came together annually for the harvest dance to give thanks to Creator for the harvest, to share food, and to participate in song and dance traditions. When the 200th rendition of the festival was held in 2004, tribal historian Wynema Morris noted, "It's a milestone and I think it speaks to our ability to endure over the centuries and to maintain our traditions and culture and it confirms us as a people with a special identity" (Linck, 2004, p. 4).

Powwow festivals are a way for Native American tribes to share their culture with others. They are also a way to demonstrate "Indianness" (Kavanaugh, 1983). When Native Americans perform publicly, they are being Indigenous as they engage in Native culture (Slater, 2010).

Competition is not a component of traditional Native American powwows. However, competition is integral to the contest powwow. The competitive aspect of the contest powwow adds additional drama and interest to the singing and dancing characteristic of the festivals.

The grandest of today's contest powwows is the GON which has been referred to as the, "Super Bowl of all Indian Powwows" (Dell'Angela, 2003, p. 2). The two-day event, preceded by the Miss Indian World contest, is held each April in Albuquerque, New Mexico. The GON involves more than 3,500 competitive dancers. Over $200,000 in prize money is awarded and it is estimated that 150,000 spectators attend the powwow each year (Nathanson, 2018). Participants in the 2018 GON represented 526 of the tribes recognized by the U.S. government and 220 Canadian First-Nations groups (Larse, 2018). Other large intertribal contest powwows include the Denver March, Black Hills Powwow, Red Earth Festival, Stanford, Eastern Shoshone Indian Days, Choctaw Labor Day Festival, Cherokee National Holiday, Manito Ahbee, Marvin "Joe" Curry Veterans, Tesoro Indian Market, Coushatta, Julyamash, and Rocky Boy. There are others. Numerous contest powwows, including the GON, are broadcast over Internet radio and video sites such as iHeart Radio, Facebook, and Powwows.c om (Gathering of Nations, 2018a; Powwows.com, 2021).

NCAA Division I Basketball Games as Festivals

NCAA Division I basketball games are cultural festivals. Sport provides human beings with a reason to congregate and an opportunity to identify with something larger than themselves (Eitzen, 2009). Thousands of college basketball fans come together to watch regularly scheduled contests. Excitement is generated through the games and their ancillary activities. Performance is found within the athletic contests themselves but can also be observed in performances of non-athletes such as cheer leaders, vocalists, and musicians. The festivals are built upon the cultural genre of sport. In sport, culture is made visible through the language spoken, foods and merchandise sold, the music played, and the sport forms on display.

According to the Council of Europe, "Sports provide young people with opportunities for social interaction through which they can develop the knowledge, skills and attitudes necessary for their full participation in civil society" (Council of Europe, 2021, p. 2). Sage et al. (2019) report that sports teach participants the values of competition, external conformity, materialism, progress, and work ethic. Each of the values is important to success in postmodern America. Competitive sport aligns with Christian values such as the Protestant work ethic in that it inculcates the importance of a time ethic, achievement of status, individualism, goal-directedness, rationalism, worldly asceticism, and demonstration of moral worth. Within the Super Bowl, and we believe in collegiate basketball contests, one can observe the value placed upon specialization, the military, financial success, personal achievement, teamwork, consumerism, patriotism, and violence (Eitzen, 2015). Eitzen (2009) also explains that sport mirrors the human experience. Victory, defeat, pain, and transcendence are experienced and observed in sport. Excellence is performed in athletic contests and spectators witness it. Sport also conveys to participants and spectators alike that the only thing certain in life is uncertainty.

The Commercialization of Cultural Festivals

In the past, festivals were small local affairs that might have been organized around cheese rolling in England, radishes in Mexico, ice sculptures in

Norway, or beer in Germany (Chang & Hsieh, 2017; Popescu & Corbos, 2012). But today, festivals can draw thousands of visitors and have become significant generators of income and tax revenues.

For any festival to generate broad appeal and grow, people outside of the community must become aware of the event, it must capture the interest of others, others must have access to the event, and visitors must enjoy themselves to the point of wanting to return. Satisfied visitors are more likely to recommend that family and friends attend any given festival (Chang & Hsieh, 2017). Festival sponsors often conduct opinion surveys to determine visitor satisfaction and the results are used to make improvements in the promotion and staging of the events.

A focus upon tourism and socioeconomic development led communities to invest in and promote cultural festivals. Cultural festivals are important in generation of individual income for vendors, performers, promoters, event staff, event administrators, and income for businesses such as hotels and restaurants. Festivals have also become important generators of tax revenues (Chang & Hsieh, 2017; Crespi-Vakkbona & Richards, 2007; Maurin & Watson, 2019).

Throughout the world, cultural festivals have become market oriented, and they are evaluated by how many people attend, how many hotel rooms are booked, and how much money visitors spend (Crespi-Vakkbona, & Richards, 2007; Shin & Stevens, 2013). Festivals are marketed as is any product.

The Contest Powwow as a Commercial Enterprise

Economics are important to the sponsorship and success of modern contest powwows. This fact has been given little attention in the existent powwow literature. Urban community leaders view powwows as important to tourism and generation of tax revenues (Arndt, 2005). Native American tribal leaders understand that public display of culture can provide income for the tribe and its members. Illustratively, the Monacan's annual powwow is the primary source of income for the tribe (Cook et al., 2005).

A significant investment of time, money, and effort are required to raise the income required to put on large powwows (Arndt, 2006). For the events to be sustainable, income must be generated to pay for their promotion and staging. Ticket sales are important to the sustainability of contest powwows. Powwow organizers often seek financial assistance from philanthropic organizations, city governments, state governments, and branches of the federal government through grants. Sales of branded merchandise help to advertise specific powwows and generate income for them (Albers & Medicine, 2005). Sponsorship funds provided by casinos, major corporations, and local businesses are also important to the financial viability of large contest powwows.

Mismanagement of funds, unsuccessful promotion, and poor staging of contest powwows can lead to significant financial losses. For example, the Seminole Tribe's annual powwow exceeded its budget by $104,000 in 1992 (Fitzgerald, 1992).

Big money is up for grabs on the powwow circuit and the amount of prize money available at specific powwows helps some dancers and singers determine what powwows they will participate in (Albers & Medicine, 2005; Ellis, 2005; Ellis & Lassiter, 2005). The GON distributes $200,000 in prize money (New Mexico Nomad, 2020). The Black Hills powwow offers $100,000 in prize money (Lockett, 2018). At the San Miguel Powwow, $250,000 in prize money is dispensed each year (Robles, 2018). Some Native American families generate their annual incomes through contest powwow winnings (Albers & Medicine, 2005).

Vendor markets are regular fixtures at contest powwows. Markets are popular with visitors and sales are an important source of income for Native American artisans and craftsmen (Gagnon, 2013; Rendon & Markusen, 2004). Tourists most often purchase Native American art at powwows. Robert DesJarlait and Jeff Savage observed that most Native Americans don't have money to purchase art (Rendon & Markusen, 2004).

Many Native American vendors complain about the cost of booths required to sell food and merchandise at contest powwows. The larger and more popular a powwow is, the more the organizers tend to charge for booths. When large numbers of vendors are present at a powwow, it becomes more difficult for craftsmen to sell their arts, crafts, and food because of the amount of competition (Gagnon, 2013). Native vendors also complain about the propriety of non-Natives making and selling Native American style crafts at contest powwows.

The IRS (n.d.) has published guidelines for Native Americans concerning reporting of income generated through powwows. Clarification concerning income declaration is offered to committee members, announcers, drummers, dancers, concessionaires, raffle winners, and others. In response to the IRS guidance, contest powwow coordinators require winners to provide social security information and the victors must complete forms that were not required in decades past. A bewildered powwow coordinator stated on Powwows.com, "A reality of some modern powwows is that you have to fill out a tax form with your social security number in order to get big prize money and head staff/host drum honorariums these days" (Powwows.com, 2005, p. 2).

Some economic impact figures have been generated for contest powwows, but they are few and difficult to find. The GON had a $22 million economic impact on the city of Albuquerque, New Mexico, in 2019 (Navajo-Hopi

Observer, 2021). The Red Earth Festival provided $9 million to the Oklahoma City economy in 2010 (Mcdonnell, 2011). Nott et al. (2018) reported that the Lumbee Dance of the Spring Moon powwow contributed $591,000 to the regional economy. Depending upon the popularity of specific contest powwows with singers, dancers, and spectators, the economic impact of a contest powwow can be significant.

Modern contest powwows are highly commercialized events; however, commercialization was not an aspect of traditional powwows in the past nor is it today. As explained earlier, the activities taking place in commercialized cultural events often depart from those of tradition. Understandably, Native American traditionalists consider large intertribal contest powwows to be inauthentic representations of Indigenous culture (Coyne, 1990). Noted Native American activist Russell Means picketed at the GON entrance in 1990. The sign he carried said, "Dancing for Dollars" (Dell'Angela, 2003, p. 18). American Indian Movement cofounder Dennis Banks suggested that the GON would be more aptly named, "Gathering of Dollars" (Coyne, 1990). Dancers such as Josef Reiter have concluded that many competition powwows are driven by profits rather than art and culture (Rendon & Markusen, 2004). Melonie Mathews, a member of the GON powwow committee, disagreed. She explained that money is required to put on the huge cultural event. But it must be exciting if the Native American values, traditions, and knowledge are to be passed on to the next generation, "Some people call it commercialism, but you have to make this culture palatable to young people or it is going to die out" (Dell'Angela, 2003, p. 13).

College Basketball as a Commercial Enterprise

The following financial summaries generated from the Equity in Athletics Data Analysis tool (U.S. Department of Education, 2020) demonstrate that college athletics, including men's basketball, at the Division I level are, indeed, businesses. The University of Texas, one of the NCAA's premiere programs, spent $149,499,361 and secured $168,023,540 in revenue. The University of New Mexico, a mid-major athletic program, spent $37,576,010 on its athletic program while generating $24,448,617 in income. The University of Texas men's basketball team had expenses of $10,494,885 and income of $13,322,731. The University of New Mexico men's basketball team spent $4,178,669 and raised $4,176,344 in income.

In hopes of increasing interest in their men's basketball program, enhancing team success, and increasing basketball revenue, the University of New Mexico hired well-known coach Rick Pitino in March of 2021. Pitino's six-year contract was guaranteed at $4,975,000. Additional income will be provided if various performance criteria are met (Fuller, 2021).

According to Banjo (2011), government leaders have come to agree that sports events are a catalyst for socioeconomic development, cultural revival, infrastructural renewal, and development of tourism (p. 416). In states such as New Mexico, the government partially funds operations of collegiate athletic programs. In other states, such as Texas, use of state money to fund collegiate athletic programs is prohibited by law.

When people buy a ticket to an athletic event, they want to be entertained (Eldridge, 2019). Although sports fans attend athletic events because of the competition, many people choose to attend sports events because of the concessions, ancillary entertainment, and opportunities to socialize (Armstrong et al., 2019).

Fan satisfaction is important as dissatisfied fans will not come back and future revenue is lost. Several activities are conducted at basketball games to maintain fan interest. Pre, post, and dead time activities such as dance team performances, cheer squad performances, band performances, and the playing of popular music and videos keeps the activity level and fan interest high as do giveaways and social media engagement activities (Pratt & Pride, 2020; Ruehle, 2017; Spiller et al., 2018; Tamari, 2017; Taylor, 2017).

It is common to see activities during breaks in which participants have an opportunity to win large cash prizes such as hole in one putting challenges and half court shots. Other activities used to fill breaks include dizzy bat races, relays, eating contests, and kiss cams. A good selection of food and beverage concessions is important to fan satisfactions as is their quality (Megargee, 2019; Ruehle, 2017; Spiller et al., 2018). College athletic departments survey fans to determine their level of satisfaction with the game day experience. Because fan satisfaction is important to a program's viability, athletic departments are always looking for ways to keep fans happy and to enhance the game day experience (UNM, 2020).

Excellence in promotion and staging are necessary if commercial success is to be achieved in any collegiate sport endeavor (Armstrong et al., 2019). Job titles related to promotion and staging of events such as basketball games include directors, assistant directors, and assorted staff in athletic administration, business, communications, concessions, creative services, event management, facilities management, marketing, ticketing, and property management (Golobos.com, 2021).

Spectacles

Festivals may range in the number of spectators from a few hundred to tens of thousands, most festivals remain local are held in small communities and have small budgets (Waterman, 1998). Small local powwows, such as the Crownpoint powwow described earlier, are small affairs. Few outsiders would have been amazed by what they witnessed at the Crownpoint powwow, and the event would not have been considered spectacular. In comparison, the GON powwow with 11,000 cheering spectators, drums rhythmically pounding and singers harmonizing at 110 decibels, and 3,500 dancers in colorful regalia filling the arena floor as one is something spectacular.

In similar fashion, small basketball games do not excite the senses and imagination in the same way as do larger events. Small college basketball games at an NCAA Division III institutions averaged 327 fans per game in 2020, but NCAA Division I institutions averaged 4,689 fans per game (NCAA, 2020). The attendance leader for 2019–2020 averaged 21,704 per game (Wittry, 2020). The grandness of well-attended Division I basketball games makes them spectacular and memorable.

Festivals in and of themselves are not spectacles. A spectacle is something extraordinary, bigger than life, striking, stupendous and grand. When people witness a spectacle, it is indelibly etched within their memory. According to Manning (1992), a spectacle is a, "large-scale, extravagant cultural production that is replete with striking visual imagery and dramatic action that is watched by a mass audience" (291).

The chariot races and gladiatorial combats of Ancient Rome were spectacles employed by leaders to entertain the masses and display the power of Rome as well as that of the sponsors (Kyle, 2015; Moore, 2001). Chariot races were viewed by as many as 150,000 Romans. Beast hunts and gladiatorial combats were watched by 50,000 screaming Romans in the Colosseum.

Today, worldwide spectacles include mega-sports events such as the World Cup and the Olympic Games. In the United States the Super Bowl, NBA Championships, and baseball World Series are mega-sport spectacles. Each event involves armies of administrators and staff, massive investments of time and money. The valued cultural activity (sport) and related activities are well-coordinated so that the production runs smoothly. The sights and sounds of the event are loud, reflective of the culture, and visually stunning. Thousands watch sport spectacles in person and millions watch them on televisions and streaming devices.

Cultural events can also be classified as spectacles. The annual South by Southwest music festival (SXSW), for example, is a music festival, but it is also a spectacle. In 2016, the event saw a total attendance exceeding 280,000, a production cost of $159.7 million, and a contribution of $317 million to the economy of Austin, TX (Theis, 2016). To make the SXSW possible, effective promotions and staging are required. SXSW is a large-scale event compared to a small local music festival involving one performer and a few hundred spectators. SXSW is an extravagant cultural production requiring great expense. It requires the participation of hundreds of musicians, vendors, and staff. Striking visual imagery is provided through the size of the crowds, light shows and pyrotechnics. Dramatic action is provided through excellence of performance delivered by musicians. Finally, SXSW is viewed by a mass audience of over a quarter of a million people.

The first goal of the current study is to determine if the GON contest pow-wow and a University of New Mexico Lobo basketball game meet the characteristics of spectacles as defined by Manning (1992). Our second goal is to determine how the promotion and staging of the GON and a New Mexico Lobo men's basketball game are similar and how they might differ.

METHODS

We employed participant observation as a tool to conduct the current qualitative research study. Our study describing the similarities and differences between the GON contest powwow and the University of New Mexico Lobo (Lobo) men's basketball game is field based and ethnographic. This method provides strong validity, objectivity, and accurate information while reducing limitations including potential research bias and generalizability of the research findings (Charmaz, 2006).

The first goal of our study is to determine if the GON and a Lobo basketball game are sport spectacles. The five characteristics of spectacles identified by Manning (1992) will be used as the criterion for making the determination. Are the events large-scale, extravagant cultural productions replete with striking visual imagery, and dramatic action, watched by mass audiences?

The second goal of our study is to determine the similarities and differences in the promotion and staging of the GON and Lobo men's basketball game. We searched for information about the events online and purchased tickets to the events online. Round-trip travel to Albuquerque, New Mexico, from Odessa took 12 ½ hours by car. Travel took place the day before and after the events. First author attended four sessions of a single GON powwow and a Lobo basketball game as a paying customer.

Observations from the field served as the foundation for assembling our findings. Field notes were taken during each event concerning each of the factors assessed and used for comparisons. Photographs were taken at the GON and Lobo game to assist in making comparisons. Use of photographs helped us develop structure and order for our findings. Photographs also assisted us to identify markers of cultural and tribal identity (Ziyanak, 2014).

Field observations concerning the Lobo basketball game were made during a home game against Colorado State University on March 2, 2019. Observation of the Lobo game involved approximately three-and-a-half hours (6:50 p.m.–10:18 p.m.) beginning with first author's arrival at the parking lot until departure from it. The game was held at UNM's facility known as "The Pit."

Observations relating to the GON were made April 27 and April 28, 2018. The GON was held at Tingley Coliseum, located on the New Mexico State Fairgrounds. First author was on the powwow grounds and at the contest powwow for eleven hours each day (11:00 a.m.–11:00 p.m.). He arrived one hour before the scheduled start of the powwow. Observations and field notes were taken from the time the parking lot was entered until the time the parking lot was exited.

Nineteen factors important in the promotion and staging of NCAA Division I collegiate basketball games were used to compare the promotion and staging of the GON Powwow and Lobo basketball game. Eighteen factors were taken from the *Champion Your City: NCAA Site Selection document* (NCAA, n.d.). All 18 factors are considered in the selection of host sites for NCAA Basketball Championship Tournament games. The importance of 15 of the 18 factors to the fan experience was further validated in publications authored by Kennett et al. (2001), Sarstedt et al. (2014), and Zhou (2015). The provision of entertainment before events and during breaks was deemed important to the fan experience by Armstrong et al. (2019), Sarstedt et al. (2014), and Zhou (2015). Pre-event and break entertainment was added to the list of factors to be assessed in the current study. The final list of nineteen promotional and staging considerations was reviewed by a NCAA Athletic Director with over thirty years of administrative experience at the Division I level. The Athletic Director agreed that the list of nineteen factors was both complete and valid. The nineteen factors evaluated in the present study are presented in alphabetical order within table 2.1.

After establishing the list of nineteen factors important in the staging and promotion of athletic events, the focus of the current study was to determine if all factors were common to both the GON and Lobo basketball game, which might be absent, and how the nature of the factors may have differed in the two settings. For example, if concessions are sold at the basketball game, are they sold in the contest powwow setting? If so, how do the concessions sold differ in variety?

FINDINGS

The first goal of the current study is to determine if the GON and Lobo basketball game meet the definitional characteristics of a spectacle provided by Manning (1992). Are the events large-scale, extravagant cultural productions

Table 2.1   The List of 19 Factors in the Staging and Promotion of Athletic Events

Factor	NCAA	ZHOU	KSH	SRRG	AD
Advertising	X				C
Cleanliness of Facility	X		FE	FE	C
Competition/Opponents	X	FE		FE	C
Food & Drink Concessions	X	FE	FE	FE	C
Event Staff	X	FE	FE		C
Game Programs	X				C
TV/Video/Radio	X				C
Merchandise Concessions	X	FE	FE	FE	C
Officials	X				C
PA Announcer and Announcements	X	FE	FE		C
Public Address System	X	FE	FE	FE	C
Parking	X		FE	FE	C
Pre-Event and Break Activities		FE		FE	C
Seating	X	FE	FE		C
Security	X		FE	FE	C
Sponsor Signage	X	FE			C
Social Media	X	FE			C
Ticket Sales	X		FE		C
Video Boards/Scoreboards	X	FE		FE	C

Note: (PS) Promotional and Staging Considerations Identified by the NCAA; (FE) Fan Experience Factors Identified by Kennett, Sneath, & Henson (KSH), Zhou, and Sarstedt, Ringle, Raithel, & Siegfried (SRRS) as being important; (C) Confirmed by an NCAA Division I Athletic Director (AD).

replete with striking visual imagery, and dramatic action, that are watched by mass audiences?

The Gathering of Nations and Lobo Basketball Games Are Spectacles

Both the GON and Lobo basketball game are large-scale events. Media specialists, designers, printers, ticket sellers, traffic attendants, concession-aires, announcers, isle attendants, security staff, administrators, and others are required to plan, promote, and conduct each aspect of the events, which thousands of spectators attend. Thousands attend both events.

The extravagance of both events is reflected by the production quality of related activities and the cost of attendance. Each aspect of the events is controlled, timed, and choreographed with the goal of providing optimal customer experiences. Lighting systems, sound systems, giant video screens, and the size and comfort of the venues are testaments to the extravagance common to the two events.

Significant amounts of money are invested and generated as the events are planned, promoted, and staged. According to the U.S. Department of Education (2021) the University of New Mexico spent $4,206,654 on men's basketball and the team generated $4,206,654 in 2019–2020. The GON reported income of $648,000 and expenses of $667,743 for the 2014 tax year (ProPublica, n.d.). The amount of money spent and generated through the GON and Lobo basketball program are evidence of extravagance.

Striking displays of cultural imagery were observed at the Lobo game and GON. During grand entries at the GON, over 3,500 Native Americans in full regalia danced into the arena and gathered on the arena floor as one to the sounds of beating drums and wailing voices. During the Lobo game, athletes, cheerleaders, dance squads, and fans wore the colors of the home team branded with university-approved logos. At times, it seemed that the Pit was awash in a sea of red. In unison, spectators sang fight songs and make hand gestures that symbolized a Lobo. University of New Mexico flags sporting a snarling wolf adorned the facility and were carried aloft by spirit squad members.

Both the GON and Lobo basketball game provided dramatic action. Competition in dance and song provided dramatic action as competitions were conducted and as dance-offs were staged to determine winners through the process of elimination. During the Lobo game, drama was noted as individuals competed in 1 on 1 match ups, as teams worked together on offense and defense, and as shots were lofted moments before the thirty-second clock expired.

Mass audiences watched the Lobo game and GON. The Saturday evening session of the GON was sold out. Tingley coliseum seats 11,571 spectators. Attendance at the Lobo game was officially 11,207. The Lobo game and GON powwow had very similar attendance numbers. Additional thousands of people viewed the Lobo game on television. On Saturday, the GON emcee announced that as of 3:45 p.m., 1.8 million viewers from sixty-eight countries had watched the powwow live over Internet feeds.

In sum, both the University of New Mexico Lobo basketball game and the GON contest powwow are large-scale extravagant cultural events replete with striking visual imagery and dramatic action that are watched by mass audiences. Both events are correctly classified as spectacles.

Promotion and Staging Similarities and Differences

The similarities and differences in the nineteen factors involved in promoting and staging the GON and Lobo game are addressed in table 2.1. We begin with how a prospective spectator might find information concerning the events, and purchase tickets. The other factors are presented in the same order that notes were taken during the events.

As a means of advertising their events, both the Lobos and the GON had a presence on the "Visit Albuquerque" (City of Albuquerque) website. The GON was also advertised on "New Mexico True" (New Mexico Tourism

Department) website. If looking for something to do in Albuquerque, information about the powwow and Lobo basketball could be found by individuals interested in attending a spectacle.

The GON and Lobos support websites that provided information concerning dates and times of events, ticket-purchasing opportunities, and information pertinent to each event. Each entity also maintains social media sites including Facebook and Twitter pages. The GON has 87,030 followers on its Facebook page, and the Lobo basketball team has 1,391 followers. The Lobos basketball team has nearly twenty thousand Twitter followers and the GON has over five thousand. Social media is used to advertise events and highlight specific stories associated with each organization.

Both the GON powwow and the UNM Athletic Department charge admission to their events and tickets are available for purchase online. In 2018, the Lobos charge $22–$40 for reserved seats with a chairback. Reserved seating with chairbacks at the GON cost $32.50 per day. Patrons who have not purchased tickets online or on the phone are able to purchase tickets at walk-up window sales points at the Lobo game and GON. The cost to attend the events is quite similar.

Parking fees are charged for patrons of Lobo games and the GON Powwow. Parking for the Lobo game is $10. Parking for the GON is $10. Parking lot attendants collected fees and directed patrons to specific spots to expedite parking activity. There is no difference in the price of parking or parking procedures.

Arenas, stadia, and concert halls are built to host spectacles. Both the GON and Lobo game are held in arenas with large seating capacities. Each venue is comfortable and clean. Seating provides good line of site for the Lobo game and GON.

Numerous event staff are observed at the Lobo game and GON. Upon approaching the venues, parking staff collect fees and direct drivers to parking spots. Staff are observed selling tickets in the box office for the Lobo game and at the GON. Staff scan tickets before entry is granted at both venues. Ushers check ticket seating assignments and escort and/or direct patrons to their assigned seats. Concessionaires and merchandise sales staff are noted on the way to purchased seats. Event staff, including public address announcers, are observed at tables on the south end of the arena during the GON and the east end of the arena during the Lobo game.

Security appears to be important at both venues. Spectators entering the Pit for the Lobo game are subjected to security screening which included a bag check to prevent prohibited items including professional-grade cameras, food, drink, and weapons from being taken into the arena. Screening for powwow patrons is more thorough. In addition to bag checks, screenings are expanded to include use of metal-detecting wands at the entrance to the fairgrounds. In both settings, security staff are visible and appear adequate in numbers considering the flow of pedestrian traffic which moves quickly through the security check points. No significant waiting is required to enter either venue.

Programs are sold at the Lobo game and GON. Programs include current information about the powwow or team, history of the powwow or team, information about participants and organizers, printed sponsor advertisements, and sponsor logos. Program sales produced income for the event organizers and enhanced the experience of the patrons by providing information germane to each event. Powwow programs were sold by high school students. The Lobo programs were sold at an area adjacent to the main entry from behind a counter. The emphasis upon program sales was greater at the powwow. I was pressured more to purchase a program at the powwow and had to ask staff at the basketball game where I could purchase one.

Sponsor signage is significantly greater at the Lobo game than at the GON. At the Lobo game, sponsors' logos are featured on the full-color digital videoboard strip surrounding the inside of the facility. At any given time only one sponsor appears. All fans can see the sponsors' logos as they look at the scoreboard or in any direction throughout the facility. Forty-six sponsors appear on the video strip on a rotating basis starting before the time of my arrival (one hour before game time) and through my departure fifteen minutes following conclusion of the game. Sponsor logos also brand the standards supporting the basketball goals.

GON sponsors do not have sponsor signage visible inside Tingley Coliseum. Branding is observed inside the arena, and the signs are permanent, but the logos are not of GON sponsors. Presumably, sponsors pay for their signs to be placed inside the coliseum and exclusivity is part of the contractual agreement. GON sponsor signage is visible within Tingley Coliseum's vestibule. Three GON sponsors have tables at which they distribute information and gifts, and their logos are prominently displayed. Signage acknowledging GON sponsors are also visible throughout the food court and outside the Indian market sales areas.

Sponsor ads appear in programs at the GON and Lobo game. The GON program includes 63 ads not placed by the powwow itself while the Lobo program includes 83 ads not placed by the University of New Mexico or its athletic department. Major corporations deem both spectacles worthy of sponsorship. UNM Athletics sponsors include major corporations such as Blue Cross-Blue Shield, Nike, Coors, Albertsons, Wells Fargo, and others. GON Powwow sponsors include Facebook, Wells Fargo, Bank of America, Whataburger, Marriott, Ultra Health, and Southwest Airlines. Sponsors also have a presence on the Lobo and GON websites.

At the Pit and Tingley Coliseum, powerful public address (PA) systems that include massive speakers and powerful amplification equipment is used to make announcements and play music. Large venues require such systems to ensure information and music can be heard by all patrons and participants.

Both the Lobo basketball games and GON include formalized entrances onto the arena floor and powwow circle respectively. Announcers and the crowd convey excitement as the GON Grand Entries take place and over 3,500 dancers fill the arena floor. Likewise, when the Lobos enter the arena floor before the start of the game, there is considerable hype, hoopla, and cheering.

Introductions and announcements are made before, during and after completion of the GON. The head male dancer, head female dancer, Eagle Staff bearer, tribal groups, dignitaries, and others are introduced by the GON announcers. Age groups, dance types, and the tribal affiliation of various performers are also announced. The GON emcees spend considerable time telling jokes, recounting history, explaining information about activities, providing information about competitors, explaining Native American traditions, and pointing out the values held by Native Americans.

At basketball games, starters and coaches are introduced by the PA announcer, as are substitutes and those charged with violations in play and after scoring. Public service and informational announcements are also made before, during, and after the game.

Veterans are honored and thanked for their service to the country over the PA system during the opening ceremonies of the Lobo game. During opening ceremonies for each session of the GON, drum groups perform a Veterans' Song to honor all veterans and the PA announcer thanks them for their service. Several times during each powwow session, veterans were thanked for their service over the PA system.

At the Lobo game, the announcer asks the crowd to stand and remove their caps to honor the American flag as it is carried on to the floor by a military honor guard before the playing of the National Anthem. The American flag is not visible during the GON opening ceremonies nor was the National Anthem sung. At each session of the GON, the Eagle Staff is carried into the powwow circle and a Flag Song is performed.

At the start of each GON session, a prayer is offered over the PA system in English or a Native American language. Prayers are not offered before the basketball game.

Copious amounts of information focused upon Native American culture are shared over the PA system by the powwow announcer throughout the GON. Information the announcer shares relates to Native American homes, reservations, reservation dogs, foods, humor, values, history, traditions, and much more. Other than thanking the military and asking people to raise for the National Anthem, nothing the basketball announcer shares is related to culture unless it is within the context of sponsor ads and university announcements.

First author measured the noise level during the Lobo game and GON with the dB Meter Pro app. The average of fourteen readings taken during dances and the grand entries is 101 dBs with a high of 110 dBs. The noise level is consistently high at the powwow and the announcer often asks for the decibel level to be turned up. On one occasion, first author experienced pain.

As the Lobo game is being played, the ambient decibel level is seventy-nine. Twelve measurements are taken immediately after interesting plays for which the crowd demonstrates excitement. The average of the twelve measurements is 93.33 dBs. Though both environments are loud, the powwow is typically louder. High decibel levels, upbeat music, powwow songs, and announcements add to the ambiance of the spectacles and helps make them bigger than life experiences.

Before Lobo games, during time stoppages, and after the contest, entertainment is provided through the playing of popular music over the PA system. The UNM pep band, cheer, and dance squads also provide entertainment in conjunction with the Lobo game. Before each session of the GON, musical entertainment is provided by Native American pop and rock performers. Ancillary to the powwow circle, the GON presents live performances throughout the day and evening on "Stage 49," located outside the coliseum. Activities peripheral to the powwow competitions and basketball game add to the interest and perceived importance of the spectacles.

Huge videoboards are located on the northern and southern end of Tingley Coliseum and the Pit that are used to show live play/dancing and replays, in addition to ancillary entertainment and promotional activities. The live stream and video-replays enhance the spectator experience and assists in making the event larger than life.

Both the GON and Lobos provide radio and video broadcasts of their events. In 2018–2019, Lobo basketball games were broadcast live on various television networks including the Mountain West, AT&T SportsNet, Fox Sports, ESPN2, ESPNU, and CBS Sports (golobos.com, 2021). The GON Powwow is not broadcast live on television networks but is streamed live on livestream.com and was made available live and on demand at Powwows .com (Gathering of Nations, 2018a). On Saturday afternoon of the 2018 powwow, it was announced that as of 3:45 p.m., 1.8 million viewers from 68 countries had viewed the powwow live over Internet feeds.

The Lobo radio broadcast is transmitted over the Lobo Radio Network consisting of nineteen stations throughout New Mexico, Colorado, and Arizona (golobos.com, 2021). The GON is broadcast over the Internet by GON Radio (Gathering of Nations, 2018a). The fact that the GON is not broadcast over traditional radio and television networks serves as a notable difference between the two events.

Competition is a component of all collegiate athletic contests. Winners and losers are determined, and results are made public by the local media. The success and failures have importance to the job security and pay of the basketball coaches and department administrators. At the GON powwow, dancers, singers, and drum groups compete for $200,000 in cash prizes in five singing and drum categories and thirty-seven dance categories. Both basketball players and dancers wear numbers as they compete. Competition is an integral aspect of the GON and the Lobo game.

Neither the Lobo basketball players nor GON Powwow competitors are responsible for officiating or judging their own events. Basketball officials make sure that published NCAA men's basketball rules are followed. Eleven powwow judges are responsible for selecting winners in dance competitions based upon traditional criteria applicable to performance of the dance, including how each dancer's regalia's beadwork, and handcrafting contributes to the overall impression of the performance (Gathering of Nations, 2018b). There are also judges for the drum and singing competitions. Officials and judges are present in both environments to make sure that the rules of competition are followed, and outcomes are fair.

Food and beverage concessions are sold by vendors at the Lobo game and GON. At the Lobo game, twenty-five different varieties of food and beverage types are sold. At the GON, food is sold outside Tingley Coliseum by numerous vendors. Hot dogs, hamburgers, chips, fries, nachos, and other typical American sports venue concessions are available in both venues. However, at the GON, traditional native foods are also offered for sale including fry bread, Navajo burgers, mutton stew, kneel-down bread, and others. The variety of concessions is superior at the GON, however, having to purchase them outside is an inconvenience. Beer is sold at the Lobo game but not at the GON.

Merchandise concessions are sold at the Lobo game and GON. At the Lobo game, merchandise including t-shirts, sweatshirts, key chains, mugs, stadium chairs, blankets, football, basketballs, foam hands, flags, stuffed animals, koozies, decals, pom-poms, and stadium cushions, and various other items were sold at the Lobo Den, a store encompassing approximately 1,500 square feet.

Typical souvenir items such as hats, t-shirts, sweatshirts, bumper stickers, key chains, and various other items are sold at the GON, but attendees can also choose from hundreds of traditional native arts and crafts such as dreamcatchers, sand paintings, handmade Native American jewelry, ribbon shirts, shawls, blankets, and more at the Indian Traders Market adjacent to Tingley Coliseum. The number and variety of vendors and objects available for sale is vastly superior at the GON.

DISCUSSION AND CONCLUSIONS

The first goal of the present study was to determine if the GON and or a Lobo basketball game are spectacles. Our findings lead us to conclude that both events encompass the characteristics of spectacles identified by Manning (1992). Each is a large-scale extravagant cultural production replete with striking visual imagery and dramatic action that is watched by a mass audience. Both events are rightly considered spectacles.

We compared nineteen promotional and staging characteristics of the GON and a University of New Mexico Lobo basketball game. All nineteen factors were used by the GON and Lobo basketball in promotion and staging of their respective events. However, twelve differences in their implementation were noted.

Five of the twelve differences we observed between the Lobo basketball game and the GON were related to staging of the events. The screening process was more thorough as patrons and participants entered the powwow grounds: metal-detecting wands were used. The emphasis upon program sales was higher at the powwow. Sponsor signage was more prevalent at the basketball game. The powwow was louder than the basketball game. Though transmission of live audio and video of the powwow occurred, it was not broadcast through traditional radio and television media as was the basketball game.

Seven of the twelve differences we noted between the GON and Lobo basketball game were culturally based. Veterans were acknowledged and thanked more often at the powwow. Notably, Native Americans serve in the military at a higher per capita rate than any other American minority group (Gover, 2015; Naval History, 2017; WTOP, 2017). This high rate of military service is often explained by the Native Americans' love of country and the cultural tradition of the warrior spirit.

The variety of food and drink concessions and merchandise concessions was superior at the GON. At collegiate and professional athletic events, concessions are important, but when traveling to basketball games across the country, concessions are highly similar. Concessions are often identified by fans as being important and in need of improvement. Intertribal contest powwows such as the GON bring together Native American vendors from throughout North America, and they sell the foods, crafts, and clothing popular with their people. In doing so, the vendors share their food and art cultures with others.

The National Anthem was not played at the GON, and the American flag was not honored. According to Flynn (2016), "From a non-Aboriginal perspective, the Eagle Staff can be compared to a national flag: it represents people, states, governments, regiments, and battle honours. Thus, it is an honoured and sacred symbol" (para. 3). The words to a Kiowa Flag Song, translated into English, may serve as an example of a Flag Song, "United States of America, the country I love. I am courageous. United States of America, its staff will always remain standing forever 'til the end of the world" (Heth & Vennum, 1997, p. 13).

Prayers were offered over the PA system at the powwow but not at the basketball game. At public institutions such as the University of New Mexico, religious activity is prohibited by law. At the GON and other powwows Creator/God is given thanks for the opportunity to celebrate and for the safety of those traveling to and from the event. As powwows are not directly sponsored by government entities, prayer is permissible.

At the Lobo game and in American athletic events generally, flag, country, and the military are celebrated before the competition begins. Americans do not have the patience to listen to lengthy presentations before a game begins, so little is typically verbalized, and presentations are short. Breaks in the Lobo games are filled with promotional activities, general announcements, and sponsor advertisements. Values and traditions are displayed at Lobo games but are not explicitly mediated by the announcer. Conversely, abundant information was shared by GON announcers that focused upon Native American tribal and Pan-Indian culture. Through the powwow announcer, values, traditions, and history are shared with all present; Native American children learn them, adults have them reinforced, and non-Natives are given the opportunity to gain a better understanding of America's first peoples.

Small traditional non-contest powwows are typically local affairs and are not highly commercialized. They are often tribal-centric, and outsiders may not be permitted to attend. However, commercialization is necessary to promote and stage large intertribal contest powwows. Commercialization in the form of advertising, admission costs, sales of concessions and merchandise, the awarding of prize money, and extensive sponsorships makes it possible to bring together vendors, dancers, drum groups, and spectators for contest powwows. Commercialization is indispensable to the creation, maintenance, and spread of modern contest powwows. Despite the presence of commercialization, culture remains central to the large intertribal contest powwow.

NOTE

1. Parts of this chapter were previously published in *International Journal of Humanities and Social Sciences* (J-HumanSciences.com) and used with permission. Aicinena, S., & Ziyanak, S. (2019). Examining the GON powwow and a NCAA Division I basketball game. *Journal of Human Sciences*, *16*(3), 875–884. https://doi.org/10.14687/jhs.v16i3.5742

Chapter 3

Contest Powwow Dancing as a Competitive Sport

The Native American powwow has served to maintain and celebrate the culture of North America's Indigenous peoples since before the arrival of European colonialists.[1] Powwows are sites in which cultural persistence, cohesion, and ritual focus are celebrated through song, dance, and social interaction (Dufrene, 1990; Kracht, 1994). Thousands of powwows are conducted each year throughout Canada and the United States (Eschbach & Applbaum, 2000). There currently exist two primary forms of the powwow, the traditional powwow and the contest powwow.

Traditional powwows are typically local events and participants generally include individuals from the same tribal group. Tribal-specific culture is emphasized at traditional powwows. As such, traditional powwows are integral to the continuity of tribal and regional cultural identity (Herle, 1994; Lerch & Bullers, 1996; Scales, 2007). Competition does not typically take place at traditional powwows and is not integral to their structure (DesJarlait, 1997; Herle, 1994).

Competition is an essential component of the contest powwow. Contest powwow dancers must register to compete; they are assigned numbers, and performances are judged and scored. Winners are selected, and cash prizes are awarded. Dancers from various tribal groups compete in numerous age categories and Native American dance styles for prize money and awards. For example, the 2017 Gathering of Nations Powwow sponsored competitions in the Fancy Shawl Dance, Jingle Dance, Traditional Northern Dance, Southern Traditional Dance, Southern Cloth Dance, Northern Cloth Dance, and Southern Buckskin Dance for females in girls, teens, women's, golden age, and elder categories. For males, competitions were offered in the Grass Dance, Fancy Dance, Southern Straight Dance, Northern Traditional Dance, Northern Fancy Dance, Southern Fancy Dance, and the Chicken Dance in boys, teens, men's, golden age, and elder categories. Boys and girls under age five competed in the tiny tots dance events. Cash prizes and awards were issued in a total of thirty-six dance categories (Gathering of Nations, 2018). Over 3,500 dancers were involved in the competitions and in excess of $200,000 in prize money was awarded.

Thousands of people pay to watch large contest powwow competitions conducted within massive arenas that typically host athletic events. Aicinena and Ziyanak (2019) demonstrated that there was a high degree of similarity in the promotion and staging of a large intertribal contest powwow and a mid-major intercollegiate basketball game. Herle (1994) described male competitive powwow dancing and female Fancy Shawl competitions as a, "type of sport" (p. 70) and equated the competitions to Indian rodeos as displays of athletic talent. However, Herle's contention was supported by neither qualitative nor quantitative data.

Native American high school athletes have competed publicly in high school sports since the 1920s and have won numerous state championships in a variety of sports (Sage et al., 2019). High school gymnasia are regularly packed with fans for basketball games at Window Rock, Chinle, and Monument Valley high schools on the Navajo reservation. The annual Lakota Invitational involves Native American high school athletes from several South Dakota reservations. The event is one of Rapid City's most impactful economic events, generating over $3.5 million over a four-day period (Penwell, 2019).

Coaches working in Native American high schools often differ from their athletes culturally and hold values and expectations for behavior reflective of the dominant American individualistic culture (Allison, 1982). Often, non-Native coaches assume that Indigenous athletes share their values and outlook toward competition. However, Native Americans participate in sport on their own terms, often harboring and exhibiting traditional collectivist attitudes and behaviors (Sage et al., 2019). The differences in competitive attitudes, values, goals, and what is deemed acceptable behavior in both Native and non-Native cultures result in conflict for coaches and athletes alike. Many outstanding Indigenous athletes choose not to participate in high school sport because of conflicts caused by differences in traditional cultural values and those of the dominant culture (Simpson, 1987).

Native Americans have embraced American sport and contest powwows share many of the characteristics of sport commonly found within the broader American culture. However, there is no published study in which data has been used to establish whether or not contest powwow dancing is a sport from the competitor's point of view, nor has a published study examined whether or not contest powwow dancing meets any definitional requirements of sport. Whether contest powwow dancing is a sport or not, dancers compete at contest powwows. To date, the competitive attitudes and goals of contest powwow dancers have not been formally assessed. Assessment of the competitive goals and attitudes of competitive powwow dancers may provide insight into the degree to which participants adhere to traditional values while competing in culturally valued dance or to those found within the dominant American culture.

In our current research, we focus on the Native American contest powwow. The purposes of the study are first, to determine if contest powwow dancing can be classified as a sport and how contest powwows dancing might reflect or differ from competitive sports found within the broader American society. Second, we strive to understand the goals and meanings of competition held by contest powwow dancers. Finally, we seek to discern the importance of the contest powwow to Native American cultural identity.

The results of this research will be of interest to sport sociologists and those interested in sport as a reflection of culture. The findings will also be of interest to scholars interested in determining how Western individualistic culture impacts the competitive experiences of Native Americans who have been characterized historically and contemporarily as collectivist in their values and behaviors. Finally, the results will supply teachers and coaches with a deeper understanding of how differences in values may cause conflict as they seek to effectively work with Native American populations.

LITERATURE REVIEW

We utilize sociological and philosophical sources to define sport. We then examine how dancing for profit, intertribalism, and American sport served to contribute to the formation of the modern intertribal contest powwow. In an effort to illustrate how Native American athletes can compete seriously in sport while adhering to collectivist values, we describe the "Medicine Game," a traditional version of lacrosse, as it is played contemporarily by the Iroquois. The Iroquois' reasons for participating, outlook toward competition, and competitive behaviors are demonstrated to differ significantly from those of athletes who have adopted the competitive attitudes and behaviors reflected within the broader American individualistic culture.

What Is Sport?

Sports are social constructions that incorporate the realm of cultural life referred to as physical culture. Sport sociologists have proposed numerous definitions of sport. Sage et al. (2019) observed that there is no universal definition of sport and define sport as consisting of activities involving physical activity and rules. Renowned sport sociologist Jay Coakley (2017) summarized the definitions of sport ascribed to scholars from throughout North America and Europe: "Physical activities that involve challenges or competitive contests" (p. 6).

Philosophers have considered sport as a topic worthy of reflection since the time of the ancient Greeks (Reid, 2011). As is true in the discipline of sport sociology, sport philosophers have tendered numerous definitions of sport (Torres, 2014). According to Devine and Frias (2020), the philosophical definition crafted by Suits (1973) is a classic one. Suits (1973) defined sport as being related to games; games consist of a goal (winning a contest), a means of winning (what constitutes winning the contest), rules (procedures one must follow in seeking victory), and acceptance of the rules of competition. Further, Suits (1973) stated that to be considered a sport, an activity/ game must involve skill, the skill must be physical in nature, the activity must have a wide following, and the activity must demonstrate stability over time.

For the purposes of the current study, we will use Coakley's definition of sport as we seek to determine if contest powwow dancing can be classified as a sport from a sociological perspective. We will turn to Suits' requirements to determine if contest powwow dancing can rightly be classified as a sport from a philosophic perspective.

Dominant and Native American Cultural Attitudes toward Competition

One of the purposes of the current study is to determine in what ways, if any, the competitive attitudes, goals, and behaviors of contest powwow dancers may align with or differ from those associated with the dominant American culture. Subsequently, we examine the dominant cultural attitudes generally held by Native Americans and those common to the dominant American culture.

It is difficult for many influenced by Western individualism, Christianity, and Western dualistic views of life to understand why, despite historic and continuing assimilation efforts, Native Americans and others from collectivist societies do not compete with attitudes similar to their own. We often heard exasperated non-Native American coaches on the Navajo reservation complain that their athletes were not physically aggressive, shied away from contact, refused to hurt others, and did not do what it took to be fully committed to achieving competitive success in sport. The shock that the coaches experienced may have been due to ethnocentrism and the mistaken belief that it was reasonable to expect athletes from a different culture to share the same competitive motives and goals.

The conflict caused by Native American collectivist values and the individualistic values of the dominant American culture within athletic settings were formally studied by Maria Allison (1980, 1982). Adherence to collectivist values and behaviors was considered by coaches to be an impediment to competitive success and to full assimilation into mainstream society. By refusing to wholly assimilate, Native American athletes demonstrated commitment to their culture's traditional collectivist values in the face of pressure to abandon them. According to Sewell (2005), the meaning of high school basketball has been transformed by Native Americans domiciled upon the reservation to meet their cultural needs. Participation affords an opportunity for them to express and retain their Native identity. Sport has often been called a microcosm of society, for sport and how it is played springs forth from culture (Coakley, 2017; Kyle, 2015; Sage et al., 2019). It is reasonable to expect peoples from different cultures to compete in sport with different goals, motivations, attitudes, and values.

Below, we use differences between organized competitive lacrosse and the traditional version of the sport known as the "Medicine Game" of the Iroquois to illustrate differences between Native Americans and non-Native Americans concerning their reasons for participating, outlook toward competition, and competitive behaviors. The Iroquois still proudly conduct Medicine Games. Our description of traditional Native American competitive attitudes, values, and behaviors is gleaned from a depiction of lacrosse when played by the Iroquois as a traditional Medicine Game (Price, 2010). The description of Americanized lacrosse is something manufactured from experiences and observations Aicinena made as a competitive athlete, youth sport coach, high school coach, collegiate coach, collegiate athletic director, and researcher over a forty-three-year period. It is reflective of the power and performance orientation toward sport crafted by Coakley (2017). The contrast in participation motivations, values, and behaviors observed in the playing of the two forms of lacrosse is palatable and must be appreciated if one is to comprehend how it is possible for Native Americans to seriously compete in sport and competitive powwow dancing while rejecting many of the competitive conventions of sport as it is commonly contested within the broader American culture.

Dominant Cultural Attitudes toward Competition

A lacrosse player adhering to the goals and values commonly associated with American sport competes in a formal league. Pick-up games are informal contests played between friends. Pick-up games are not real lacrosse, and they are discouraged by coaches who believe all games are to be played in the correct manner or not at all. Competitions are scheduled well in advance.

Boys, girls, men, and women are segregated and grouped by age and or gender. It is only right that girls and women play, for they should have opportunities equal to males in all sport activities.

The game is played with a manufactured hard rubber ball on finely manicured or artificial fields adorned with regulation goals and markings. Players compete with factory-manufactured lacrosse sticks typically consisting of an aluminum or composite material shaft, plastic heads, and nylon webbing. Athletes believe that technology improves athletic equipment and their performance. When the game is played, referees enforce codified rules.

The ultimate goal of playing is to achieve success. Victory is to be gained through the employment of all necessary means. Winning is everything. To the victors go the spoils and individual worth is proven through competitive success. Standing above the crowd is an important goal of participation.

To the truly committed, it does not matter if cheating or violence is used to elevate one's standing. "Whatever it takes." Injuries are often attributed to cheap shots taken by opponents who purposely injure others as a competitive strategy. An appearance of religiosity may be seen during ubiquitous pre-game prayers but during play, religious mandates for reciprocity are discarded in the name of victory. God is thanked for victory often tainted.

If a lacrosse stick is broken during play, it is discarded, and another is purchased to replace it without a second thought. The world is filled with disposable things made of resources we take and use at our will. The world belongs to humankind and we are in control of it. After the game, a trip to McDonald's is taken to celebrate the day's glory or to anguish over a competitive failure.

Individualism is characteristic of cultural groups within which individuals focus upon the self rather than others (Beckstein, 2014). Members of individualistic cultures are motivated by their personal needs and desires (Triandis, 2018). American, European, and other Western cultures tend to highly value individualism (Sampson, 2000). Individualism has long been associated with modernity, is highly compatible with economic development, and has been associated with the Westernization of Indigenous peoples (Kagitçibasi, 1997). Achievement, recognition, acquisition of possessions, and acquisition of wealth are highly valued goals within individualistic cultures. Mainstream American culture encourages individualism and individualism is reflected ubiquitously within competitive American sport.

Native American Attitudes toward Competition

The traditional form of lacrosse is central to the Iroquois culture and tribal members are reluctant to discuss the traditional form of the sport with outsiders (Price, 2010). It is known as the "Medicine Game." Medicine Games can be organized any time during the year and are called whenever a tribal member is in need of comfort or healing. Medicine Games are often held in conjunction with funerals and lacrosse sticks are frequently buried with the dead, for it is believed that those who pass will play on through eternity. The game itself is a gift from the Creator. All players are recipients of the good medicine supplied by the Creator through competition. Playing is viewed as a means to thank him for blessings provided.

Games are held in the traditional manner, sometimes until three goals are scored and at other times to five goals. Unmarked open fields sport two posts wedged into the ground that serve as goals. An unlimited number of males from age seventy down to age seven take the field at the same time. Handmade deerskin balls used to play the game are given to individuals who are suffering, for they are considered good medicine.

Only traditional handmade wooden sticks can be used in Medicine Games. The wooden lacrosse stick is believed to be a gift from Mother Earth. A good stick may take more than one year to craft. Its webbing is made of cow gut. Through the stick, the spirit of the sacrificial tree becomes one with the player and the spirit requires that the Medicine Game be played in a spiritual manner: with humility and with calm. When a stick breaks, its caretaker may shed tears of grief.

Dirty play is considered disrespectful. To injure another intentionally is contrary to tradition and reason. As a consequence of tradition, women are not allowed to play the Medicine Game, and in fact, they are not allowed to touch a stick. The typical Iroquois sees Medicine Games and formal lacrosse competitions as a means to commune with the Creator, not to prove himself number one. The people are one with the Creator as they play and, following the game, as they feast communally.

Collectivism is a cultural arrangement in which members of a group are interdependent and other-focused (Beckstein, 2014; Triandis, 2018). Collectivists are motivated to adhere to social norms. They value connectedness and harmonious relationships. The group is held paramount in collectivist societies and its success holds precedence over personal accomplishment. The culture of Native American groups has been and continues to be described as collectivistic in nature (Hossain et al., 2011; Kitayama & Markus, 2000). Native Americans have maintained collectivist values despite hundreds of years of the dominant American culture's assimilation efforts (Heine, 2008). Collectivist values are reflected in how the Medicine Game is played.

The documentary film *The Medicine Game: Three Brothers, One Goal* (Korver, 2013) tells the story of a contemporary professional lacrosse player and his brothers. Miles Thompson, a member of the Onondaga Nation, is a two-time winner of the Tewaaraton Award which is bestowed upon the

NCAA's best lacrosse player. He was drafted into the National Lacrosse League and played in the Major League Lacrosse league.

Thompson was taught by his father never to play for the name on the front or back of a jersey, but instead, for the Creator. He explains, "It should never be about yourself. . . . It should be about affecting someone else. . . . It's about being thankful for everything I have been given already." His people believe the Creator provides everyone with a gift, and he believes his gift is the ability to play lacrosse.

Thompson deems that in lacrosse and in life, the goal should always be the same: being a good person with a positive mind. During competition, he keeps in mind that the game is sacred, "So. I would say the Creator's happy when I'm playing the game." Playing is a joy and players should have fun. Thompson's outlook toward playing lacrosse as a collegiate and professional player is reflective of how the Medicine Game is played among the Iroquois. Thompson also serves as an example of how modern Native American athletes can compete successfully at the highest level of sport while adhering to traditional values and beliefs.

Jim Thorpe

Jim Thorpe, who was educated within the Indian boarding school system, may be the embodiment of the ideal Native American competitive athlete. He has been considered by many sport historians and writers to be the world's greatest athlete (Wheeler, 1979). The cable television sports channel ESPN placed Thorpe seventh on its list of the twentieth century's North American top 100 athletes (ESPN, 1999). Thorpe is enshrined in the Professional Football Hall of Fame, played professional baseball for six years, and won gold medals in both the Olympic pentathlon and decathlon during the same Olympiad. Did Thorpe compete in a way that aligned with Native American collectivist values, or individualistic values common within the dominant culture?

A former teacher described the humility Thorpe demonstrated in light of his athletic accomplishments, "He was offhand, modest, casual about everything in the way of fame or eminence achieved" (Wheeler, 1979, p. 139). How did Thorpe's Carlisle Boarding School classmates respond to his competitive success? He was, "liked by all rather than venerated or idolized" (Wheeler, 1979, p. 139).

Thorpe did not seem to have competed in order to stand out above others, "My earning days in athletics are at an end and while sports have been my livelihood, I have really played for the love of competition" (Pro Football Hall of Fame, 2019). He stated in another interview, "I played with the heart of an amateur—for the pure hell of it" (Willis, 2017, p. 30). Finally, Thorpe claimed outright that he competed simply because it was fun, "I have always liked sport and only played or run races for the fun of the thing" (Thorpe, 2020, p. 2).

Did Thorpe compete to benefit himself financially and live a comfortable life? When he went into the hospital to have surgery to remove cancer on his lip late in his life, Thorpe's wife confessed, "We're broke. Jim has nothing but his name and his memories. He has spent money on his own people and given it away" (Jenkins, 2012, p. 28). Did Thorpe compete with a win at all cost attitude? He recalled, "I played clean, but I played hard" (Willis, 2017, p. 78).

Thorpe competed for the enjoyment of it in alignment with traditional Native American goals of competition. He did not compete for wealth. What he earned; he gave away as is expected in traditional communal societies. He did not compete with a win at all cost mentality. To do so was a concept foreign in traditional Native American communities. The spiritual and physical well-being of others was of greater importance in his traditional upbringing. It appears that Thorpe rejected mainstream sport's calling for competitors to compete for fame and wealth and to use any means possible to do so. Efforts to assimilate Thorpe into the dominant culture seem to have failed. Was Thorpe an anomaly concerning his competitive goals and attitudes?

High School Basketball: A Celebration of Native American Identity

Contrary to assimilation goals, Native Americans use sport to celebrate their identity and autonomy as a people. "The Northern Arapaho and Eastern Shoshone have transformed the meaning of basketball to suit their cultural needs, rendering it a new method of expressing Native identity and resistance, both on and off the court" (Sewell, 2005, p. 29). On the Wind River reservation, the run and gun style of basketball play is a part of Indian identity. The history of running throughout Arapaho and Shoshone history is used by the people of the tribe to explain their success or failure in sports. For example, after a disappointing loss, a player's father blamed the poor performance on the failure to implement the run and gun style of play, "They are Indians, and they should play like Indians" (Sewell, 2005, p. 35).

Identity is also strengthened at basketball games played on the Wind River reservation as tradition is combined with sport. Native American culture is reinforced as traditional giveaways are conducted, when native foods are sold in the concession stand, and as the Arapaho flag song is performed by traditional drum groups before tip-off. On the Wind River reservations and other reservations throughout North America, sport has come to serve as a site in which Native Americans have an equal chance at winning the battle against whites for cultural relevance (Sewell, 2005).

The literature enables us to conclude that Native American athletes can seriously compete in sport. Yet, the literature also demonstrates that Native Americans do not always compete in ways that align with those expected within the broader American culture. The goals, experiences, and perceptions of contest powwow dancers have yet to be investigated by researchers. The question of whether contest powwow dancers compete in a way that aligns with traditional or dominant American culture has yet to be determined. Finally, it has yet to be determined through any formal data collection process if contest powwow dancers consider their events as sport. These voids in the literature led to the development of our research questions.

RESEARCH QUESTIONS

In this chapter, we have addressed the following questions:

1. What are the goals, experiences, and perceptions of contemporary competitive powwow dancers?
2. Do competitive powwow dancers embrace the dominant culture's individualistic values when competing or do they adhere to traditional Native American collectivist values?
3. Do contest powwow dancers consider contest powwow dancing a competitive sport?

METHODOLOGY

For this project, we sought to systematically determine how competition in contest powwows might reflect and differ from that common to established American sports in the lived experiences of our participants. We employed qualitative methodology techniques including interviewing, coding, and developing themes as practical tools to conduct and analyze semi-structured qualitative data (Bryant & Charmaz, 2007; Corbin & Strauss, 2015). Use of qualitative methodology enabled the researchers to develop a deep understanding of the lived experience of competitive powwow dancers (Bryant & Charmaz, 2007; Corbin & Strauss, 2015).

In her seminal work *Decolonizing Methodologies: Research and Indigenous Peoples*, Linda Smith (2008) raises numerous concerns about non-Indigenous peoples (colonizers or imperialists) conducting research with Indigenous peoples. As neither of this paper's authors are Indigenous, some may question our motives and perhaps the ethics of our research. Smith provides guidelines for non-Indigenous researchers to follow when conducting research with Indigenous peoples including respect the people, conduct your research face to face, look at your participants, listen and speak with your participants, be cautious, do not trample over the mana (life force/spiritual energy) of people, do not flaunt your knowledge, and share and host participants while extending generosity. We intentionally endeavored to adhere to Smith's guidelines throughout the process of completing our study.

Smith (2008) declares that, "Indigenous peoples want to tell our own stories, write our own versions, in our own ways, for our own purposes" (p. 28). However, to date, no research has been conducted upon Native American contest powwow dancers and no published study has examined the relationship of the contest powwow to sport. It is our sincere hope that Native American scholars expand upon our humble research efforts in the future for we believe the contest powwow to be important in the lives of many Native Americans. We state here that we harbor neither an "Imperial" agenda nor a decolonizing agenda.

Participants

Fourteen Native American competition powwow dancers were interviewed in order to understand and describe the goals, attitudes, and behaviors they held while competing in the world's most prestigious contest powwow. We employed a purposeful sampling technique to select our participants in order to maximize the depth and richness of data (Creswell, 2015; Creswell & Plano, 2011). We utilized three criteria to identify potential participants to ensure that they were, indeed, contest powwow dancers at the time of the interviews. Individuals were only approached and asked to participate in the study if they appeared to be at least eighteen years old, wore regalia, and wore an official Gathering of Nations powwow competitor's number. Participants were informed verbally and in writing as to the purpose of the study and the participation requirements.

Thirty-two competitive dancers were approached by Aicinena and asked to participate in the study. Those approached wore regalia, wore a Gathering of Nations competitors' number, and appeared to be at least eighteen years of age. Seven of ten females approached agreed to participate. Seven of fifteen males approached agreed to be interviewed. Seven potential participants approached did not meet the minimum age requirement for participation.

The participants traveled to the powwow from various regions of the United States (Northwest, Northern Plains, Southern Plains, Southwest, Midwest, Northeast, and Pacific Islands) and Canada and represented eighteen Indigenous tribal groups including Cheyenne, Chippewa, Cochiti Tewa,

Colorado River Indian Tribes, Cree, Crow, Dakota Sioux, Hidatsa, Lakota Sioux, Mandau, Navajo, Ojibwe, Potawatomi, Pueblo, Shoshone, Sioux, Tututni, and Zuni. Some participants stated affiliation with more than one tribal group. The sample of participants represented an array of tribes. Participants held differing degrees of contest powwow dancing experience. Six participants had zero to ten years of competitive experience, four had eleven to thirty years of competitive experience, and four had twenty-plus years of competitive experience. Participants also reflected a wide range of ages. Six participants were aged twenty to twenty-nine, five participants were between thirty and forty-nine years of age, and three ranged in age between fifty and eighty-one. There were equal numbers of male (seven) and female (seven) participants.

Data Collection

We obtained Institutional Review Board (IRB) approval from The University of Texas Permian Basin for the project. Besides, we also obtained additional written consent to conduct interviews from the Gathering of Nations administration before data collection commenced.

Data were collected at the Gathering of Nations which has often been referred to as the, "Super Bowl of All Indian Powwows" (Dell'Angela, 2003, p. 2). The two-day competitive cultural event is held each April in Albuquerque, New Mexico. It involves more than 3,500 competitive dancers. Over $200,000 in prize money is awarded, and it is estimated that 150,000 people attend the powwow each year (Nathanson, 2018). Participants in the 2018 Gathering of Nations powwow represented 565 tribes recognized by the U.S. government and 220 Canadian First-Nations groups (Larse, 2018). We chose the Gathering of Nations powwow as the site for data collection because it is the premiere contest powwow in the world.

Interviews were conducted on the New Mexico state fairgrounds and within Tingley Coliseum which served as the site of the powwow. The coliseum is located within the state fairgrounds. Interviews were conducted on April 27 and April 28, 2018. Each day, Aicinena arrived at the fairgrounds by 10:30 a.m. and departed at 10:30 p.m. A special media pass was granted to him by the Gathering of Nations organizers which afforded him access to all areas of the arena and powwow grounds.

Data collection began with the conduction of semi-structured interviews. Semi-structured interviews allowed us to ask prepared questions and to gather unexpected data through follow-up questions (O'Leary, 2017). We were interested in identifying participants' personal experiences within the traditional powwow, contest powwow, and established American competitive sport (e.g., basketball, ice hockey, volleyball). Second, we were interested in determining participants' competitive goals and the value they placed upon competition and winning to determine if they aligned with traditional collectivist cultural orientations, or those of the dominant individualistic culture. The researchers worked together to formulate semi-structured interview questions used in the interviews. Questions were based upon our review of literature. In broad terms, we were interested in determining, in the experience of contest powwow dancers, if contest powwow dancing is a sport, how contest powwow dancing and competing in established American sport may be similar or different, what is required to be a successful competitive powwow dancer, and how it might be similar or different from what is required to be a successful athlete, and how competitive powwow dancing serves to reinforce or supplant traditional Native American collectivist values.

Several steps were taken to help participants feel comfortable before interviews commenced. Aicinena wore a shirt displaying the university's logo and offered them a university business card. He shared with each participant that he had been a teacher and coach at Crownpoint High School for seven years and that he worked with Navajo students. It was disclosed that his wife was Navajo. He also engaged in informal and unrecorded talk with participants before they reviewed the informed consent form and signed it. After informed consent was given, he began the semi-structured interview. The formal interviews were electronically recorded with an iPhone 6 Plus.

In order to gather an in-depth understanding of the powwow dancers' involvements and to evaluate transformation of the powwow as a sport activity, we conveyed overarching questions such as, "What does powwow mean to you? What differences have you observed in the traditional and contest forms of the powwow? What are your primary goals for competing? How do you feel when you win and lose a contest powwow event? In what ways do you believe contest powwow competition mirrors athletic competition? In what ways do you believe contest powwow competition mirrors sport?"

Interviews ranged in length from fifteen to ninety-eight minutes. The shortest interview involved a participant who was participating in her first competition powwow. She was not a high school athlete, did not care for competition, and belonged to a Pueblo tribe that seldom performs dances off the reservation. She competed in dance during the powwow as a component of the Miss Indian World contest, which is in and of itself a competitive event. Though her experience in competitive dancing and her responses were brief, we believe that her voice needed to be heard. The longest interview involved a participant who was eighty-one years of age. He served as Chief of his tribe and participated extensively in competitive sport both as a high school student and as an adult. He wanted to tell stories not directly related to our study, but respectfully, we allowed him to share them with us. Thirteen interviews were conducted outdoors in a large concession area adjacent to the coliseum in which the dance competitions took place. One interview was conducted in an outer hallway of the coliseum while seated with the participant. Aicinena attempted to conduct as many interviews as possible over the two days of the powwow. Each participant was interviewed once. By the eleventh interview, the receipt of similar responses from participants indicated that sufficient information was gathered in order for other researchers to replicate the study. However, we sought additional participants in order to have a reasonable representation of sexes, ages, and levels of contest powwow dancing experience. For example, the last three interviews were conducted with male participants, and their participation yielded equal representation of male and female voices in the study.

Data Analysis

Interviews were transcribed completely within two weeks following data collection. Transcripts were read a minimum of three times in their entirety before data analysis commenced. Data analysis began with open coding in an effort to determine whether or not the participants considered competitive powwow dancing as a sport (Corbin & Strauss, 2015; Creswell, 2015). In this stage, the researchers concentrated upon transcribed documentation from interviews (Elliott, 2018; Soyer & Ziyanak, 2018). Any participants' comments that seemed to be associated with the research questions were provided a code. We categorized each line with codes articulating concepts related to the lived experience of competitive powwow dancers. This process yielded fifty codes. For example, initial codes included: contest powwow dancing is a way of respect to the elderly, the purpose of contest powwow dancing is winning, contest powwow dancing provides healing, contest powwow dancing provides enjoyment, and the main reason to dance in contest powwows is to visit family and friends.

In the second stage of data analysis, axial coding was employed to identify key concepts to address our research questions. We utilized associated concepts and categories to expose codes and subcategories within our participants' messages to identify similarities and differences between contest powwow dancing and commonly sponsored American sport. In particular, we sought to identify codes which yielded data regarding direct comparison between competitive powwow dancing and sport. Some of the codes overlapped, and after examination, we collapsed them into 14 axial codes including, for example, the primary purpose of contest powwow dancing, contest powwow dancing is a sport, the importance of winning in contest powwow dancing, and dancing provides healing.

During theme development, we reviewed our evidence for each theme. Reorganization of the themes was based upon linked codes observed to exist within and between codes. Each code associated with a theme was reviewed to ensure that it had a clear relationship to the theme within which it was embedded. In this phase, we identified crucial themes such as preferred type of powwow, primary goals for dancing in contest powwows, importance of winning, powwow dancing as a sport, direct comparison between competitive powwow dancing and athletics, and the spirit of sportsmanship. We determined it was logical to collapse the themes, "Do the participants view competitive powwow dancing as a sport?" and "Powwow dancing is a sport" into one theme, "Contest powwow dancing is a sport."

FINDINGS

In this study, we sought to determine the goals, experiences, and perceptions of contemporary competitive powwow dancers. We assayed whether the participants' competitive goals reflected the dominant culture's values toward sport and success. Finally, we determined whether or not the participants considered competitive powwow dancing to be a sport. Our data analysis led to the findings of six themes and four subthemes. The discussion presented here addresses each of the following:

1. The role of competition and dancers' preferred type of powwow
2. Primary goals for dancing in contest powwows
3. How important is winning?
4. How do participants feel when they win and lose?
5. Powwow dancing is a sport
6. Direct comparisons between competitive dancing and sport
   6.1 *Competition and winning*
   6.2 *Precompetition emotions*
   6.3 *Physical preparation for competition*
   6.4 *Sportsmanship*

The Role of Competition and Dancers' Preferred Type of Powwow

Traditional powwows and large intertribal contest powwows differ in size (small vs. large), primary purpose (unity vs. competition), and degree of organization (low vs. high). Traditional powwows are described as being devoid of competition. As Native American cultural groups have been described as collectivist historically and contemporarily, a lack of emphasis upon competition in traditional powwows serves to reaffirm traditional cultural values. However, competition is ubiquitous within individualistic American society. Our findings demonstrate that competition impacts the participants' contest powwow participation experience as well as their preference for either traditional or contest forms of the powwow.

We asked the participants if they prefer contest powwows or traditional powwows. Our findings show the majority of our participants enjoy each type of powwow equally or state a preference for contest powwows. Participants also make it clear that they enjoy competition. Participants shared that the opportunity to win money and prizes is a reason for preferring contest powwows. Abe notes, "Traditional powwows have fewer people and there is no money available." Frank prefers competition powwows because he has the opportunity to compete for money, and at contest powwows, dancers are required to "dance hard."

In contest powwow settings, dancers must dance hard, with intensity, if they are to find competitive success. Success is a lusory goal in competitive activities, as it is in the contest powwow. From the participants' point of view, the traditional powwow is similar to a recreational, informal, volleyball game conducted between individuals who play to socialize and have a good time. This differs from a volleyball competition, for example, in which participants are competing for championships or monetary rewards. The level of seriousness is lessened in the recreational setting, and the environment would be considered more relaxed.

During data collection, we observed that dancers were frequently encouraged by the announcers to "Dance hard!" The call to dance hard was indelibly embossed within our minds as observers. A common exhortation in modern sport is to "play hard or go home." The researchers perceive the expression, "Dance hard!" to have the same meaning. If contest powwow dancers are not putting forth their best effort, they should not bother to compete at all.

We asked participants expressing a preference for traditional powwows why they held such a preference. Amy believes that by dancing in traditional powwows she is supporting and helping others. Freda prefers traditional powwows because, "They are closer to my home and I am representing my tribe." Disdain for contest powwows is not expressed, but rather an affinity for tribal identity, solidarity, and a collectivist's concern for others. Participants who prefer the contest powwow do so because they are competitive and because they enjoy being within the competitive environment.

This study's participants note people behave differently at traditional and contest powwows. Abe believes the large number of participants at contest powwows increases the level of stress and aggravation, and that results in increased levels conflict. Freda and Bill suggest that the large number of contestants and tight scheduling simply do not afford the same opportunities for people to socialize and make friendships; thus, making conflicts more likely. Freda attributes the conflict she observes at contest powwows to an overemphasis on winning, "It is all about winning for some people." Chuck provides additional insight to explain why conflicts increase at contest powwows, "A lot of people come here, and they all can't win."

The participants expressed that conflict and problems between competitors are greater at contest powwows. Although they viewed the conflicts occurring at contest powwows as being undesirable, most of our participants still prefer the contest powwow over the traditional powwow. The contest powwow offers dancers large crowds, excitement, and the opportunity to test oneself in competition that the traditional powwow does not.

Primary Goals for Dancing in Contest Powwows

We asked the participants what the primary goal of their competitive powwow dancing is and why it is important. Winning is identified as the primary goal of competing by a small number of participants. Illustratively, Amy and Geneva declare emphatically that they are dancing, "To win first place!"

Additional participants share that enjoyment, or having a good time are primary motivators for competition. Others assert the primary goal of dancing is to carry on the traditions of their ancestors. Betty explains, "Contest powwows are modern, but they keep me connected to our traditions."

Visiting family and friends is the primary consideration for dancing in contest powwows for several of the participants. Chuck notes that he participates, "mostly to visit and see relatives. You only compete in two to four events at each powwow." Participants also compete to stay healthy, to dance for those who cannot dance, to provide meaning and significance to life, and to receive healing. The powwow announcer often reminds the dancers and spectators that healing takes place within the powwow circle.

Showing off and receiving recognition from others is important for some participants. Gill competes to, "impress my idols, older chicken dancers, and hear from them that I did well." Dave dances in competitions, "to be recognized by other tribes; to let others know about my tribe and that we are still here." Freda dances to show off her style.

A multitude of reasons are used by athletes to describe why they participate in popular forms of American sport. They include winning, enjoyment, social opportunities, belonging to a group, because the family is involved in sport, proving competence, and gaining attention (Coakley, 2017). In this study, contest powwow dancers provide similar reasons for their participation. However, it is notable that only three of the study's participants identified winning as their primary participation goal.

How Important Is Winning?

Success in athletic competition is broadly measured in terms of victories and losses. Twelve of the fourteen participants state they have won at least one contest powwow event. We asked each participant how important it is for them to win dance competitions. None of the participants state that it is highly important for them to win.

When we asked participants why winning was not ultimately important, a variety of responses were given. Frank notes that there could be over a hundred competitors in one dance competition, yet only one can win, and few are able to place high enough to win prize money. Gill notes being new to a competitive age group places him at a disadvantage and focusing upon winning is an unreasonable thing to do. It is better for him to focus upon improving. Geneva strives for excellence in her performances. She views winning as a confirmation of her ability.

Historically, the powwow has been viewed as a place where one dances for healing, for the ill, for the dead, and for those to come. "Because I am dancing for others" is expressed by several participants as a reason for discounting the significance of winning. Winning is not of paramount importance to Dave, Chuck, Eric, Betty, or Eva because by dancing they are giving thanks to their ancestors, family, and nation. Even within the throngs of competition, participants dance for others.

Betty makes it clear that when competing, she is representing her family and tribe. Participants also express that various social aspects of the contest powwow are more important than winning. Enjoyment, family, social interaction, creating a pleasant competitive environment, and dancing for others takes precedence over winning. As such, the group is more closely aligned with collectivist values than those of the dominant individualistic culture in which winning is held in highest regard.

How Do Participants Feel When They Win and Lose?

The researchers asked the twelve participants who claimed to have won a contest powwow event how they felt after being named champion. Betty explains she felt, "alright . . . but it was always stressed to me that the money was there, but that's not why you dance." Extrinsic rewards are not as important as intrinsic rewards to Betty.

Bill seems acutely aware of the temporal nature of victory: "You feel good for a few minutes, then it's on to the next one." His understanding serves to keep the significance of winning and losing in perspective. To Bill, it is reasonable to strive for competitive success, for a championship is an achievement that not all can obtain. Perhaps more importantly, he sagely conveys that winning has no eternal significance.

Participants indicate that personal competitive success reflects well upon their tribal groups. Illustratively, Freda is pleased when she is victorious because, "I feel like they picked all of us, all of my tribe, when I win." In like manner, Frank explains, "Winning makes it fun because you're representing your family, tribe and culture." Carla experiences a sincere state of pride after victory: "I feel a sense of pride because it encourages others to be good too."

Following a winning performance, Eric feels as though he has been, "traveling with the spirits." Frank is euphoric after winning a contest: "It's the same as winning in hockey when you play hard ass!" As Geneva shares with us her litany of successes, she speaks quite pragmatically about winning. She is both grateful and thankful when she wins: "I can pay the bills and feed the kids!" The kids she refers to are her children and grandchildren. The goal of sharing with others is a traditional Native American and collectivist imperative. Geneva once gave a car that she won at a California powwow to a family member who needed one more than she did.

The participants do not hold competitive success in highest regard. Winning is something to be strived for and appreciated when achieved. Participants consider the trappings of victory as blessings they do not seem to believe they deserve. When victory escapes them, the participants find solace within the experience of participation and the social benefits they derive from joining together with others at the contest powwow.

Not one of the participants indicates that failing to win a competition is vexing. As noted earlier, Amy states winning is not important, so there is no disappointment when victory escapes her. She is sincerely thankful for the opportunity to dance. Participants note that not everyone can win, so feeling badly after a loss is unreasonable. Winning in order to prove superiority is considered a primary objective of competition by three of the participants. Even for them, losses are discounted as winning is understood to be ephemeral.

The views of participants concerning winning and losing are contrary to slogans commonly bantered about in mainstream American society such as "Pain is temporary. Winning is forever," "Second place is First Loser," "When you lose, you die a little," and "Winning isn't everything, it's the only thing." The ethos of competition present within the contest powwow functions in reaffirming and enhancing the dancers' collectivist Native American identity.

The participants of this study do not adhere to the performance ethic in which winning is everything. Collectively, they believe winning is a goal to be strived for; however, other reasons for participation are more important. Specifically, they value more highly participation in the production and transmission of culture and in the establishment and reinforcement of relationships.

Our findings show that for our participants, winning dance contests is simply an outcome of seeking excellence in performance, not efforts to prove superiority. When participants did win, often it was acknowledged that the honor reflected positively upon their family and their tribe. An emphasis upon the group and others is characteristic of collectivism. In turn, Native American identity and traditions are reinforced through participation in contest powwows.

Contest Powwow Dancing Is a Sport

We sought to determine if the participants viewed contest powwow dancing to be a sport. The majority of participants competed as high school athletes in the sports of volleyball, ice hockey, basketball, softball, soccer, baseball, and track and field. While attending high school, Chuck did not compete in high school athletics because he traveled too often to powwows. He explains that he viewed the contest powwow as an opportunity to compete in a sport. On the other hand, Eva declares she was never interested in sports because she detested competition. Two of the female participants did not have the option of competing in interscholastic sport because sports were not offered for girls when they were in school.

Given that the great majority of participants were athletes, they are able to share how traditional sports are similar to and different from competitive powwow dancing. Even the four participants who were not high school athletes are inundated with mediated sporting events, sports highlights, and sports terms used frequently within the broader society. They readily make reasonable comparisons as a result.

Our findings reveal that the overwhelming majority of participants believe contest powwow dancing is a sport. In describing the similarity between mainstream sports and competitive powwow dancing, they utilize terms commonly used by coaches including "mindset," "focus," "winners and losers," "competitors," "skill," "dedication," "precision," "poise," "tribe vs. tribe," "perfect," "do my best," "compete," "sportsmanship," and "competitive spirit." In the following pages, the participants identify similarities and differences that exist between the contest powwow and mainstream athletic environments.

Comparisons between Competitive Dancing and Sport

Participants provided direct comparisons between sport and competitive powwow dancing. They specify that in sport and contest powwow dancing winning and competition are important, that they experience precompetitive emotions, that they mentally and physically prepare for competition, and that sportsmanship is important.

Competition and Winning

Participants expressed that competing and striving to win are common to sport and contest powwow dancing. For Bill, "The size of the competitive powwow events brings out the competitive spirit. You have to dance with the same mindset you have when you play hockey." Dee recalls, "I played softball and was a cheerleader. It is a lot the same. I learned to always do my best, and to me, that is winning." Gill explains that to be successful, "You have to be focused. There are winners and losers."

Precompetition Emotions

Before dance competitions, participants experience a variety of emotions similar to those experienced when preparing for athletic contests. For Gill, the feeling is, "no different than when I am getting ready to play a game." Dave recalls, "I feel excitement, just like before I played basketball. When I'm putting on my regalia, it's like putting on my uniform to get ready." As Frank puts on his regalia and prepares to compete, it makes him, "feel alive and good."

Carly professes mental and physical precontest preparation are identical in sport and competitive powwow dancing: "We have prayer and meditation to focus." Participants share that they experience adrenaline rushes, nervousness, and stage fright just as they did before basketball, softball, hockey, and volleyball games.

Physical Preparation for Competition

In competitive sports, athletes are expected to train for competitions. Half of this study's participants state they practice dancing as a means of preparing for competitions. Half state they do not practice because they dance so much in competition, they keep their skill set up to a desirable level. Though Bill does not physically practice on a regular basis, he explains, almost apologetically, that he engages in mental practice several times a day.

Twelve participants indicate that they engage in fitness training, which involves walking, running, and/or strength training to prepare for dance competitions. Those who do not, explain that dancing often at powwows keeps them fit enough to compete. Abe explains why conditioning is necessary. You have to be in condition before competitions, "especially for the fancy dance." Sometimes, competitors must dance four songs in a row or more and doing so can be physically exhausting. Those who do not engage in physical conditioning explain that dancing often at powwows keeps them fit enough to compete.

Most of the participants engage in physical conditioning on a regular basis as a means of preparing for competition. Half of the participants practice dancing skills regularly. Within the dominant American culture, competitive athletes are also expected to train physically and to practice before competitions.

Sportsmanship

During the current study, the researchers observed competitors wishing one another good luck before competition, just as athletes do before athletic events. After dances concluded and judges had completed their work, competitors walked toward each other in lines and shared handshakes, hugs, and fist-bumps as do athletes following basketball, baseball, and soccer games. They did so in the spirit of sportsmanship. During powwow competitions, sportsmanship is considered important. Carla notes, "We compete with a spirit of sportsmanship."

DISCUSSION

In our research, participants make direct comparisons between sport and contest powwow dancing, and they use terms commonly associated with sports competition as they do. They directly link dancing to competing in sport and state that they experience the same emotions while dancing as they did before athletic contests. They practice and train physically for competitions. They take competition seriously and compete with a spirit of sportsmanship. The majority of our sample of contest powwow dancers considers contest powwow dancing to be a competitive sport, yet they do not hold winning to be the most important reason for competing. Instead, by dancing in competitions they remain connected to their traditions, help to carry on traditions, bring healing to themselves and others, receive validation from elders, demonstrate respect for elders, and buttress relationships with family and friends.

Competitive powwow dancing is a competitive contest, comprised of physical activity in which only one individual is selected as the competition's winner. As such, competitive powwow dancing can be classified as a sport per the sociological definition provided by Coakley (2017). Contest powwow events provide competitors with a goal (winning). The participants in the current study express they hold goals of winning and or performing well. There is a stated means to winning a contest powwow dancing event. Victors are judged to be the best dancer in consideration of established characteristics of the dance, as well as the quality and appropriateness of their regalia. Dancers are required to adhere to rules during competition, and point deductions are made for rule violations (Pow-Wow.org, 2019a). Contestants must accept the rules of competition as they compete. Skill is required for dancers to win competitions, and contest powwow dancing is a physical skill (Pow-Wow .org, 2019b). Contest powwow dancing exhibits stability as dance styles included in competitions have existed for hundreds of years in most cases and since the twentieth century in others. Finally, contest powwow dancing has a wide following as evidenced by attendance and online viewing of events such as the Gathering of Nations. Over 150,000 individuals attend the Gathering of Nations powwow each year and over 1 million people throughout the world view the event on the internet as it happens. Given the totality of this evidence, we conclude that contest powwow dancing meets the philosophical definition of sport provided by Suits (1973). The evidence we glean from our interviews in combination with the fact that contest powwow dancing meets all of the definitional requirements of sport identified by Suits (1973) and Coakley (2017) leads us to conclude that contest powwow dancing is a competitive sport.

We noted several factors within the context of the powwow that served to illustrate the importance of sport and competition among Native Americans at the Gathering of Nations powwow. Powwow announcers, who are Native American, serve several important functions. They are participants in the powwow, actors who manage and interpret what transpires during the event. On numerous occasions, the powwow announcer lets the crowd know that dancers and the children of honored individuals are athletes. For example, the men's junior head dancer is introduced as a, "dancer and a baller." The head women's junior head dancer was introduced as, "a scholar and an athlete." The second announcer's son, the audience was told, "was a college athlete." As we toured the food court and the powwow grounds, athletic logos were ubiquitously present, indicating that Native Americans have embraced American sport and value competition.

With a focus upon individualistic goals and behaviors, there often comes an increase in antisocial behavior as individuals strive to reach the upper echelons of competitive success. Therefore, antisocial behavior should be expected to increase at contest powwows as cash prizes grow larger, as the number of contest powwows proliferates, and as more dancers attempt to make a living on the powwow highway. Our participants report that they observe higher levels of conflict at contest powwows than they do at traditional powwows. Based upon our findings, we argue that conflict is more frequently observed at contest powwows than it is at traditional powwows because of the great chasm which exists between traditional Native American collectivist values and those of the dominant individualistic American culture. Members of individualistic cultures view competitions as zero-sum events. The only competitor who can benefit is the winner, and it is functional to serve the self at the expense of others. From a collectivist perspective, as individuals compete in an effort to achieve their potential, they can acknowledge that all involved in the competition are important, that individual success is achieved through the actions of the many, and that success is a testament to the importance of them all. Such an orientation is conducive to the creation of a state of personal and collective peace. Perhaps those responsible for creating conflict in contest powwow settings as described by this study's participants have, as individuals, adopted individualistic attitudes toward competition and winning.

The participants involved in the current investigation competed on their own terms in a way that aligned with their traditions and values. The powwow circle has always been considered a place for healing in times of sickness, in times of trouble, and in times of conflict. The powwow announcer reminds the crowd, "There's a lot of healing that goes on out there in the circle, in spite of the competition."

CONCLUSION

Despite the efforts of the dominant culture to force Native Americans to assimilate over a period of hundreds of years, this study's participants demonstrated commitment to traditional collectivist values as they sought competitive victory. The contest powwow affords Native Americans an opportunity to compete in an intertribal event that serves to maintain important aspects of their traditional culture. Although the number of problems and conflicts caused by professionalization of the contest powwow is likely to increase, many participants will seek to overcome them through a commitment to their traditional collectivist values.

Individuals who choose to teach and coach in Native American communities may be helped by the findings of this study. If they assume their athletes will hold the same motivations, goals, and attitudes toward sport as they do, they might be wrong. An enhanced understanding of collectivist culture and how one can seriously compete with a different set of goals, attitudes, and values than those common within the broader American culture may lead to enhanced competitive success and fewer conflicts in the athletic setting.

This study has a number of limitations associated with the data collection process. First, we focused only Gathering of Nations powwow in Albuquerque, New Mexico, in 2018. Our findings were limited to only one contest powwow. Second, we collected our participants in Albuquerque, New Mexico. It is possible that competitors from areas not represented at the powwow or in our pool of participants may have expressed different views. Third, we did not examine the traditional form of the powwow. Fourth, because we are not from a Native American background, we must acknowledge a bias unknown to us which may have impacted our research. Finally, over 3,500 dancers participated in the powwow, and they represented over five hundred tribal groups. Fourteen participants cannot speak for all Native Americans.

In particular, this study increases the understanding of the contest powwow, Native American identity, and Native American orientations toward competition. This study suggests further research is needed to more completely understand the importance and function of the contest powwow in modern Native American culture.

NOTE

1. Parts of this chapter were previously published in *The Qualitative Report* and used with permission. Aicinena, J. S. and Ziyanak, S. (2021). Contest powwow: Sport and Native American culture. *The Qualitative Report*, 26(1), 27–51. https://doi.org/10.46743/2160-3715/2021.4517

Chapter 4

The Contest Powwow Announcers

Mediators of Culture and Traditions

Native American powwows, also referred to as doings or gatherings, consist of two basic forms (Albers & Medicine, 2005). The traditional powwow celebrates tribal-specific traditions and typically is restricted to members of the tribe and specific invited participants. As there are over 574 tribal groups in the United States (Indian Affairs, 2020), traditional powwows often differ. Traditional powwows are typically quaint events taking place in settings such as arbors or school gymnasiums (Gelo, 2005).

Song and dance traditions of the Blackfoot, Comanche, Dakota, Kiowa, Lakota, Ojibwa, Pawnee, Ponca, and other tribes inhabiting the Great Plains region of the United States were the foundation from which the contemporary contest powwow evolved (Hoffmeyer, 2015). They are the product of interaction between tribal groups and the influence of non-Native culture (Howard, 1955). According to Scales (2007) activities observed at contest powwows have been standardized for several decades. Powwow announcer Howie Thompson observed that at nontraditional powwows throughout the United States and Canada: "The songs are all the same, we all dance the same, we all pray the same way, we all honor the drum the same way, and we go to the same circle" (Schilling, 2013, p. 22).

Since World War II, academics have described contemporary powwows, particularly contest powwows, as social events, or secular ceremonies (Callahan, 1993; Crawford & Kelley, 2005; Gamble, 1952; Howard, 1983; Lurie, 1971). Dancers have also acknowledged that the spiritual focus of the powwow has been lessened as the events have become more commercialized and voyaged from reservations into mainstream America (Rahimi, 2005).

Contest powwows celebrate traditions and values common to many North American tribal groups and are considered Pan-Indian or intertribal events.

Dance and drum contests are open to all Native Americans, and the events are open to all people who wish to spectate regardless of race or tribal affiliation. The culturally rich spectacles are:

> an amazing opportunity for education of the non-Native community on Native traditions and cultures and may serve as one of the only chances that . . . spectators have to interact with Native peoples in a modern and culturally relevant setting. (Keene, 2010, p. 7)

Contest powwows are often held in large venues including convention centers and coliseums built to host NCAA and professional sporting events. Over fifteen thousand spectators attend the largest contest powwows such as the Gathering of Nations held each April in Albuquerque, New Mexico.

One of the most prominent and notable individuals associated with any contest powwow is the powwow announcer. Powwow announcers are also referred to as powwow emcees. Depending upon where a contest powwow is held, announcers may be referred to as an announcer or an emcee. Throughout this chapter, we will use the two terms interchangeably. Powwow announcers are important to the smooth running of any contest powwow, but they also serve an important social role in Native American culture.

REVIEW OF LITERATURE

In this chapter, we examine the scarce literature focused upon powwow announcers. First, we present the history and function of sports announcers as they developed around the time that powwow announcers became common. Sports announcers perform some of the same functions that emcees execute. Our discussion then turns to the history of Native American powwow announcers. We then explore the research on powwow announcers conducted by Gelo (2005). Finally, because academic studies concerning powwow announcers are limited, we examine interviews of powwow announcers supplied through published interviews conducted by newspaper and freelance reporters to gain first-person accounts of their preparation for and entrance into the role of emcee, perceived event-specific social functions, challenges, goals, and objectives.

History and Function of Sports Public Address Announcers

Modern contest powwows are competitive events reflective of modern sports spectacles (Aicinena & Ziyanak, 2021). Although most Americans are familiar with sport and the function of stadium and arena announcers, they may not be familiar with the function of contest powwow announcers. The history, responsibilities, and social functions of the two types of announcers differ in very significant ways.

Public address announcers are a part of most North American sporting events staged by high schools, colleges, and professional sport franchises. Sporting event public address announcers were reported to have been active as early as 1889 (The Brooklyn Citizen, 1889). Fred Burns, the "silver voiced announcer" who worked for the Brooklyn Athletic Club, made public announcements in conjunction with a boxing event. Burns also announced changes in baseball lineups through a megaphone for the New York Giants in 1894 (The Brooklyn Daily Eagle, 1894).

The amplified voice of the public address announcer in contemporary professional sport venues has been likened to the voice of God thundering from the heavens (Rushin, 2012). Sport public address announcers identify corporate sponsors, make public-service announcements, and read scripted information before games, during breaks in play, and after contests. They inform the crowd of starting lineups, substitutions, time outs, and other information specifically germane to the contest.

During sporting events, public address announcers utilize their amplified voices to create excitement. They consciously attempt to endear the home team to fans, but seldom do they offer the crowd historical information, nor do they explicitly share information about values aside from statements associated with color guards and the playing of the national anthem. Though traditional American values are reflected in American athletic contests (Coakley, 2017; Sage et al., 2019), public address announcers do little to explicitly promote or reinforce American values and traditions to those attending sporting events.

Sporting event public address announcers should not be confused with sports broadcasters. Television sports broadcasters, for example, have been found to convey traditional American values such as individualism and achievement through their commentary (Bailey & Sage, 1988). A mediator serves to bring about reconciliation and agreement between people. In the United States, sports broadcast on radio, television, and streaming services are mediated in that broadcasters convey values and beliefs traditionally held by Americans including individual effort, competition, teamwork, and others (Coakley, 2017; Sage et al., 2019).

History of Powwow Public Address Announcers

Contemporary contest powwow announcers have not always existed as the contest powwow itself is a historically recent Native American cultural institution. The role of contest powwow announcers is believed to have been influenced by several factors. Historically, important information was shared within Native American communities by camp criers such as the Comanche's *tekwawapi*, who served as assistants to tribal chiefs (Gelo, 2005). Today's powwow announcers also evolved, in part, from the "whip men" who served to keep activities and individuals at traditional powwows and gatherings moving. According to Gelo (2005), powwow announcers serve many of the same functions as do rodeo announcers and it is likely that the evolution of the powwow announcer was impacted by rodeo announcers as many Native Americans participated in and attended rodeos in the late 1800s and early 1900s. Also influential in the institutionalization of powwow announcers were barkers and announcers associated with traveling circuses and carnivals active in the same period. It has been and is still rare for females to serve as powwow emcees (Koefnagles, 2012).

Gelo's Powwow Announcer Research

Gelo's (2005) research on powwow announcers was based upon observations and tape recordings made over a fifteen-year period at powwows conducted in rural and metropolitan areas of Oklahoma, East Texas, and North Central Texas. The research primarily involved five Native American tribal groups. At the time of this chapter's publication, Gelo's was the only academic work focusing upon powwow announcers or powwow emcees in the EBSCO Host database published between 1900 and 2021. Accordingly, Gelo's research is referenced frequently within the powwow literature.

According to Gelo, the powwow announcer is a key figure in the proceedings of any powwow. The announcer is, in effect, the powwow's voice of authority functioning to:

1. Entertain the crowd before the Grand Entry.
2. Call in Dancers for Grand Entries.
3. Coordinate activities to keep the event on time.
4. Oversee and comment on presentations of special guests, giveaways, awards, and specials.
5. Express thanks to sponsors, dancers, drums, security, crowd, etc., on behalf of the powwow's organizers.
6. Conduct raffle drawings.
7. Inform those in attendance of logistical and security issues.
8. Publicize upcoming events.
9. Tell jokes.
10. Recognize others (powwow committee, princess, etc.).
11. Say prayers or introduce people giving the prayers.

12. Share history, myths, culture, and traditions with the crowd.
13. Provide commentary.

Powwow announcers are further expected to tell jokes and to entertain those attending powwows. Most jokes are understood by the Native Americans at the powwow but not by those who are culturally unenlightened. Jokes told by announcers reinforce status differentiation and social control (Gelo, 2005; Lowie, 1954; Wallace & Hoebel, 1952).

Through their voice, powwow announcers influence and shape Native American social structure and ideology. They remind Native Americans in attendance of their own ideals and share them with non-Native onlookers. Tradition and values important to Native Americans identified as "our way" are explained and emphasized by announcers. Examples of "our way" include the honoring of elders and the emphasis placed upon sharing, family, and traditions within Native American communities. The verbalization of "our way" serves to unity those within earshot. Powwow announcers are also concerned with establishment and maintenance of harmonious social interactions.

In effect, it appears that powwow announcers function as cultural mediators. Their activities serve to help those participating in the powwow agree as to what has been important to Native Americans, what is important to Native Americans, and why what has been important should continue to be important. The primary purpose for conducting the current study is to determine whether contest powwow announcers believe they are purveyors of culture who mediate what takes place within the contest powwow and how they act to bring about agreement and reconciliation through their efforts.

Before moving on, we wish to make it clear that at very traditional celebrations, such as a Ponca Hethuska Warrior Society Man Dance, information is shared quite differently than it is at larger traditional powwows or contest powwows.[1] Man Dances tend to be small events, and dancers are limited to members of the society for the bulk of the event. Spectators consist primarily of dancers' family members and invited guests. Announcements are not made with the aid of amplification systems and no one person makes all announcements. There is no announcer per se. The whip man and Head Man of the host chapter of the society make brief introductions of the participating dance groups and special guests, say prayers, make announcements before each session begins, during break periods, and at the conclusion of the gathering. Events such as the Ponca Hethuska Man Dance are at the far traditional end of the powwow spectrum and contest powwows such as Gathering of Nations are on the far nontraditional end of the powwow spectrum. The roles and the responsibilities of those charged with verbalizing information are quite different at powwows on the two ends of the spectrum.

Reporter Interviews with Powwow Announcers

As noted earlier, published academic papers focused upon powwow announcers are limited to that of Gelo (2005). Notably, Gelo did not include interviews of powwow announcers in his work. What do powwow announcers have to say about what they do and why they do it? Before formulating semistructured interview questions used in the current study, we turn to websites for additional insight.

We analyzed the content of seven selected powwow announcer interviews conducted by reporters that have been published in newspapers and on powwow websites (Chavez, 2010; Head, 2016; Green, 1999; Martin, 2009; Place, 2017; Rice, 2015; Schilling, 2013). Prominent powwow emcees participating in the interviews included Raymond Whitstone, Rob Daugherty, Vince Beyl, Tommy Christian, Tom Phillips, Howie Thomson, and Dennis Bowen. We did not conduct an extensive and formal content analysis as doing so is not the purpose of our current study. The information presented here provides insight into experiences of powwow announcers as told by powwow announcers to reporters. We used the information, in part, to formulate semistructured interview questions used in our study.

It is considered both an honor and a great responsibility to serve as the emcee at a powwow (Green, 1999; Place, 2017). The best announcers are in high demand and are booked solid through the summer months to work powwows throughout the United States and Canada (Schilling, 2013). Ultimately, announcers must do their best to serve the powwow's organizers (Place, 2017). Top announcers must work hard to stay at the top and remain in demand (Green, 1999).

Interviewees first had an opportunity to serve as a powwow announcer for a variety of reasons. Two announcers were asked to fill in for someone who did not show up to work the powwow they were at (Martin, 2005; Rice, 2015). Raymond Whitstone first emceed when he filled in for an announcer who became fatigued (Green, 1999). Howie Thomson got his first break because the emcee working the powwow was considered "weak" and he was asked to replace him (Schilling, 2013). Tommy Christian began his career when he was asked to say a prayer during a powwow and participants were impressed with him (Head, 2016).

Announcers interviewed typically attended powwows as youths and often participated in powwows as singers and or dancers. Spending time in the powwow environment helped the emcees learn the values, traditions, and protocols important to Native Americans and the powwow (Head, 2016; Martin, 2009; Rice, 2015; Schilling, 2013). According to announcer Tom Phillips, growing up within the powwow culture taught him the real values of his culture as well as dances (Rice, 2015). Tribal and family elders were also considered by the emcees interviewed as important teachers of Native American culture, values, history, and traditions represented in powwows (Chavez, 2010; Green, 1999; Head, 2016). Raymond Whitstone explains, "Today I use all of the stories and happenings I learned from the Elders . . . I try to pass that on, our ways, our traditions, our powwow" (Green, 1999, p. 34).

Emcees capable of speaking a Native American language are most desirable (Chavez, 2010; Green, 1999). When announcers use local Native languages, it makes tribal elders participating in the powwow happy (Green, 1999). Many announcers make a conscious effort to learn at least a few words and phrases in languages that are foreign to them.

Powwows are founded upon Native American culture and a respect for its traditions (Head, 2016). An important function of powwow announcers is to teach others about Native American history, values, and traditions (Rice, 2015). Effective announcers understand powwow protocols that may differ from one part of the country to another. Examples of such differences include how to break a tie in a competitive dance event and what actions are required when an eagle feather is dropped (Green, 1999).

Powwow protocols serve as unifiers of ritual and celebratory practices and are often Pan-Indian in nature. They are expected to be followed though they are often unwritten. Participants are expected to learn powwow protocols through observation. Adhering to protocol is considered a sign of respect and failure to adhere to protocol is disrespectful (Owen, 2008). Non-Natives are often unaware of protocols until they break one. Announcers serve to explain many of the protocols important in the contest powwow setting.

Many emcees believe that expressing respect and gratitude to others during the powwow is important (Martin, 2009). It is disrespectful to drum groups for the announcer to speak while they are performing (Green, 1999). Further, it is disrespectful and unacceptable for announcers to pick on people (Green, 1999). It is inappropriate for announcers to use their microphone to impose their traditions on others (Head, 2016; Martin, 2009).

Though serving as an emcee is considered an honor, those interviewed consider announcing to be a job and they take it seriously (Chavez, 2010). They must work at their craft and continually learn if they are to achieve and maintain excellence. For example, powwow announcers may work to improve their voice or take lessons from radio announcers and experienced powwow announcers to improve their performance (Green, 1999). A good voice is considered a plus for powwow announcers (Martin, 2009). After assuming the role of announcer, individuals are often mentored by family members and prominent emcees (Chavez, 2010; Head, 2016; Place, 2017).

Experience is perhaps the most important factor in achievement of excellence in powwow announcing (Martin, 2009).

Laughter is a healing component of the powwow. When people come and laugh, for a short time, they forget their pain. It helps them to heal (Schilling, 2013). A good sense of humor is important in the art of powwow announcing (Chavez, 2010; Green, 1999). Popular announcers have the knack of knowing when to tell jokes (Green, 1999). People want MCs who are a bit crazy yet keep jokes and comments clean (Schilling, 2013). Announcer Rob Daugherty mixes being serious with humor during the powwow but does not like telling a lot of jokes. Jokes, he says, often offend people (Chavez, 2010).

Announcers set the tone for the powwow beginning in advance of the grand entry. The goal of emcees is to raise the crowd's level of excitement and anticipation. Raymond Whitstone believes that nothing is worse than a dead grand entry (Green, 1999). It is also the powwow announcer's responsibility to keep the event moving (Martin, 2009). To do so, emcees must be brief with commentary, observations, jokes, and the sharing of history and traditional values (Chavez, 2010; Green, 1999).

Announcing a powwow is like riding on a roller coaster. Emcees go from telling jokes, to being serious, and asking the crowd to demonstrate respect (Place, 2017). It is imperative for announcers to ensure that there is never a period when nothing is going on (Schilling, 2013). During periods of "dead air" the interest in a powwow may wane. An important goal for announcer Vince Beyl is to make sure everyone leaves powwow celebrations with good feelings (Martin, 2009). Keeping things moving and entertaining the crowd helps to make sure that he meets his goal.

The powwow announcer study conducted by Gelo (2006) is valuable in understanding the practical and social functions of powwow emcees, but it was limited in two ways. First, the bulk of Gelo's work focused upon traditional powwows or powwows on the traditional end of the powwow spectrum taking place in arbors and small facilities. Second, interviews were not conducted with the powwow announcers he studied. In seeking to hear the voices of powwow announcers, we reviewed interviews conducted with powwow emcees that were published in newspapers and on powwow websites. The interviews examined during our literature review did provide great insight into the role of the powwow announcer during the powwow, their socialization into the role, their challenges, and their perceived and social functions.

The purpose of the current study is twofold. First, we seek to expand knowledge concerning the contest powwow. Second, we seek to determine if contest powwow announcers consciously serve as mediators of culture and, if so, how they accomplish the goal.

METHODS

This participatory study allows the researchers to qualitatively determine and describe socialization factors important in motivating the study's participants to become powwow announcers, social factors influencing the participants' development as announcers, social factors impacting the participants' verbal behavior during a contest powwow, and their perceived role in the socialization of powwow participants and spectators. We also seek to determine whether the participants serve all 13 functions of powwow announcers identified by Gelo (2005).

The contest powwow serving as the focus of the current study is referred to throughout this chapter as the North Plains Contest Powwow (NPCP). The NPCP has been referred to as one of the premiere contest powwows within the northern plains. Nine hundred and forty-two contest powwow dancers from throughout the United States and Canada participated in the NPCP at which our field notes were recorded despite heavy snow and dangerous conditions on roads of the northern plain region of the country in the days preceding the event.

We utilize grounded theory technique to collect qualitative data through semi-structured interviews to qualitatively determine and describe socialization factors important in motivating the study's participants to become powwow announcers, social factors influencing the participants' development as announcers, social factors impacting the participants' verbal behavior during a contest powwow, and their perceived role in the socialization of powwow participants and spectators.

Interviews are conducted in advance of the powwow. Interviews with the 2 participants average 85 minutes each and are digitally recorded. Notes are taken during interviews and during the six sessions of the powwow. Recordings are transcribed for analysis upon return to campus. Observations are made and field notes are recorded during four sessions of the NPCP.

We obtained The University of Texas Permian Basin Institutional Review Board approval to conduct the current study. Signed informed consent was received from both participants. We attest that their participation in this study is confidential and anonymous. Both participants are assigned pseudonyms as was the powwow and the city within which it was held. We refer to the city hosting the contest powwow as North City and the contest powwow as NPCP.

In our efforts to gather qualitative data used to determine and describe socialization factors important in motivating the study's participants to become powwow announcers, social factors influencing the participants' development as announcers, social factors impacting the participants' verbal behavior during a contest powwow, and their perceived role in the socialization of powwow participants and spectators, we conduct semi-structured interviews. Examples of primary research questions included, for example, why did you become a contest powwow announcer? What factors influenced you to become a contest powwow announcer? What is important in becoming a successful contest powwow announcer? How do you determine what to say during a contest powwow? Follow up questions were posed to secure additional clarification, and insights when deemed appropriate. Through our interviews, we seek to determine if contest powwow announcers consciously serve as mediators of culture and, if so, how they accomplish the goal.

We employ open coding to evaluate composite data. During this phase of data analysis, our focus is upon transcribed interviews and field notes (Soyer & Ziyanak, 2018). We generate key concepts through axial coding such as challenges for announcer, scripts, humor, history, and inspiration. Our findings concerning each theme and subtheme are examined and reorganized. The selective coding stage concludes the coding process. The process of mapping is utilized to organize the data into a coherent form (Corbin & Strauss, 2007; Aicinena & Ziyanak, 2021). The present study is focused upon announcers working at a large contest powwow and not a traditional powwow. It cannot be assumed that our findings are fully applicable to announcers working at a traditional powwow.

The Participants

Robert is forty-one and has served as one of two announcers at the NPCP for the past ten years. He grew up on various reservations in the northwestern United States. For as long as he can remember, Robert has participated in traditional powwows and he competed in contest powwows as a dancer for four years. For fourteen years, Robert has served as an announcer at traditional and contest powwows. Robert is one of the most sought-after powwow announcers in the country, working year-round throughout the United States and Canada. Announcing powwows has become Robert's full-time business. Robert's son has been a champion contest powwow dancer. Robert speaks his tribal language and holds a bachelor's degree. He receives compensation to serve as an announcer at the NPCP and considers the event to be one of the premiere powwows held in the northern plain region of the United States.

Walter is a resident of North City and is forty years of age. He is a member of the local chamber of commerce and is the first Native American to have been elected as its Chairman. He serves on numerous community and state organizations that focus upon helping others. Walter was raised by his grandparents on a reservation near North City in a "very traditional" manner. Walter began his participation in powwows at the age of two and for twenty years danced in contest powwows. Walter's grandfather taught him to play the drum and sing. He became a member of a drum that traveled often to sing at traditional and contest powwows as a teen. He sang and danced in the NPCP for most of his life. To him, the event is special. For ten years, Walter has served as a member of the powwow's head staff and as one of its two powwow announcers. Walter works both contest and traditional powwows throughout the Great Plains region of the country and is in high demand. Though he has stopped competing in singing and dance competitions, his wife continues to compete as a dancer. Their children have participated in contest and traditional powwows. One of their daughters was highly successful in the contest powwow circuit and won many championships. Walter holds a bachelor's degree and speaks his Native language fluently.

RESULTS AND DISCUSSION

During the four sessions of the NPCP, the study's participants performed all thirteen functions identified by Gelo (2005). They called in dancers for grand entries, coordinated activities which assisted in keeping the event on time. They oversaw and commented during presentations of special guests, giveaways, awards, and specials. They expressed thanks on behalf of the powwow organizers (sponsors, dancers, drums, security, crowd, etc.), conducted a raffle drawing, informed those in attendance of logistical and security issues, publicized upcoming events, told jokes, and recognized individuals including powwow committee members and the powwow princess. The emcees introduced the people giving the prayers, shared history, myths, culture, and traditions with the crowd. They also provided commentary throughout the powwow.

The themes yielded through analysis of our interviews provide insight into the how and why behind what our participants share over the public address system during contest powwows. The following themes are presented and discussed here:

- Factors influencing the participants to become contest powwow announcers.
- Attributes of effective contest powwow announcers.
- Contest powwow announcers influence others.
- It is important to recount Native American history.
- Announcers are expected to adhere to contest powwow protocol.
- It is important to entertain the crowd before and during the contest powwow.
- It is important to bring energy to the contest powwow.
- It is expected for contest powwow announcers to be humorous.
- The participants do not use scripts during the contest powwow.
- Factors influencing the participants to work at the NPCP.

Factors Influencing the Participants to Become Powwow Announcers

Growing up on reservations was instrumental in motivating the participants to become powwow announcers and teaching them the philosophy of the powwow. Each participant was surrounded by family and community elders as they matured. They were immersed within traditional Native American culture within and outside of powwow settings. Both participants had close family members who worked as powwow announcers and served as role models to them. Walter shared a glimpse into the socialization process that resulted in his participation in contest powwows as an announcer:

> When I was a little boy growing up, my grandfather would always talk to me about what the announcers were saying and why they were saying it. My grandfather was the one who taught me how to sing and dance and he made my outfits. He taught me. He sat me at the drum at a young age and taught me how to sing. He took me around to powwows all the time, in the summertime espe-cially. He and my other grandmother, his sister, my grandmother, they would always make us get up at our family gatherings and introduce ourselves and tell the people our traditional tribal names. My grandmother was just as strong as my grandfather in terms of our traditional ways. As I started to get older, my grandfather would ask me to get up to speak for him to share some things that he wanted to relay to them at the gathering.

Robert was most inspired to become an announcer by his great uncle:

> Now my dad's mom's brother, which is my dad's Uncle, which is my grandpa, his name is Jack Yellowstone. . . . He was, for many years, our home MC. He spoke the language. He knew protocol. He knew our home and he was our home MC for years up until he passed. . . . Until he couldn't do it anymore. I still remember listening to him on the mic when I was a young boy. But I really wasn't sitting with him at the announcer stand and taking notes and learning, but I knew what he did there, and it was always there in my mind.

The first time Walter got up and served as an emcee, it seemed like a natural thing for him to do. He felt as if he had prepared to do so since his youth:

> The first time that I got up and announced was because my grandfather was hurt-ing. I got up and I just took over. All the things that he used to tell me to do, he no longer had to tell me. At that point I was ready.

Robert shared that when he attended powwows or competed in dance contests that he detested poor announcers and believed they were responsible when events were something less than they could have been. He wanted to become an announcer to bring excitement to powwows:

> I knew that being a singer and a dancer sitting at powwows that they could be better if the MC could be rocking it. . . . Why did I want to be an announcer? Because it felt good, it felt natural, and it gave me the chance to bring light to a lot of other areas that weren't being highlighted at powwows . . . and it also gave me a chance to Hype it up. . . . To hype it up!

Both participants were taught powwow protocol, traditions, values, and history by family. Each was further influenced and taught implicitly and explicitly by others as they participated in powwows as dancers and singers. The participants believe that when the opportunity came for them to work their first powwow that they were prepared to do so. They relish the opportunity to impact others as they provide the voice of tradition to the activities taking place during the powwow.

Attributes of Effective Announcers

According to the participants, a good voice, understanding what excites powwow participants, knowledge of the powwow, and knowing how to gain and maintain a crowd's attention are all important factors that lead to an announcer's effectiveness. Walter explains that a good announcer must have many tools that can be used during the powwow:

> It just sucks the life out of the powwow, celebration or gathering you're at if you do [the same thing] all the time, it then becomes redundant. But like I said, having all these different tools, using them at the right time, knowing when to talk and share, and when not to say anything is important.

Because Walter and Robert are serious about being good announcers, they are still honing their craft, and that requires continual learning. Walter explains that he must examine himself, his knowledge, and his abilities while remaining willing to learn and accept new things. He must be teachable and willing to adjust what he brings to a powwow.

Robert encourages other emcees to develop their own style, voice, and creativity. He developed his style of announcing by listening to announcers he admired during powwows and as he watched sporting events, but he believes good announcers have a "gift" that poor announcers do not. He provides an example:

> Michael Buffer . . . remember him? When that microphone would drop down in the middle of that arena and had that cool ass voice. He had that cool voice and his classic, "Let's get ready to rumble!"

Those with the gift provided by "Creator" must work to make the most of it as they develop their style. Part of the development of announcer's unique style includes the use of specific terms or "tag lines":

> See you got to have a tagline. You've got to have something that makes you unique. And over the years I've created a lot of taglines. I've created, "Uh hu, yeah!," "Say it loud and proud!," "Good from the hood!," "Save me a lead!" . . . I've created, "A ho!" I've created a lot of them . . . little taglines. . . . Little sound bites.

Robert keeps up with current events and national news and incorporates some of the day's information before and during the powwow:

> You also have to understand what's going on in current events. I'll turn on the news and just watch CNN for a while and listen to Trump . . . what he said . . . this and that. What's going on there and what he's trying to do there? Do I use a lot of that? Maybe . . . Do, you know, who's passed on recently? What kind of current events are going on? What's going on out in the real world? So, you can incorporate those things.

Both announcers inform the crowd of upcoming powwows, what type of powwows they will be, some of the specials that will be sponsored, who the sponsors of the powwows and specials are, and where the events will be held. Sharing such information helps to fill dead time during the powwow in which there is no music, dancing, or other activity. It also conveys to those present that the events have importance.

As Gelo (2005) noted, powwow participants and committee members continually evaluate the performance of emcees. Effective contest powwow announcers use a variety of tools. Their voice is a tool and effective emcees use their voice to command attention. Knowledge is a tool. Effective announcers are knowledgeable of traditions and protocol important to Native American culture and to the powwow. Effective emcees are familiar with current events, understand how to keep the powwow moving, recognize when it is appropriate to share information and when it is important to be quiet. Announcers understand that to become and remain effective, continual learning is required. Finally, effectual emcees must be able to fill a powwow's dead time with verbal activity that gains and maintains the attention of those present. Failure to fill dead time effectively makes them inferior announcers, decreases their marketability, and reduces the number of events they can work. When powwow committees hold high expectations for announcers regarding their ability to explain, exhibit, and maintain tradition, they assist in maintaining important cultural characteristics.

Powwow Announcers Influence Others

Walter is positive that his announcing influences others and he relishes the opportunity to do so. He understood at a young age that cultural and powwow traditions were important and that announcers impact others in important ways:

> My grandfather had a way of getting behind the microphone and telling it like it is. It really bothered him when people weren't doing things the right way traditionally. As he got older, he would ask me to get up and speak for the family or for him and to share information with people. So, that's where it started for me, even though I didn't become an announcer until later in my life. But that's when I started to think about how, when I spoke, how does that have an impact on people?

Walter believes his powwow experience, his education, and the fact that he was trained as a teacher have prepared him to serve as a leader and to influence others through the powwow. Robert believes that announcers have more impact upon those participating in powwows than any other facet of the powwow.

Walter consciously seeks to inspire spectators to pay attention to and enjoy what's going on during the powwow. Robert purposely tries to influence and inspire others to be athletes, to get an education and to "be somebody." The powwow provides him with a platform to share his beliefs, "Where else am I going to get that platform?"

Both participants share the powwow's schedule of events with those in attendance and identify the dancers competing within the circle. They often share history, information concerning dances, Native American traditions, and the Native American way of thinking or viewing situations. Walter explains that there are always non-Natives in the crowd and if he does not share what has gone on in the past and what is going on at the powwow, "they will never get it."

When announcing at powwows, Walter serves as a translator. Spectators, dancers, and drummers often ask him to share information over the public address system in his Native language. Part of the effectiveness of an announcer, in his opinion, is being able to change the words, yet convey the original meaning of the information. According to Robert, "The powwow announcer has a big influence on the crowd. I believe you definitely watch what you say. You definitely choose your words carefully."

A goal for both Walter and Robert is to introduce singers and dancers in such a way that they share the passion the competitors have for singing and dancing. Often, the participants show respect for singers and dancers through their introductions. Robert explains:

My style of emceeing is different than any other MC and I've noticed a lot of things since I started. I like to remember people's names, their tribe, where they come from. It gives me a challenge, but it also gives those dancers recognition too, especially if a dancer's been dancing for a lot of years and he's earned some respect, and he's earned some notoriety. You know who he or she is especially if he's a champion dancer. During Grand entry I give them shout outs. It's more personal. It gives them a sense of pride, a sense of respect, when they get noticed.

The participants' verbal activity during introductions serves to excite the crowd. After performances, both announcers provide praise to singers and dancers for their performance. As they do, appreciation and excitement are conveyed.

In what ways do contest powwow emcees influence others? When traditions such as the "giveaway" are conducted during the powwow, announcers explain that giving is important to the people, that giving and sharing with others is something that is and has always been important in the Native community. In retelling history and emphasizing the importance of traditions and values associated with the Native American way of life, emcees encourage powwow participants to reflect upon what is heard. Perhaps reflection upon differences between the Native American collectivist "way" and that of the dominant culture assists in maintaining the unique qualities of Native American life, its traditions, and its values in opposition to the winds of change which continue to encourage assimilation and their disappearance.

It Is Important to Recount Native American History

Robert gained historical knowledge of his people formally in college. He was also taught in the traditional way by elders, through non-formal means. He also learned by listening to announcers when he participated in powwows as a singer and dancer. Native American history was also a part of Walter's formal college studies. He too learned history from his elders and while participating in powwows as a drummer, singer, and announcer.

Recounting Native American history during powwows is deemed important by both participants. Non-Natives and many Natives often lack an awareness or understanding of the history of the people. Robert believes that an understanding of the peoples' history encourages young Native Americans and reminds them of what their ancestors went through to survive. It helps them appreciate how far they have come. Walter believes that it is important for Native Americans to know who they are. He asserts that knowing the history of the ancestors' struggles is necessary for them to appreciate how their culture, traditions and values survived in the face of forced assimilation efforts. When Walter shares history, he is cognizant of the fact that some Caucasians in the audience may feel guilty as he celebrates his ancestors:

I pointed out that there were 50 to 100 million of our ancestors here a long time ago and at the end of the 1800s only 250,000 remained. And then I talked about the Black Hills and the Black Hills Act. Gold was found here, and Custer came along. You know, our ancestors never sold the land. We never signed that agreement. We've never agreed to sell it. . . . So, I shared that history and then said, "We're all here! We're remembering who we are! And we're memorializing those Warriors that stood up at a time that we needed them." And so, when I shared it that way people kind'a understood. And people in the arena, man, the energy . . . it was awesome!

During the powwow, Walter often expressed that the elders should be held in high regard for it was because of them that the Native American way of life survived. It was they who maintained the language when they were forced to learn English and it is because of them that traditions and Native American values survived when it was expected for the ways of the colonizers to be adopted.

Robert trusts that if he can educate Natives and non-Natives in attendance about Native American history, it may give them a little better understanding of, "why we do the things we do . . . you know . . . why we value our family and our culture so much." In the day of the Internet, cell phones, and a focus upon the present, Robert and Walter believe it is more important than ever to teach the history of their people.

Robert believes it is important to share historical information specific to the tribal groups that are hosting a powwow:

If I'm in an area I'll talk about a certain chief from that area . . . Chief Numaga from Reno Nevada, Chief Wa Walvolka, Chief Sitting Bull, Chief Two Moons. . . . Maybe I'll go up to Blackfoot country and talk about Chief Carry the Kettle. . . . We've got Chief Pound Maker and all these different Chiefs. And you wonder who they are.

By opening minds to wonder, Robert believes people become motivated to learn and to better appreciate their history.

Recounting history during the contest powwow helps Native Americans better understand who they are. They also grow to appreciate how and why they think and behave differently from those in the dominant culture. When announcers share Native American history, cultural outsiders in attendance can also better understand Native American values and behaviors.

Contest Powwow Protocol

Protocols are likened to social etiquette. Etiquette may be described as expected behavior in various areas of social life. For any social group, protocol is based upon its established values and traditions. Because culture differs between social groups, values and traditions often differ between groups. So, too, do protocols differ in various cultures. For example, we note that pointing with fingers to indicate direction or place is considered impolite in Navajo culture. It is expected to point with the lips. Protocol for indicating direction in the dominant culture is to use the fingers. In adhering to traditional powwow protocol, contest powwow announcers reinforce the importance of protocol in Native American culture.

The lessons Walter learned concerning powwow protocol have made protocol something he is especially cognizant of as he announces:

> I think I always have my grandfather and my grandmother's voices in my head telling me, "Make sure you do these things. Make sure you follow these protocols." Some announcers, maybe they don't care. They're going to do what they do and that's just the way that it is. But I think for me, because I've been trained, it feels like I've been brought up to do things a certain way . . . and the right way.

Walter believes that it is always important to follow protocol. For example, traditional protocol calls for announcers NOT to talk while drum groups are performing. Robert learned this aspect of powwow protocol early in his announcing career:

> I remember, one time I was making an announcement loud over the intercom and it was at the end of a song. And this dancer, one of the older dancers, got upset. He said, "Hey, I'm trying to hear the end of this song and there you are talking." So, the older dancers just got upset about it.

The incident illustrates how troubled elders made sure to inform Robert of proper powwow protocol. Talking over the drum made it difficult for the dancers to hear the drum. Part of a competitive dancer's score is based upon stopping on the last beat of the song and they were justifiably upset when Robert talked during the dance. The sanctions supplied by the elders ensured that Robert would avoid talking over the drum in the future.

Powwow committee members often request that specific information be shared over the public address system. When asked to do so, Walter and Robert share the information when and how they believe it should be shared. Experience guides each of them as to what is appropriate. They are receptive to the requests of the committee members, but not all announcers are. Walter observes that some announcers, "are maybe like, 'No! I'm the announcer. I'm down there and I'm going to do what I want.'" Announcers are expected to meet the needs of the powwow committee whenever possible.

Sometimes singers, dancers or spectators ask Walter to share specific information with the crowd in a specific manner. They often fail to realize that the request or the way they want the information to be shared is inappropriate considering protocol. He must serve as a filter concerning what is shared:

> If you don't filter information, it can come across the wrong way and it takes some of the energy out of the building.

Walter credits elders with teaching him what is appropriate to say during the powwow and what the appropriate way to share information is. It is contrary to protocol, for example, when announcers utilize vulgar language or make jokes about specific individuals.

Traditional contest powwow protocol was taught to our participants and is reinforced by elders and other powwow announcers. During contest powwows, announcers committed to preserving and adhering to protocol serve to keep traditions and values intact as they verbalize and pass them on explicitly and implicitly.

Entertain the Crowd before and during the Contest Powwow

Both participants acknowledge that as powwow announcers, part of their job is to entertain the crowd. Their work and the duty to entertain begin as much as two hours before the scheduled start of the grand entry. They advertise upcoming events, share current events, and share jokes with those who come to the powwow in advance of its scheduled starting time. At any given time before the grand entry, a portion of the crowd could be seen looking at the announcers during announcements and laughing in response to their humor.

Before the grand entry of one session, Robert called upon drum group members to participate in a "slow motion" football play competition. Each of the thirteen drum groups divided up its members into offensive and defensive units and ran a play of their own creation in slow motion and then performed a choreographed touchdown celebration. The crowd voted for the drum group presenting the best celebration through its applause. Running the impromptu competition was a way to engage and excite the crowd before the powwow officially commenced. The activity was a parody of the football celebrations drum groups witnessed on television.

If the energy level is high before the Grand Entry, the participants believe the event will be enhanced. Their efforts to bring energy to the event must, however, continue throughout the event. Robert believes that people come to the powwow to be entertained and that places the responsibility of entertaining the crowd firmly upon him:

> The crowd . . . if they're paying an admission to be there then you best believe if they're going to fork out 10 . . . 20 dollars, then they want to be entertained. They want to be entertained. They want to know what's going on. They want to know that things are going smoothly, that there's no dead air, that it's not boring, that they're aware of things that are going on . . . but mainly they want to be entertained.

The participants make it clear that they are expected to entertain those attending the contest powwow. Announcers feel an obligation to entertain and keep the attention of those in attendance. Creativity is necessary to create entertainment because repetitive verbal behavior as well as trite and unremarkable commentary cannot hold the attention of those participating in the powwow.

Bring Energy to the Contest Powwow

Both participants agree that through the effective use of their voice and by sharing interesting and entertaining information they can infuse energy into the powwow. High energy levels and excitement, they contend, results in a higher quality experience for singers, dancers, and spectators. Walter believes that when he brings energy to the powwow, it makes people feel good. Robert explains that he pays attention to the level of interest and energy level of the spectators and responds when it seems to be low:

> Once in a while I'll do like a 7th inning stretch if I noticed the crowd getting sleepy and tired and the energy's low. I'll get people to stand up but that just comes from my creativity. Again, that's just me being me. It's my creativity. It's my sense of noticing stuff.

Robert feels a responsibility to make the powwow committee look good because it works very hard all year to put on the powwow. Bringing energy to the event helps the committee look good:

> The powwow committee works hard all year, you know what I mean? They raised the money. They got donations. They got everything ready to go. They mowed the lawn. They fixed their campgrounds. They put their lights up and they built their arbor. It's all ready to go. Hundreds of dancers come, and a bunch of drum groups come. And if the announcer up there is kind of boring, no disrespect, but the whole energy, the whole powwow is like ee eee eeee. But if you've got a rock'en announcer, boom man! Boom! Boom! Yep!

According to Walter, keeping up the energy at a contest powwow is one of his biggest challenges. When announcers bring energy to the powwow and keep energy levels high, people have a better experience. The powwow committee "looks good" when energy levels are high, and the event is more likely to be considered successful.

Expected to Be Humorous

Walter notes that humor is a huge part of the Native American culture and it has always been. During the difficult times Native Americans faced throughout history, humor was one thing that served to help them persevere. Laughter helps people feel good and that is why it is important for announcers to interject humor into the powwow. Robert makes it clear that humor is always a part of Native American gatherings, whether an announcer is making jokes or not:

> And I think singers and dancers, when they're out there, when they're around the drum, and out there dancing, they're making each other laugh. They're sharing stories. They're telling jokes. They're teasing each other. . . . That's already happening there.

Walter believes that when he observes something humorous at a powwow and jokes about it, it helps with energy and the positivity of the powwow. He tells fewer jokes today than he did in years past and depends less on scripted jokes. He prefers to share humorous observations and jokes based upon what is going on at the powwow at any given moment, "I tend to get more laughter from more people, no matter what race, cuz there are some things are funny no matter what race you are."

Some jokes at powwows are told that Native Americans can relate to. In some cases, the non-Natives at the powwow may not understand the joke. Robert explains:

> If there's a joke or a story about six or seven Indian cars parked around the house on blocks with dogs living under them, everybody's like, "Oh yeah, yeah! That's just like my aunt's house!" "Just like my house!" But the non-native that's there just to watch the powwow and experience it for a couple hours, then go back to the suburbs to their big rich house and to their two big Escalades that are parked out in the front. . . . They don't know anything about that. And it's not so much about money or finances or upper-class middle-class poor class or whatever, it's just being able to relate.

Walter agrees that when some jokes are funny to some and not understood by others it is because of different degrees of cultural awareness. When

Walter anticipates that some at the powwow will not understand a joke or humorous incident, he provides additional context through commentary, a cultural bridge, so that non-Natives will better understand the point of the joke. In doing so, he helps others appreciate the Native American way of thinking.

Robert often likes to tell jokes about himself because by doing so, he does not offend anyone else. People can laugh at such jokes because they can relate to the situation and because it is humorous. He observed, "I know myself and can tease myself and I'm not going to get mad at myself." It is contrary to powwow protocol to offend others.

Robert contends that it is especially effective to tell jokes that are meaningful to the people living in the area where the powwow is being held. The jokes and banter become more meaningful to the powwow participants when he does:

> In Northwest Montana and Blackfeet Country, [the Natives are] known for their red wieners and their boiled eggs. Out here in Lakota country, you know, and even back home in my Cheyenne country, we like to tease around about eating dogs and the one-legged dog, different stuff like that. You go down southwest, maybe you want to talk a little bit about sheep, or sheep herding, or mutton, or something like that. You just need to know where you are out in that country. If you're up in the northwest, maybe you want to have some fishing jokes or salmon jokes, you know?

The powwow is not all fun and games. It is inappropriate to joke around constantly. Robert notes,

> There are different jokes that are appropriate at times and I always tell people timing is key. You gotta know when to joke and when to be funny but you also need to know when to be serious and you need to know how to balance both.

According to both participants, good announcers know when to be serious and when it is okay to be humorous. Understanding the time and place for humor contributes to the effectiveness of announcers. Understandings result from instruction as well as immersion within the powwow culture. As they tell jokes during contest powwows, the participants implicitly teach the accepted protocol.

Scripts Not Used during the Contest Powwow

The participants were asked if they are required to follow a script when they serve as announcers. They are not provided with scripted material and are given little formal instruction as to what they are to say by powwow organizers. Neither participant brings a self-created script with them when they announce. They are typically given a schedule and it is up to them to determine what is to be shared over the public address system and how to say it. Robert explains that everything is, in his "noggin" and a script is not required. He also notes that during the powwow, people often ask him to make announcements:

> There are times when I get so many requests for different things. People will text me . . . email me . . . Facebook message me. . . . Somebody wants their special for next weekend announced to invite the chicken dancers over there cuz' they're doing a memorial chicken dance and special for someone. This is the prize money. This is what we're giving out. Can you please give me a shout out? And I'll do it as a good favor.

Robert and Walter honored veterans during grand entries and many other times during the NPCP. The information shared is not scripted. It comes from their knowledge of the history of Native American participation in the military, the importance of the warrior spirit, and the importance placed by tribal groups upon protecting the Native American peoples, their traditions, their freedoms, and values. Robert shared that he is often asked for copies of the script he used when sharing how Native Americans have fought for the American flag and their country. He apologizes and tells them that he does not have a script.

Because the participants are not required to adhere to scripts, they are permitted to improvise during the powwow. Through improvisation, they can better insert their personalities and spur of the moment observations and commentary into the contest powwow. When they do, it helps make the event unique from others.

Seek to Make the Powwow Enjoyable to All

Both participants want to make sure that their announcing assists in making the powwow something that all involved can enjoy. Accordingly, Robert and Walter state that it is important not to offend others. Walter explains,

> You want to be careful in how you translate things, or how you communicate things. Because if you don't do it in the right way, you can offend somebody. I think there are certain announcers that either can be too obnoxious or maybe not fun enough or maybe not energetic enough, or maybe are too negative.

Although Walter and Robert want those participating in the powwow to enjoy themselves, the goal is often difficult to achieve. According to Robert, "The big challenge? It's being able to satisfy everybody in attendance. It's hard. That's the biggest challenge."

Will the jokes be funny? Will voices be utilized effectively? Are the stories and myths told during the event meaningful and do they have a direct connection to what is going on when they are told? Is there dead time in which nothing is going on? Is protocol being followed, or are people upset because something stated breaks from it? Each of these questions must be addressed through the choices made by announcers and their resultant verbal behavior. As such, the contest powwow announcer serves as a mediator. Successful choices are requisite for creation of an enjoyable event.

Factors Influencing the Announcers to Work at the NPCP

As is common at contest powwows, the NPCP uses two announcers during the four sessions of the powwow. For periods of time mutually agreed upon, they alternate handling announcing duties. Both participants are in high demand on the powwow circuit. Throughout the year, they emcee at traditional and contest powwows. Each participant was asked why he chose to serve as an announcer at the NPCP.

Walter grew up on a reservation near North City and he participated in the powwow for many years as a singer and dancer. The event served to inspire him and his involvement with the powwow gives him an opportunity to help bring about changes in the Native and non-Native communities most impacted by the powwow. The president of the powwow committee was also important in Walter's initial involvement in the powwow, "Stanley and I worked together at a youth mentoring program previously. So, we had a connection." Once becoming involved in the powwow, Walter took it upon himself to actively promote the powwow through social media, to talk with people in the area about powwow, and he served to educate community members and area elementary school children about powwow traditions and dances through an educational program he refers to as "Powwow 101." The program is a means to educate others on the history of the powwow, dance, regalia, as well as traditional values and traditions.

Robert chooses to participate in the NPCP for several reasons. He views the event as one of the premier contest powwows in the northern plains and believes the powwow committee works hard to make the powwow bigger and better each year. Robert also is impressed by the educational activities conducted by Walter and the powwow committee within the community and public schools.

The participants chose to work the NPCP because they believed in the powwow's ability to educate others concerning Native American history, values, and traditions. The event was viewed as important by both participants and they relished the opportunity to announce at an event that inspires others to retain traditional values and traditions. Finally, relationships served to bring and keep the emcees as regular fixtures at the NPCP.

CONCLUSION

The purpose of the current qualitative study was twofold. First, we sought to expand knowledge concerning the contest powwow, particularly as it related to the social role and function of announcers. Second, we sought to determine if contest powwow announcers consciously serve as mediators of culture and, if so, how they accomplish the goal.

Uniquely, this study focused upon announcers working at a large intertribal contest powwow. During the NPCP, our participants performed each of the thirteen functions of powwow announcers identified by Gelo (2005). As Gelo's work was focused upon announcers serving at traditional powwows, within our review of literature we turned to newspaper and blog interviews to identify how high-profile powwow announcers became emcees, what they did as announcers, what was expected of them as announcers, and why they believed announcers were important in the powwow environment. We sought to determine if our participants shared their goals, beliefs, and experiences through the employment of semi-structured interviews.

As was true with prominent powwow announcers interviewed for newspaper articles and blogs, this study's participants were in high demand. They spent a significant amount of time in the powwow environment as youths and were mentored by elders and others as they danced, sang, and spectated. Both participants understand and embrace their role as teachers of Native American culture, values, history, and traditions. Powwow protocol was informally taught to the participants by announcers, elders, singers, and dancers as they attended and competed at powwows as youths and young adults.

Similar to other prominent announcers, this study's participants are committed to making the powwow enjoyable for all in attendance. They acknowledge that they are entertainers. Both participants believe that it is their responsibility to bring energy to the contest powwow by filling dead periods with interesting and meaningful commentary. The participants understand that humor is important within the powwow milieu. During contest powwows, they provide humorous commentary, stories, and jokes that are especially meaningful to local dancers and spectators. Often their comedic commentary is focused upon Native Americans and the Native American experience.

Commentary the participants bring to the powwow is unscripted and is the product of their years of experience, study, and conversations with local powwow committee members. Effective commentary requires creativity and hard work. Both participants believe in the powwow's ability to educate others concerning Native American history, values, and traditions.

The second purpose of the current study was to determine if contest powwow announcers consciously serve as mediators of culture and, if so, how they accomplish the goal. We found the participants of the current study shared goals for their announcing activity that aligned with those of other high-profile powwow announcers. Like them, our participants felt a responsibility to pass on Native American culture, values, and traditions through their announcing activity. Maintenance of powwow protocol maintained high importance as they performed in the role of contest powwow announcer.

Both participants believe they assist in the maintenance and continuation of traditional Native American values and traditions by serving as contest powwow announcers. How the contest powwow relates to Native American history and tradition, and how the contest powwow unites Native Americans in attendance is made clear to all by the announcer. Announcers provide meaning to the songs, dances, traditions, and values common to the contest powwow that urban Native Americans and non-native Americans might not know, understand, or appreciate on their own. In doing so, announcers serve as cultural mediators who help Native American traditions, values, and history live on.

NOTE

1. Aicinena was invited to attend a Hethuska War Dance in White Eagle, Oklahoma by a member of a Hethuska Warrior Society. The information presented is based upon notes and observations he made during the event.

Chapter 5

Is the Contest Powwow a Spiritual Ceremony?

Black Elk, a Lakota Sioux, has been identified by historians as the pre-eminent holy man of the Sioux (Mails, 2012). He lived at a time when the Lakota were at war with the American government to retain their traditional way of life and fight confinement to reservations. The holy man's story as told by Neihardt (2008) provides unique insight into the daily life of Native Americans during his lifetime. Within Black Elk's story the role of dance in both the secular and sacred realms of Sioux society are recounted.

During Black Elk's life, from 1863 to 1960, sacred dance was ceremonial in nature and purposefully directed toward Wakan-Tanka, the Creator of all things, or toward Wakan-Tanka's Helpers. Ceremonial dance was a key component of the religiously[1] significant Horse Dance, Buffalo Dance, Sun Dance, Elk Dance, and Ghost Dance. Dancing was also a component of healing ceremonies performed by Black Elk as he called upon Wakan-Tanka and the Helpers.

Social dances serving no religious function also took place among the Sioux. Social dances were celebratory in nature and often functioned as a communal expression of joy. Black Elk described social dancing taking place after successful hunts, following a boy's game to count coup, after the killing of an enemy (victory dance and scalp dance), after recovery from illness, and following naming ceremonies for children. Social dances were also conducted after preparations had been completed for religious ceremonies such as the Sun Dance. At times, feasting and celebratory dancing took place by open fires all night long. Black Elk recalled, "Those were happy times" (Neihardt, 2008, p. 44).

Dance continues to be important in contemporary Native American culture. The people might dance for social reasons, for fitness, for prizes, or for others who are themselves incapable of dancing. Some Native Americans continue to dance in conjunction with sacred ceremonies such as the Sun Dance which continues to be conducted among the Sioux and other tribal groups (Andrews & Olney, 2007; Ellis, 2003).

Dance and song are primary components of Native American cultural gatherings known as powwows (Albers & Medicine, 2005). Through the central elements of the powwow, Native American culture is maintained and reproduced. The people forge and recommence relationships, renew cultural traditions, and celebrate a common past, future, and present (Dufrene, 1990; Foster, 1991; Kracht, 1994; Roberts, 2002). The powwow serves as an educational and cultural contact zone in which youths learn tribally valued songs, dances, and traditions (Hsiu-Yen Yeh, 2006). The gatherings provide a context within which cultural practices that might otherwise disappear are maintained and reinterpreted (Burke, 2000; Ellis, 1999).

Public powwows provide a bridge for cultural exchange between disparate Indigenous cultures, and between Native Americans and non-Natives (Hsiu-Yen Yeh, 2006). Keene (2010) describes the powwow as one of the only places that non-Native spectators can interact with Native Americans in a culturally relevant setting. Yet, powwows also serve as an important marker of alterity for Native Americans (Andrews & Olney, 2007; Wightman, 2012).

Traditional powwows are locally based events that may include activities such as local tribal business, local politics, and ceremonies important to tribal members. Dance and song typically follow these community-based activities. Some dances performed at traditional powwows are considered sacred. The gatherings are believed to foster spiritual connections to the Creator and each other (Albers and Medicine, 2005; Andrews & Olney, 2007; Fowler, 2005).

Some traditional powwows include no sacred activity. For example, the Iroquois have public gatherings they refer to as "socials." Socials are public affairs that anyone can participate in. The twenty songs and dances performed during Iroquois socials are devoid of religious significance (Krouse, 2001; Logan, 1993). Iroquois religious dance and ceremonial activity are conducted in settings that are not open to the public.

Contest powwows are competitive events at which dancers and drum groups vie for prizes or cash awards. Dance contestants compete in various age groups and different styles of dance, wear a number, must adhere to rules as they compete, and receive scores from judges. Contest powwows are typically intertribal in nature as they often involve individuals from multiple tribal groups, traditions, and regions of the country. Because contest powwows are not tribal or community-centered events, Pan-Indianism or Intertribalism is fostered and reinforced between participants from various tribes. Contest powwow participants celebrate traditions shared by Native Americans collectively. Examples of commonly shared traditional Native American values include family, generosity, humor, dance, song, honoring of elders, and honoring of veterans. Contest powwows may be no less important than traditional community dances or ceremonies in expressing and maintaining Native culture and identity (Ellis, 1999).

Disagreement exists among dancers as to the role of tradition and religion[1] in contest powwows. Andrews and Olney (2007) studied the dance culture of the Nez Perce and Kwakwaka'wakw tribes in the Pacific Northwest region of the United States and southwestern Canada. One of their participants explained that when dancing in a contest powwow, he must disconnect the dances from their traditional and spiritual meaning. Participants viewed contest powwows as social events because local culture and spirituality are replaced by a focus upon money and competition. The contest powwow is not a place a place where traditional spiritual dances can be performed. Most participants, however, noted that dancing in contest powwows can involve cultural traditions and spiritual practice on a personal basis.

Powwow dancers have stated that contemporary powwows, both the traditional and contest forms, are more celebratory than spiritual (Rahimi, 2005). Sociologists and anthropologists have also described powwows as social events or secular ceremonies since the 1940s (Callahan, 1993; Gamble, 1952; Howard, 1983; Lurie, 1971). However, the belief that contest and traditional powwows are devoid of religious significance and character may be incorrect.

The level of religious significance and activity associated with any individual powwow may be high or low. Traditional powwows are more likely to be characterized by religious activity, yet not all would be. Large intertribal contest powwows as publicly performed sporting contests would be expected to include little explicitly religious activity. Features of each individual powwow overlap in different ways to various degrees depending upon the specific gathering (Scales, 2007). Figure 5.1 illustrates the continuum of religious character upon which any specific powwow might fall based upon its specific characteristics.

Hundreds of thousands of spectators are drawn to contest powwows each year through an interest in Native culture. Yet, many Non-Natives and Natives who identify with Christian religious denominations choose not to attend powwows because they are perceived as ceremonial gatherings in which traditional Native American religions are celebrated and practiced (Kelley, 2012; Wenger, 2011). When we discussed our research agenda with friends and colleagues, we found that few knew anything about powwows and those with limited knowledge frequently asked, "Isn't the powwow a religious thing for the Indians? Aren't they worshiping strange gods and stuff?"

If contest powwows are crucibles for Native American religious tradition and ceremony, perhaps it would be reasonable for devout Christians to shun attending contest powwows to avoid the worship of "false gods" and engaging in idolatry (King James Bible, 2021, Exodus 20:3, Exodus 34:14, 1

Traditional and Contest Powwows: A Continuum

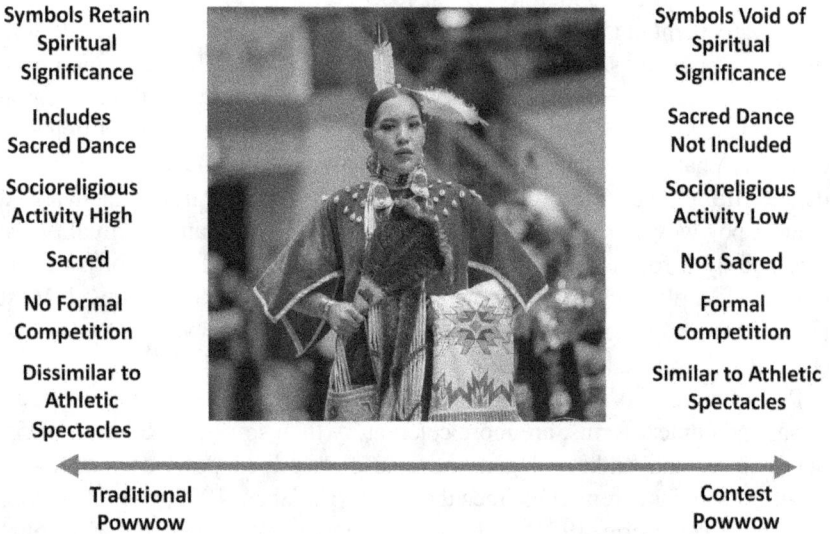

Symbols Retain Spiritual Significance	Symbols Void of Spiritual Significance
Includes Sacred Dance	Sacred Dance Not Included
Socioreligious Activity High	Socioreligious Activity Low
Sacred	Not Sacred
No Formal Competition	Formal Competition
Dissimilar to Athletic Spectacles	Similar to Athletic Spectacles

Traditional Powwow   Contest Powwow

Figure 5.1   Traditional and Contest Powwows: A Continuum.

Corinthians 10:14, 1 Corinthians 10:20, Jeremiah 10:2-5). If, however, it can be demonstrated that the contest powwow is not a religious event in which sacred religious rites and ceremonies are commonly practiced, perhaps more Non-Natives will choose to attend the celebrations and learn more about Native Americans, their history, and the richness of their traditional culture.

It has been demonstrated that explicitly religious activity is not uncommon in traditional powwows, however, our review of published literature yielded no study in which researchers sought to determine what explicitly religious behavior might be observed in a large contemporary intertribal contest pow-wow. Further, we located no study in which those involved in the organization and conduction of a large contest powwow were asked to assess the level of Native American religious behavior existing within contest powwow. Because individuals who plan and conduct powwows are instrumental in what occurs within the event, their views are especially important to consider when assessing the role of religion in the contest powwow.

In the current study, we first seek to determine what individuals involved in the planning and staging of a large intertribal contest powwow think the role of religion and Native American spirituality are in the contest powwow. Second, we seek to determine what explicitly religious behavior is present in a large intertribal contest powwow.

REVIEW OF LITERATURE

In this review of literature, we define religion. We then turn our discussion to the basic tenants of Christianity and those of Native American spirituality. Doing so is imperative as Christianity and Native American spirituality reflect significantly different worldviews. We examine the Doctrine of Discovery which sprang forth from Christianity and was used by explorers, colonialists, and expansionists throughout North America to justify the murder and cultural genocide visited upon Native Americans and other Indigenous people groups across the globe throughout history. Christianity will be shown to have been instrumental in governmental efforts to eliminate dance and traditional religious activity from the lives of Native Americans. Efforts made by Christians to prohibit dance led, in part, to secularization of many traditional dances and their festive cultural gatherings. Finally, we utilize existing literature to demonstrate that symbols and ceremonies commonly observed in conjunction with contest powwows share similarities with Christian symbols and ceremony existent in the broader American culture.

What Is Religion?

According to sociologist Émile Durkheim, religion is a means by which society collectively self-validates itself through ritual and myth. Durkheim (2001) defined religion as:

> a unified system of beliefs and practices relative to sacred things, that is to say, things set apart and forbidden—beliefs and practices which unite into one single moral community called a Church, all those who adhere to them. (p. 46)

Cultural traditions widely recognized as religions include Islam, Christianity, Buddhism, Daoism, Judaism, Confucianism, and others (Taliaferro, 2019).

Scholars hailing from numerous academic disciplines have provided definitions of religion (Bruce, 2011; Durkheim, 2001; Falassi, 1987; Taliaferro, 2019). Despite the best efforts of academics, a definitive definition of religion remains elusive (Nath, 2015; Oppong, 2013). We define religion as a collection of scriptures or oral traditions that informs a culture's members of the existence of a higher power or spiritual path, how the higher power or spiritual path is evidenced on earth, how the higher power or spiritual path is accessed, what actions are deemed moral, how one atones for misdeeds, what rituals or actions are required of believers, and how one achieves a life fulfilled.

A Brief Description of Christianity

We address Christianity in this chapter rather than other recognized religions for two reasons. First, Christianity is the predominant religion in the United

States, with 76 percent of Americans identifying with various Christian denominations (Pew Research, 2020). Second, forms of Christianity are common in reservation communities. Sixty-six percent of 3,084 Native Americans who were members of two large tribes in the southwestern United States polled by Garroutte et al. (2014) identified as Christians. Further, 75–82 percent of Native Americans living on reservations indicated that Christianity had salience in their lives (Kosmin & Keysar, 2006).

The following description of Christianity is based upon that provided by Wilson (1991) in *World Scripture: A Comparative Anthology of Sacred Texts* and scriptures gleaned from the King James Bible (2021). All Christian scripture presented in following pages was taken from the King James Bible (2021). For ease of communication, the books of the Bible, chapter, and verse will be used as citations throughout the remainder of this chapter. For example, Genesis 1:3 = Genesis (book) 1 (chapter):3 (verse).

Christianity shares traditions and sacred scriptures with Judaism. The Old Testament is considered important in Christianity as it is believed to contain prophecy foretelling the coming of Jesus, the Christ, and the reconciliation of believers with God, the Father. The Old Testament served as the core scripture for the Jewish faith as well as for Jesus and his disciples. The New Testament of the Christian Bible includes accounts of the life of Jesus, who is considered the Messiah and savior of humanity, and writings of the apostles that were important in the growth of the church. Christianity is considered a monotheistic religion. Most Christian denominations hold that God exists in three forms (Father, Son, and Holy Spirit), as the Holy Trinity.

Christian Account of Creation

God is the Creator of the universe. God is omnipotent and therefore sovereign over the world. Human beings are God's final creation, and they were created in the very image of God:

> 26 And God said, Let us make man in our image, after our likeness: and let them have dominion over the fish of the sea, and over the fowl of the air, and over the cattle, and over all the earth, and over every creeping thing that creepeth upon the earth. 27 So God created man in his own image, in the image of God created he him; male and female created he them. (Genesis 1: 26-27)

Mankind is the pinnacle of God's creation.

The Presence of God in Christianity

Christians believe God to be omnipresent (Jeremiah 23:24; Isiah 43:2; Job 34:21; Proverbs 15:3; Hebrews 4:13).

7 Whither shall I go from thy spirit? or whither shall I flee from thy presence? 8 If I ascend up into heaven, thou art there: if I make my bed in hell, behold, thou art there. 9 If I take the wings of the morning, and dwell in the uttermost parts of the sea; 10 Even there shall thy hand lead me, and thy right hand shall hold me. (Psalm 139:7-10)

However, in the Christian view, humans are separated spiritually from God because of sin. Salvation from sin and reconciliation with God is achieved when believers accept the saving grace offered through the death and resurrection of Jesus who paid the debt of sin to reconcile sinners with a Holy God. At the time of salvation, the Holy Spirit of God comes to reside within the believer to provide guidance in life. Though God's existence is evidenced through creation and all of nature, Christians do not believe that the spirit of God resides in anything other than human beings.

Christianity and Nature

Human beings are commanded by God to rule over every earthly creature and to subdue the earth itself,

28 And God blessed them, and God said unto them, Be fruitful, and multiply, and replenish the earth, and subdue it: and have dominion over the fish of the sea, and over the fowl of the air, and over every living thing that moveth upon the earth. (Genesis 1:28)

Transmission of Christianity

The "Great" Commission to share the Gospel with the world was given to the disciples in Matthew 28:18-20:

18And Jesus came and spake unto them, saying, All power is given unto me in heaven and in earth.19Go ye therefore, and teach all nations, baptizing them in the name of the Father, and of the Son, and of the Holy Ghost: 20Teaching them to observe all things whatsoever I have commanded you: and, lo, I am with you always, even unto the end of the world. Amen.

According to Hackett and McClendon (2017), Christianity is currently the largest world religion encompassing 31.2 percent of the world's population and 2.3 billion members. The Great Commission was vital to the growth of the early Christian Church and continues to be for many Christian denominations today.

We now turn our discussion toward Native American "religious beliefs." In doing so, we strive to convey how very different they are from the dualistic form of Christianity that was brought by colonizers to the New World and its Indigenous inhabitants.

Native American Spirituality

There are currently 574 federally recognized Native American tribes in the United States (Bureau of Indian Affairs, 2020). There is a great variance in the specifics of each tribal group's traditional sacred beliefs and practices; however, there is a marked similarity in their cultures' core beliefs and philosophy (Rhodes, 1991). According to Silverman (2015), "Indians across space and time have shared certain religious elements, such as shamanism, the notion of spiritual guardianship, and belief that spiritual power courses through the world and the things in it" (para. 2). According to McNally (2000), Native American traditions may be better characterized as lifeways rather than religions.

Native Americans often use the term "spirituality" in place of the term "religion" when describing their beliefs and practices. In the Lakota language, the words *wicohan* and *wakan* translate into "the way we do things"; and "holy," "sacred," or "powerful" respectively (Riggs, 1890). Wakan-Tanka refers to the Great Spirit or Great Mystery, the supreme deity and Creator of the Sioux (Leeming, 2005).

To traditional Native Americans, the thought of separating daily life from Creator and worship is nonsensical. A word such as "religion" was neither conceived nor needed by traditional Native Americans. Illustratively, there is no word for religion in the Lakota language (Owen, 2008).

Native American Accounts of Creation

Native American creation stories are at odds with Western anthropocentric thought which views humankind as God's special creation (Rhodes, 1991). Black Elk summarized the Lakota's creation story:

> It is the story of all life that is holy and is good to tell, and of us two-leggeds sharing in it with the four-leggeds and the wings of the air and all green things; for these are children of one mother and their father is one Spirit. (Neihardt, 2008, p. 1)

Wakan-Tanka is the Creator of all things and His power is found in all things created. All of creation enjoys a spiritual relationship (Hendry, 2003; Jocks, 2004).

The Presence of Creator in Native American Spirituality

It is impossible in Native American spirituality to differentiate between the profane and the sacred as is common in Western dualistic thought (Hendry,

2003; Mails, 2012). In the Western world, the act of worship is often isolated as a discreet component of one's individual and social life. Contrarily, to Native American traditionalists, spirituality and acts of worship permeate every aspect of their lives (Rhodes, 1991; Talbot, 2006). Lakota holy man Fools Crow (Mails, 2012) explains, "In the old days my people did not separate their daily life in the world from the spiritual life. Everything was spiritual. We were soaked with it. It is only now that we see a difference" (p. 37). Barney Old Coyote in testimony before the United States Senate astutely observed, "This oneness of Indian life seems to be the basic difference between the Indian and non-Indians of a dominant society" (Abourezk, 1978, p. 87).

Native American Spirituality and Nature

In traditional Native American life, activities were undertaken prayerfully, and the people held a profound reverence for humans, animals, and the earth. According to Osage, Francis La Flesche, all things, both animate and inanimate, are given power by the Creator:

All life is Wakan [sacred]; so also, is everything which exhibits power, whether in action, as the winds and drifting clouds, or in passive endurance, as the boulder by the wayside. For even the commonest sticks and stones have a spiritual essence which must be reverenced as a manifestation of the all-pervading mysterious power that fills the universe. (Fewkes, 1925, p. 186)

Traditional Native Americans believe they need the assistance of other forms of life for survival (Deloria, 1994). Other forms of life are viewed as other "peoples" rather than insensitive things (Deloria, 2003). All creatures are respected and activities such as hunting are considered spiritual adventures. Lame Deer, a Sioux medicine man, provides elucidation:

When we killed a buffalo, we knew what we were doing. We apologized to his spirit, tried to make him understand why we did it, honoring with a prayer the bones of those who gave their flesh to keep us alive, praying for their return, praying for the life of our brothers, the buffalo nation, as well as for our own people. . . . To us, all life is sacred. (Callenbach, 1996, p. 67)

Transmission of Native Spirituality

Unlike religions based upon sacred scriptures, no theological treatise or sacred scriptures outline Native American spirituality. Whether labeled Native American religion or spirituality, the "road" or "path" is correctly described as being a way of life not a codified set of rules, beliefs, and behaviors (Owen, 2008; Weaver, 1998). Native American spirituality is, "transmitted to others by the proper behavior of the possessors of the tradition" (Deloria, 1999, p. 134).

Spirituality is the consequence of a collective experience that is shared and within which the sharing of oral traditions and sacred ways are indispensable (Talbot, 2006). The proper way to behave and to view the world is learned through observation and informal instruction rather than through purposeful individual study of sacred texts, or formal instruction in Sunday schools, mosques, synagogues, and churches.

Christianity and the Doctrine of Discovery

An attitude of love and reciprocity was advocated in the teachings of the Christ. When asked what the greatest commandment was in Mark 12:30-31, Jesus replied,

> 30 And thou shalt love the Lord thy God with all thy heart, and with all thy soul, and with all thy mind, and with all thy strength: this is the first commandment. 31 And the second is like, namely this, Thou shalt love thy neighbour as thyself. There is none other commandment greater than these.

Reciprocity is required of Christians. Reciprocity employed logically leads to peace.

Between the time the great commission and calls for reciprocity were given by Jesus and the middle of the fifteenth century, how one was to go about spreading the Gospel and treat others was significantly altered. The Romanus Pontifex of 1455, later known as the Doctrine of Discovery, issued by Pope Nicholas V implored Christians to:

> invade, search out, capture, vanquish, and subdue all Saracens and pagans whatsoever, and other enemies of Christ wheresoever placed, and the king-doms, dukedoms, principalities, dominions, possessions, and all movable and immovable goods whatsoever held and possessed by them and to reduce their persons to perpetual slavery, and to apply and appropriate to himself and his successors the kingdoms, dukedoms, counties, principalities, dominions, possessions, and goods, and to convert them to his and their use and profit. (McLaren, 2016, p. 77)

According to the World Council of Churches (2012), "The Doctrine [of Discovery] mandated Christian Europeans to attack, enslave and kill the Indigenous Peoples they encountered and to acquire all of their assets" (p. 3). The Doctrine of Discovery was employed by the British, Spanish, Portuguese,

Dutch, and French explorers and colonists as they expanded their respective empires. It served as a license to perform genocide on all non-white, non-Christian nations (McLaren, 2016). In America, the Doctrine of Discovery supported the ideology of Manifest Destiny which served as justification for Christian Caucasians to murder Native Americans, to steal their traditional homelands, and to commit cultural genocide during periods of exploration, colonialization, and westward expansion (McLaren, 2016).

One quote well illustrates the thoughts of some Christian soldiers during this dark period of American history. John Chivington, a Methodist Minister and Military Leader, argued that the murder of Indians was within the will of God:

Damn any man who sympathizes with Indians! . . . I have come to kill Indians, and believe it is right and honorable to use any means under God's heaven to kill Indians. . . . Kill and scalp all, big and little. (Masich, 2017, p. 219)

It is important to note, however, that not all Americans embraced Covington's beliefs. Kit Carson, a well-known Indian fighter himself, was quite critical of the Doctrine of Discovery and its impact upon Native Americans. In describing his reaction to the Covington-led Sand Creek massacre of 1864, Carson expressed his outrage:

Jist to think of that dog Chivington, and his dirty hounds, up thar at Sand Creek! Whoever heerd of sich doings "mong Christians!" that durned miscreant and his men shot down squaws and blew the brains out of little innocent children—pistoled little papooses in the arms of their dead mothers, and even worse than this!—them durned devils! . . . And you call such soldiers Christians, do ye? And pore Indians savages! (Ellis, 2013, p. 14–15)

In regard to inhumane treatment of Native Americans by the American government, Carson asked, "What der yer 'spose our Heavenly Father, who made both them and us thinks of these things?" (Ellis, 2013, p. 14). Carson also lamented over the confiscation of Native lands:

Pore things! Pore things! I've seen as much of "em as any man livin," and I can't help but pity 'em, right or wrong! They once owned all this country, yes, Plains and Mountains, buffalo and everything, but now they own next door to nuthin, and will soon be gone. (Ellis, 2013, p. 16)

Carson's prognostication was partially incorrect in that Native Americans still exist. Native American population in the area that became the forty-eight contiguous states fell from an estimated 5 million before first European contact to 375,000 around 1900 (Thornton, 1987).

In recent years, acknowledgment of the atrocities visited upon Indigenous peoples throughout the world has increased. The World Council of Churches (2012) denounced the Doctrine of Discovery and its enduring impact on Indigenous peoples, "as fundamentally opposed to the gospel of Jesus Christ and as a violation of the inherent human rights that all individuals and peoples have received from God" (p. 10). The council calls upon churches, "to reflect upon their own history to seek a better understanding of the current plight of indigenous peoples" (p. 14). Numerous American Christian denominations including the Presbyterian Church, United Church of Christ, Christian Reformed Church, and United Methodist Church have endorsed the resolution. At the time of this book's publication, the Catholic Church has not endorsed the resolution.

The belief that it was just to have taken what once belonged to Native Americans is still commonly held by non-Native citizens of the United States. American movie legend John Wayne articulated their thoughts:

> I don't feel we did wrong in taking this great country away from them...our so-called stealing of this country was just a matter of survival. There were great numbers of people who needed land, and the Indians were selfishly trying to keep it for themselves. (Addis, 2018, p. 1)

Toward Christianization of the Indians

Roman Catholics, Episcopalian, Lutherans, Methodists, Church of Jesus Christ of Latter-day Saints, Pentecostals, Jehovah's Witnesses, and representatives of other denominations have sought to evangelize Native Americans since the arrival of explorers to the New World. At times, religious groups served as tools of the government in its efforts to eradicate traditional Native American religions and culture (Bowden, 1981; Larsen, 1963).

Colonists and expansionist held an expectation that Native Americans would think and behave as they did because it was what "normal" people did (Twiss, 2015). Problems surfaced when it was discovered that what was normal in the lives of the colonists was not normal in Indigenous cultures. It was with great disappointment that Pastor John Shay (1857) described the frontier as a place where, "pure unmixed devil-worship prevailed throughout the length and breadth land" (p. 25). Words such as "heathen" and "savage" were used by colonists and American expansionists to describe Native Americans who existed in a "debased" state. The air of superiority grew from the Doctrine of Discovery which referred to "other" people groups as pagans. Technological superiority also provided the invaders with a sense of hubris.

The view of Native Americans as pagan savages set the stage for churches and the American government to make concerted efforts to destroy their religious practices. It was believed that following the destruction of Native American religion and culture, assimilation into the dominant culture and acceptance of the true religion would be facilitated. Attacks upon the religious beliefs and practices of Native Americans have been regarded as the most damaging factor in the demise of Native American culture (Niezen, 2000; Rhodes, 1991).

When Native Americans were relegated to reservations, churches intensified efforts to supplant Native religious beliefs with Christianity (Deloria, 2003). Missionaries understood that dance was an important part of the religious and social life of the people and soon demanded that Indian agents ban Native religious ceremonies and dance.

Unsuccessful Conversion

Religious efforts to universally Christianize Native Americans failed in part because of the Christian's linkage with politics and concerted efforts to expropriate their ancestral lands (Baird-Olson, 2005; Miller, 2006, Newcomb, 2008). The linkage remains a reason why some Native Americans continue to view Christianity with contempt (Martin, 2001).

When Christian evangelists made gains in Native communities, it was at the expense of traditional Native American spiritual practices. Where Native traditional practices remained, missionaries counted their efforts as a loss (McNally, 2000). At times evangelists felt like, "spurned lovers or disobeyed parents. So much was offered and so little received or reciprocated" (Michaelson, 1983, p. 670).

Before the arrival of Europeans to North America, syncretic behavior was common with Native Americans as they frequently incorporated religious traditions from other tribal groups that fit with their own. Because aspects of Christianity were compatible with many Native American traditional beliefs, some Indians made commitments to both belief systems (Bowden, 1981; Csordas, 1999; Heidenreich, 2005; Tucker & Grim, 2001).

Native Americans often appropriated Christian and Catholic symbols and rituals into their traditional religious ceremonies. To them, this syncretic behavior was a natural thing to do. To the missionaries, the practice was considered sacrilege, even in cases where belief in the Christian message was genuine (Weaver, 1998). For example, rosary beads were worn by the Abitagezhig and other Christian converts as they danced to the beat of a drum while chanting Catholic hymns (Vecsey, 1997). The Native American Church, or Peyote Way, which blends Christian teaching with Native traditions is another example of syncretism. Christians recoiled at the blending of traditions and described syncretic belief systems as inauthentic (Garroutte et al., 2009).

How many Native Americans currently identify with traditional spirituality? On and near two large reservations, Garroutte et al. (2009) found that 86–91 percent of the respondents indicated that traditional religious beliefs were somewhat important and that about half considered them to be very important. However, Kosmin et al. (2001) report that in a national survey only 3 percent of the Native American respondents, which comprised just under 2 percent of the total Native sample population, reported an affiliation with Indian or tribal religions. Thirty-seven percent of the respondents identified as Baptist or Catholic. It appears that Native Americans living on and near reservations have enhanced access to traditional religions and are more likely to adopt some of their beliefs and practices. Notably, 78 percent of Native Americans lived off of reservations at the time of the 2010 census (United States Census Bureau, 2012).

Thou Shalt Not Dance!

Although much has been written concerning efforts made on the part of Christian groups and governmental agencies to quell Native American ceremonial dancing, we have not seen it mentioned that a significant amount of effort was also made by Christian leaders to eliminate dance from mainstream American culture during the same period. In the following pages, we explore the attacks made upon dance in Native and non-Native America.

Dance was looked upon favorably in Biblical scripture when it involved acts of worship or expression of joy in the Lord (Exodus 15:20; Judges 11:34; Samuel 18:6; Second Samuel 6:14; Second Samuel 6:16; Psalm 30:11; Psalm 149:3; Psalm 150:4 and Jeramiah 31:4; Luke 15:21). Scripture presents dance in a negative light when it is associated with idol worship and other sinful behavior (Exodus 32:6; Exodus 32: 19-25; Exodus 15:20; Second Samuel 6:12-16; Matthew 14:6).

Formal efforts to eliminate Native American dancing began in 1671 when it was made illegal for Indians to, "Powwow or perform outward Worship to the Devil or other false God" within the Massachusetts Bay Colony (Brigham, 1836, p. 298). Native American and Africans' slave dance practices were particularly loathed by early American Christians. The dance practices were designated as heathenistic, especially when pelvic movements were involved (Andrews & Olney, 2007; Stuckey, 1995).

Wild dancing taking place within Native communities conjured up within Protestant settlers, "fears of bloody revolt" (Summers, 2014). Further, the act of dancing was believed by clergy to interfere with the Natives' ability to accept Christ and that the activity impeded assimilation into the dominant society. Native Americans were expected to give up dancing as a sign of true commitment to Christianity.

Throughout the nineteenth- and early twentieth-century America, which encompassed the period of the Indian wars and relegation of Native Americans to reservations, social dance within the broader American culture was also looked upon with disfavor by Christians. Efforts to curtail the popularity of dance upon moral grounds intensified. Reverend Jacob Ide (1818) noted in *The Nature and Tendency of Balls* that dances were expensive, wasteful, prone to make participants slothful, and to behave in ways that were contrary to scripture. Wilkinson (1860) stated in *The Dance of Modern Society* that ballroom dances of the time were likened to a, "massing together of a jostling crowd of mute or merely gibbering animals" (p. 41). B. M. Palmer (1849) reported in a sermon that dancers are depraved, fallen, and subject to wicked passions.

Despite unremitting condemnation of dance by the clergy, participation in the social dances of the day continued within polite American society. Laws were enacted, however, to prohibit Native Americans from participating in traditional ceremonial and social dancing. This was possible because Native Americans were not granted American citizenship until 1924 (United States Congress, 1924).

In 1882, Secretary of the Interior H. M. Teller outlined the need for laws to control the Indians and how the government might act to destroy their heathenistic way of life in the *Rules Governing the Court of Indian Offenses* (Price, 1884). By 1883, the Sun Dance, Scalp Dance, War Dance, and other religiously significant dances were outlawed in addition to feasts, polygamous marriages, and practices common to Native American medicine men. Bureau of Indian Affairs agents were instructed to stop any observed or planned feasts or dances. A Court of Indian Offenses was created on each reservation to deal with violations of the prohibitions. Punishment associated with violations included short-term imprisonment and temporary loss of government doles. Native Americans were not permitted by law to participate in traditional religious activity, including sacred dance activities, until 1978 with the passage of the American Indian Religious Freedom Act (Abourezk, 1978). Sanctions led Native American groups to modify the meaning and purposes of their dances and rituals.

Secularization of Native American Dances

Native Americans took steps to maintain their dance culture in the face of governmental oppression (Ellis, 2003). Tribal leaders thought of innovative ways to maintain their dancing culture. At times, dances were held in secret at remote locations to avoid detection by government agents. In some cases, Native Americans told new Bureau of Indian Affairs agents that they had been given permission by previous agents to hold dances. Requests were made by Native Americans to conduct dances on American holidays such as the 4th of July. Requests were also made to conduct dances that honored military veterans when they returned home from fighting in World War I. Some Native leaders stated to agents that dances would be held simply out of historical interest as displays at fairs and exhibitions. Not infrequently, agents granted permission for dances to be held in the interest of fostering good relationships with the Indians. Through the process of negotiation and accommodation, many Native American dances became secularized, and they lost their religious significance. The Omaha Dance, also known as the Grass Dance, is a dance that has been secularized over time. The Grass Dance is typically included in contest powwows as a competitive dance category.

Ellis (1999) was told by a member of the Cheyenne tribe, "We don't do dances the same way as a long time ago, but we hold on to the ideas, the thoughts that those old people taught us" (p. 147). Similarly, remnants of the symbols and rituals of the elders can be observed in modern contest powwow culture.

Native American and Christian Sacred Symbols

Symbols are ubiquitous within the Native American powwow. The powwow itself is a, "portable, universal symbol of Indian identity and cultural involvement" (Gilley, 2006, p. 224–225). The contest powwow has come to represent Pan-Indianism, especially for tribal groups that have forgotten their traditions over time (Thomas, 1968). Illustratively, the powwow became the only symbol of the Monacan tribe because all of its traditions had been lost through forced assimilation, the passing of elders and their general disuse (Cook et al., 2005).

Religious symbols can mean different things to different people. For example, the Star of David, cross, and star and crescent symbols are associated with well-known world religions. Yet the symbols mean nothing more than what they appear to be to anyone unfamiliar with the religions: a stylized star, a cross, or the depiction of a star cradled by a crescent moon. Removed from the cultural context within which they hold meaning, religious symbols hold no religious significance.

Jensen (2017) observed that the cross of Christianity takes many forms. It is considered holy by some but an idol by others. The cross might be something that holds great spiritual significance and meaning, or it can have no spiritual significance what-so-ever.

The cross has been used as a symbol by Native Americans for thousands of years and has different meanings to members of various Native American tribal groups (Carus, 1880). The cross has symbolized stars, clouds, rain, birds, men with outstretched arms, the four winds, the four caverns of the soul, and even virginity. In some Indigenous cultures, the cross holds spiritual significance, yet in others, it simply represents things observed in daily life.

Adherence to Native American spiritual traditions and the level of understanding of traditional symbols have waned at an increasingly high rate of speed within Native America (Goertzen, 2005). Because of the loss of traditions, symbols associated with powwow culture have become ambiguous (Kavanagh, 1982). The powwow circle symbolizes life in many Native American traditions (McCluskey, 2009). The drum symbolizes the heartbeat of the people, and the eagle staff symbolizes sovereign Native American tribal nations (Barker, 2010; 116th Congress, 2019). Symbols worn during contest powwows can represent specific tribes (DesJarlait, 1997; Kavanagh, 1982). However, to some contest powwow dancers and spectators, the circle is a place to dance, the drum provides a beat to dance to, the eagle staff is equated to a drum major's baton, and symbols on regalia are simply adornments.

Symbols once holding significance in Native spirituality can be seen on the regalia of contest powwow dancers alongside the logo of the Pittsburg Steelers or Mickey Mouse. According to McClusky (2009), the design of each individual's regalia has symbolic meaning to the individual owner and the meaning is individually determined, not culturally prescribed.

The eagle is considered by some Native American tribes to be a messenger that travels between humans and the spirit world. As such, eagles and their feathers are an important component of religious ceremonies such as the Sun Dance of the Lakota (Davidson, 2009). Black Elk stated that the eagle feather is symbolic of Wakan-Tonka (The Great Holy One). He also explains that the eagle feather reminds the Lakota that, "our thoughts should rise high as the eagles do" (Neihardt, 2008, p. xxv). Wambli Sina Win (2012) lamented that after hundreds of years of acculturation, "cultural erosion has diminished the value of eagle feathers for they have become commonplace" (p.12).

In the tradition of some tribal groups, if an eagle feather falls to the ground, the powwow is paused, and a ceremony is held to retrieve it. A prayer may be given, and or words may be shared with the dancer who dropped the feather concerning its symbolic significance before it is returned. In some tribal traditions, a Pick-Up the Feather Dance also is performed when a feather is dropped. In other powwow traditions, a Pick-Up the Feather Dance is not conducted at all (DesJarliat, 1997).

To the Christian unfamiliar with traditions related to the eagle, the fallen eagle feather ceremony may seem odd and to be a distinctly religious ceremony. However, the eagle feather does not necessarily serve as a religious symbol during contemporary Native American powwows for three reasons. First, the eagle feather serves as an important symbol of Pan-Indian identity as respect for the eagle is common in Native America (Owen, 2008). As symbols, the eagle and eagle feather serve to unite Native Americans. Second, in some Native American traditions, the eagle feather is symbolic of the warrior (DesJarlait, 1997). A fallen eagle feather is symbolic of a fallen warrior and stopping the powwow to reverently acknowledge the loss is an act of respect (Burke, 2000, p. 23). Finally, eagle feathers are awarded to individuals of some tribal groups in honor of special accomplishments such as graduation from high school or college. The eagle feather in these situations does not serve as a religious symbol. Contest powwow dancers may include eagle feathers as a part of regalia out of tradition while harboring no belief that they have a connection to Creator.

Within the broader American society, the eagle serves a symbolic function. The United States Congress in the Bald and Golden Eagle Protection Act described the bald eagle as being not simply a bird, but instead, a national symbol of freedom and American ideals (United States Forest Service, 1993). The statute prohibits individuals from taking, possessing, or selling eagles or their parts. Exceptions are allowed under certain circumstances for Native Americans because of the eagle's importance to their religious activities and traditions. Exceptions are granted only to members of federally recognized tribes, and most exceptions are granted to tribes rather than to individuals.

During the Catholic Holy Sacrament, should particles or wine fall to the floor, the area is to be cleaned with a spirit of sadness and tenderness as the beloved Christ has fallen to the floor. His body and blood are to be treated with all due reverence as the sacraments are cleaned up (Kosloski, 2018, p. 8; USCCB, 2020). In the ceremonial activity of taking communion in many Protestant churches, the blood of Christ is represented by grape juice and his body is symbolized by bread (Van Willigen, 1987). In the Catholic Church, the juice and bread are believed to become the blood and body of Christ during the Holy Communion (USCCB, 2020). However, the faithful would not consider bread and wine or juice to be sacred outside of ceremonial communion. They are simply bread and wine or juice. Similarly, if eagle feathers are not being used in conjunction with religious ceremony, it should not be assumed that religious significance is attributed to them by Native Americans.

The Native American practice of "smudging" (making smoke) most frequently involves the burning of sage, juniper, lavender, sweet grass, tobacco, or other herbs to ritually purify people, places, and things (Portman & Garrett, 2006). Medicine man Fool's Crow explained that smoke, "carries prayers and requests up to [Creator]" (Mails, 2012, p. 135). The site of a powwow is typically smudged for purification and prayers may be offered in conjunction with the smudging before the powwow begins. As the smudging ceremony is conducted in advance of a powwow, those not involved in the ceremony would not observe it nor know that it had been conducted.

Within the Catholic Church, incense is used in a sacramental manner to venerate, bless, and sanctify (Peterson, 2018). When the smoke rises, it conveys the presence of the Lord and links heaven with earth. It is also believed that the smoke of the incense helps prayers reach heaven:

The Church sees the burning of incense as an image of prayers of the faithful rising to heaven. The symbolism is mentioned in Psalm 141:2: "Let my prayer be incense before you; my uplifted hands an evening offering." (Peterson, 2018, p. 4)

Though Native American smudging rituals at one time would have carried prayers to Creator, today they often carry Christian prayers to God. In other traditions, smudging can be used during purification ceremonies to send prayers to the Thunder People in hope of securing their blessings (Baumann, 2019). The target of prayers offered during smudging ceremonies is dependent upon who is offering the prayers and their religious or spiritual background.

In the current study, we first seek to determine what individuals involved in the planning and staging of a large intertribal contest powwow believe the role of religion and Native American spirituality are in the contest powwow. Second, we seek to determine what explicitly religious behavior is present in a large intertribal contest powwow.

THE CURRENT STUDY

Qualitative data are obtained from Native American and non-Native powwow organizers and officials who possess extensive experience in organizing, participating in, and staging a large intertribal contest powwow taking place in the Northern Great Plains region of the United States. Observation data collected over a period of four days are also utilized to provide depth to our investigation and to assist in validation of our findings. Our participants included the president of the Powwow Association, the powwow's announcers, the facility director, the president of the local chamber of commerce who also served as one of the two announcers, the CEO of the chamber of commerce, and two civic leaders who worked on the North City powwow advisory committee. Three of the participants were Native Americans and four were not. Pseudonyms were assigned to participants to protect anonymity. The pseudonym given to the contest powwow serving as the site of our inquiry is Northern Plains Contest Powwow (NPCP) and the name assigned to the host city is North City. For additional information concerning the methods used in this study, please see chapter 1.

This research is unique in that no published study has examined the extent of religious and spiritual activity in the contest powwow. Further, no study

could be identified in which those involved in the organization and staging of a large contest powwow were asked to share what the role of Native
American religious and spiritual behavior is within their powwow.

FINDINGS AND DISCUSSION

In the current study, we first seek to determine what individuals involved in
the planning and staging of a large intertribal contest powwow believe the
role of religion and Native American spirituality are within the contest powwow. Second, we seek to determine what explicitly religious and spiritual
behavior is present in a large intertribal contest powwow.

Analysis of our data yields nine themes. Native American spirituality Is
not an Important Aspect of the Contest Powwow, Get the Word Out: The
Contest Powwow Is Not a Religious Event, Persistent Resistance: I Would
Never Go to a Church that's not Mine, Just Enjoy the Spirit of the Song
and Dance, Powwow 101 and the Pre-Powwow Blessing Ceremony, The
Youth Day Symposium: Pray as You Wish and the Four Directions Song,
The Contest Powwow's Opening and Closing Prayers, Nonverbal Evidence
of Prayer, and The Dropped Eagle Feather. Each theme is discussed in the
subsequent pages.

Native American Spirituality Is Not an Important Aspect of the Contest Powwow

Participants were asked what the meaning of the NPCP is to Native
Americans. Participants attributed a myriad of meanings to the NPCP. The
NPCP means spending time with family, renewing and formulating friendships, celebrating as a community, demonstrating excellence in singing and
dancing, securing income, demonstrating excellence in crafting regalia, maintaining culture, experiencing Native American music and songs, recounting
Native history, emotional healing, participating in valued ceremonies (grand
entry, giveaways, honoring of elders, etc.), provision of a cultural event for
the community, provision of a site for communal focus, teaching and maintenance of protocol associated with traditional activities, teaching expectations
for behavior, maintenance of health and fitness, providing passion to live, and
maintaining traditional languages. None of the participants identified religion
or spirituality as a meaningful component of the NPCP.

In short, the participants state that contest powwows provide all who attend
and participate an opportunity to experience culture. Kristi states, "There's
plenty of culture to be seen. I think it's absolutely thrilling. I just kind of get
overwhelmed." Ricky explains,

Everything is in books and stuff. People can read and see all these videos and everything about the powwow on the internet but once they come and they see it live and they see some real dancing and get right up to the drum and feel that energy, that's . . . an eye-opener! And hopefully an awakening!

Get the Word Out: The Contest Powwow Is Not a Religious Event

Participants are asked if they are aware of people who will not attend the NPCP because they believe it to be a Native American religious ceremony. All participants state with conviction that a significant number of people avoid attending contest powwows because they consider them to be religious gatherings at which sacred ceremonies are conducted.

June believes it is important for the Native community, "to get the word out and dispel the belief. It is a celebration open to all." Stan, president of the Powwow Association, echoes June's words, "The contest powwow is not only something for Native Americans to attend. It's not a religious ceremony." He explains that the contest powwow is a social gathering that emphasizes song and dance, and stresses that the NPCP is a competition, not a religious ceremony. Stan would also like to see an end to the inaccurate belief that the contest powwow is an environment in which religious ceremony is conducted. All people are welcome to attend.

Ricky is exasperated by people who want to argue that contest powwows are religious gatherings. He explains that at contest powwows, people do not discuss heaven and hell or debate about what religion is true. The people avoid those types of discussions at the contest powwow and just enjoy being with each other. They relish and soak in the good feelings provided by the song and dance that reverberates throughout the arena.

Persistent Resistance: I Would Never Go to a Church That's Not Mine

Participants unanimously convey that a lack of understanding and tolerance serve to restrict Natives and non-Natives affiliated with Christian religions from attending contest powwows. Walt believes that the undesirable outlook some harbor toward Native American ceremonies and traditions, including the contest powwow, are negatively influenced by history:

> Americans have never been educated about traditional Native American culture. Before they even got off the boat, they were already told Native American cultures were evil. Right away! That was painted into the minds of the settlers when they first came here and that's why it led to the boarding schools. That's why it led to the termination era.

Walt believes that people often fear the unknown. The unknown prevents the fearful from attending the contest powwow and from gaining a better understanding of Native American culture. In his efforts to enhance relationships between the Native and non-Native communities, Walt invited a group of townspeople to the NPCP. He was met with persistent resistance. After numerous efforts were made to get the townspeople to agree to attend the powwow, "I just flat-out asked them, 'Why don't you go to powwows? Can you be honest with me so we can have a dialog?'" After a period of silence, one of the townspeople confessed, "I won't go to a powwow because I feel like it's like going to another church. I would never go to a church that's not mine. I never would."

Ricky declares that when non-Natives do attend a contest powwow, "They really don't know what's going on." What is actually happening is left to their imagination. Ricky describes the contest powwow as a two- or three-day celebration characterized by singing, dancing, and feasting. It is not, he emphasizes, a church.

According to June, "crazy Christian evangelicals" believe that by attending a contest powwow they are committing a sin. She describes their view as ridiculous and likens the contest powwow to a sporting event. She then claims the dancers and singers, "are just trying to win some money." She asks, "If attending a powwow is sinful, wouldn't attending a professional sporting event be a sin?"

Stan acknowledges that there are sacred and religious components to his culture's religious practices including the Sun Dance, Bringing out the Pipe, and similar ceremonies. Then, he emphasizes that these ceremonies, nor others like them, take place within the NPCP.

Kristi acknowledges that spiritually significant ceremonies are conducted within Native communities. She has attended several such ceremonies at the invitation of families and has often been the only non-Native to be present. Kristi emphasizes that spiritually significant ceremonies are private, and family centered. At the NPCP, everyone is welcome and, "People don't know that."

Dave believes spiritually significant traditional Native American ceremonies should remain distinctly and exclusively Native American:

> There are things Indian people don't want non-Indian people to be involved in. I mean if you want to go to a Sun Dance you can probably find someone who will let you go to a Sun Dance. But there are things that they're just real "Indiany" and they should probably stay real "Indiany" . . . it's family stuff.

According to our participants, the NPCP is not one of those "Indiany" things.

Just Enjoy the Spirit of the Song and Dance

The majority of our participants did not use the term "sacred" during their interviews. "Sacred" was used by Dave to discuss places considered holy to Native Americans, but not in the context of the powwow. Walt explains that the powwow's song and dance provides a sacred energy that he described as a special feeling that moves through the environment. He clarified that the special feeling was not something that should be considered religious or spiritual in nature.

Stan uses the term "sacred" in describing the ceremony used during the NPCP when an eagle feather falls to the floor. Through the ceremony, he explains, the warriors who have fallen in battle are being symbolically respected, making the ceremony something sacred. Stan emphasizes that though the ceremony is something sacred, it should not be associated with something religious. Sacred is likened to reverence and respect.

June believes that there may be something "spiritual" with a dance at the contest powwow but suggests that we ask Walt or Stan because she really does not know enough about it. Stan uses the term "spiritual" when discussing his grandfather who, "was a leader in the community: a spiritual leader, pastor, evangelist, and missionary." "Spiritual" refers to his grandfather's Christian evangelistic activities, never in conjunction with his descriptions of the powwow.

Kristi explains that Native peoples have suffered on reservations due to loss of culture but, "the powwow, native spirituality, and the practices of ceremony, are helping the native cultures. It is healing!" The point Kristi makes is that traditions provide identity, strength, and purpose. In her view, the loss of traditional practices has resulted in a void in the lives of many Native Americans that government programs, modern consumerism, and individualistic values fail to address. The powwow is one Native American cultural institution that supplies identity and strength to individuals.

Ricky believes that people should just enjoy the "spirit" of the song and dance and being together as human beings when they are at a contest powwow. He does not link spirituality with the contest powwow. Ricky makes it clear that religion is the cause of many arguments and should not be considered to be a part of the contest powwow.

Powwow 101 and the Pre-Powwow Blessing Ceremony

The evening before the powwow commences, a dinner, awards presentation, and an informational program called "Powwow 101" highlighting what goes on at the powwow is held for a group of sixty-two people. Many in attendance are donors and volunteers who had given donations of time and money in support of the powwow. Various community business leaders were also in attendance. Aicinena was invited to attend by the powwow committee's president Stan, after our interview the day before the event.

The group is welcomed by Stan. Special awards are presented to community members who were instrumental in making the NPCP a success. Awardees include three of this study's participants: June, Dan, and Kristi.

Following the presentation of awards, Aicinena joins forty-four of the attendees as we form a circle within the center of the arena where the powwow is to be held. Stan's grandfather, a tribal elder, then commences to perform a "Blessing Ceremony." The purpose of the ceremony is to bless the arena in which the powwow would be conducted. The ceremony begins with Stan's grandfather saying a prayer in Lakota. Stan translates the prayer into English, "He thanks God in the name of Jesus for the powwow, for the opportunity to come together, and for the safety of those traveling."

Stan's grandfather then sets a sage rope afire, allows it to burn for a few seconds within an abalone shell, then blows it out. The sage smolders as Walt plays a hand drum and sings the "Four Directions Song" in Lakota. He explains to the group that the song is a prayer for safe travels offered for those traveling to the powwow.

Traditionally, the Four Directions Song is a plea for Wakan-Tanka, the grandfathers from the four cardinal directions, and grandmother who resides upon the earth to hear the prayers of the people (Bullhead, 2018). The Four Directions Song is equated to a doxology that is used during worship services in some Christian denominations.

When the song is completed, a veteran holds the shell and smoldering sage rope as Stan's grandfather smudges himself by gracefully pulling the rising smoke to and around his head and body. The veteran, who serves as Stan's grandfather's assistant, then smudges. Each person in the circle is given the opportunity to smudge as Stan's grandfather travels counterclockwise around the circle and fans the smoke toward each participant with an eagle feather fan. A small number of people standing in the circle refuse to participate, and the minister respectfully moves on. Aicinena is the last member of the circle to smudge. Stan's grandfather then walks through the entire arena, smudging as he walks. As Stan's grandfather completes the smudging of the arena, we are asked to be seated for dinner. Once the entire arena has been covered, the Blessing Ceremony ceases.

As a sign of respect, individuals over the age of sixty are asked to serve themselves first. Walt jokes, "If there are any bull riders in the crowd, you can go with the seniors. You all walk so slow; we don't want you holding up the lines."

Following the meal, Walt presents a short educational program he calls "Powwow 101." Basic information about powwows is presented and local youths give demonstrations of the various dance styles that are included in the NPCP. Each dancer wears full regalia. Walt explains what goes into making of regalia. One female dancer makes the sign of the cross on her chest as is the tradition of Catholics after performing. Stan describes to those present the importance of the eagle feather in his tribe's culture. He explains that eagle feathers must be earned and that they serve as a symbol of achievement and honor.

After the presentation of awards, all guests are asked to join once again in a circle within the center of the arena. A microphone is passed around to each person in the circle. We introduce ourselves, state any role we have in the powwow, and share where we are from. Most explain why they came to the NPCP and/or why the powwow is important to them. Walt thanks Aicinena publicly for attending and specifically states that he hopes Aicinena's work will help people better understand the NPCP and other contest powwows.

All in the group then hold hands as we participate in a traditional community dance. Then a group photograph is taken. The Blessing Ceremony ends with a Christian prayer offered by the powwow's security director in English. He thanks God for all of those who participating in the evening's event. He thanks God for the upcoming powwow, asks for travel mercies for those traveling to the powwow, and for the success of the upcoming powwow.

Aicinena asks Stan, a devout Christian, if the Blessing Ceremony is a religious activity. He asserts that the Blessing Ceremony is, "an important part of the powwow, but it's not like we are there worshiping spirits." In his view, the ceremony is not different than Christian prayers.

The Blessing Ceremony is only open to invited guests. Those who attended the powwow the next day would be unaware that it had taken place. Nor would they know what transpired during the event.

The Youth Day Symposium: Pray as You Wish and the Four Directions Song

Each year, the NPCP committee hosts a Youth Day Symposium to share Walt's "Powwow 101" program with children from the local schools. Approximately 4,000 children are present for the Powwow 101 program on Friday morning. The event is conducted in the Civic Center which will serve as the site of the powwow.

There is no formal prayer offered before the Youth Day Symposium began. However, before the "Four Directions Song" is performed, those present are asked by Stan to worship as they wish and to ask for safe travels for those coming to the powwow. He also asks that the crowd pray for a great weekend of powwow activities.

Walt then takes over as the emcee for the event. Eleven singers sit at the drum and play as the powwow princess sings the Four Directions Song in

Lakota. A Flag Song is performed by the drum group as the Eagle Staff and American flag are carried around the arena floor by a group of veterans. A Veterans song is then performed. The traditional meaning of the Four Directions Song is not explained to those present.

Various speakers address the audience, including a former local football player who won the Heisman Trophy. The Heisman Trophy is awarded to the best collegiate football player in the nation each year. The speaker also went on to play football professionally. He encourages the children to pursue their dreams and to always work hard to achieve them. He exhorts the children with religious fervor, "Make yourself better every day! Be in it to win it! That way, you and your family will get a portion of that TRILLION dollars!" The football player tells numerous jokes. A student asks him to talk about the time he was hit the hardest he had ever been hit. After pausing a moment, the football player responds, "When was I hit the hardest? Hmmmm. . . . It was the time I took the money out of my mom's cookie jar. . . . My mom whipped my ass good! That's the hardest I've ever been hit!"

Exhibitions of some of the dances that will be seen at the NPCP are performed by school-aged children. Many of the children performed at the previous evening's event. The youths perform the Northern Traditional Dance, Jingle Dress Dance, Grass Dance, Fancy Shawl Dance, and Fancy Dance. An intertribal dance is also performed for the spectators.

A hoop dancer performs a hoop dance with numerous hoops. The hoop dancer's performance is followed by a renowned Native American rap artist from the immediate area. He performs to the great delight of the young crowd. Then he speaks to the crowd in English and Lakota. Art and music, he explains, are things that there are no words for in his culture, because art and music permeate it. Walt encourages the children to come back with their parents for one of the powwow sessions sometime during the weekend. The event then ends.

Stan's request for the crowd to pray in their own way for safety and blessings for a good weekend, and the performance of the Four Corners Song were the only noted religious activities, behaviors, or words noted during the Youth Day Symposium. Neither Christianity, nor traditional spiritual beliefs were mentioned in Stan's request for prayer. To be clear, the traditional meaning of the Four Directions Song was never explicated. The Four Directions Song was not performed during the contest powwow.

The Contest Powwow's Opening and Closing Prayers

During his interview, Stan states, "We open [the powwow] with a prayer and end it with a prayer." Participants explain and Aicinena observes that when a prayer is given in a native language, the master of ceremonies (announcer) lets everyone know what was said in English.

Walt explains that the prayer offered at the start of the powwow is, "no different than if you go to a football game and there's a prayer said before they run onto the field. They pray for the safety of the people and for their health."

Ricky describes the content of prayers given at the powwow in a similar vein:

If you really listen to a lot of those prayers interpreted, when they speak in their language, they're giving thanks for this host tribe that gives us a weekend to all come together and be among family and friends and the singing and the dancing. That's the celebration part of [the powwow].

Dave chides, that if the prayer offered during the powwow's opening ceremonies is bothersome, "You shouldn't go to a city council meeting."

We report here that the prayers offered in conjunction with the NPCP were indeed akin to those made before athletic events. God is thanked for the event, for safety provided during travels, for the opportunity to come together for the powwow, and He is petitioned for the provision of His blessing during the event. At the conclusion of activities, He is thanked for the opportunity to come together for the event, for those who helped organize the powwow, and for travel mercies for all traveling back to their homes.

The opening prayers associated with the first of the powwow's four sessions are made by Stan's grandfather in the name of Jesus. During the close of the first session and at the beginning and end of the powwow's other three sessions, the speakers do not identify their religion and speak in Lakota. During translations, the term "Creator" is used in reference to God. And it is explained that the prayers are offered by all of us. According to Stan, this is done to be inclusive of all people present.

Opening and closing prayers were given in English and in Lakota. In some, Creator was thanked and petitioned. In others, God and Jesus are thanked and petitioned. Some present may have viewed God and Creator as the same entity. Others may have differentiated between them, and the chasm caused discomfort. Some Christians would state that the Creator, spoken of in the prayer, is not the God of the Bible and such prayers are to be avoided.

Nonverbal Evidence of Prayer

Aicinena observes three behaviors that appear to be associated with prayer. First, on occasion, dancers cross themselves as is the custom of the Catholics. Second, following dances, a few dancers point to the heavens in celebration as do professional athletes after an excellent performance. Third, on occasion, dancers bow their heads for a few moments as if in silent prayer following performances. None of the observed behaviors differ in form from those observed in athletic settings. Importantly, we cannot ascertain the religious affiliation or spiritual beliefs of athletes or powwow dancers engaging in the same rituals. Prayer is common within sport settings (Aicinena, 2017; Czech et al., 2004). It is used to enhance performance, to increase team cohesion, as a part of routines, as a petition for safety, and to give thanks.

The Dropped Eagle Feather

A ceremony takes place each time an Eagle feather falls from a dancer's regalia during the powwow. Special accomplishments are acknowledged through the presentation of eagle feathers. The feather, according to Stan, is likened to a military medal. To earn one is a special honor. For example, they are bestowed upon individuals when they graduate from high school and college and to those who have served in the military.

According to Stan, the eagle feather's symbolic importance is taught to Lakota children at young age. It is not permissible for an eagle feather to touch the ground for it represents the warriors of the tribe and their collective spirit. When a feather falls from a dancer's regalia to the ground during the NPCP, all activity is stopped, and a ceremony is held.

On the first night of the powwow, Aicinena notices a man appearing to be over 6'4 and 300 pounds. The majestic and imposing man enters the powwow circle in full regalia for a dance competition. Aicinena's gaze turns to other competitors as the drum beats, the singers sing, and the dancers dance.

When the song concludes, all the dancers exit the powwow circle except for the mountain of a man who stands alone, weeping. Individuals who appear to be his parents enter the powwow circle and embrace him in an unsuccessful effort to console him. An eagle feather had fallen from his regalia during the dance. His shame and embarrassment are clearly displayed through the shedding of tears, in his facial expressions, and by frequent and violent sobbing. He refuses to lift his gaze from the floor.

The powwow announcer explains to the crowd that an eagle feather has fallen, and that the powwow will be stopped. He reminds the crowd that no photos or videos can be taken as the veterans address the situation. Stan notes, "It's really emotional for some of the dancers that drop a feather. They feel so bad, embarrassed."

A small contingent of veterans carrying tribal flags is led into the circle by a veteran hoisting the Eagle Staff. The group surrounds the fallen eagle feather. An elder veteran offers tobacco and sprinkles it around the feather, then picks the feather up lovingly. The elder holds it in front of the gaze of the man who dropped it. The elder says a prayer or shares words of comfort and instruction with the bereaved dancer. Aicinena could not hear the communication because of his location in the arena.

Once the instruction was given, the weeping mountain of a man nods in the affirmative, dries his eyes, and takes the feather from the extended hand of the elder veteran. Dozens of people come down from the bleachers to extend comfort and support to the distraught dancer, who continues to cast his gaze downward.

When the well-wishers stop streaming toward the dancer, the family walks to the drum that was performing, and places a cash gift upon it. Then they present a cash gift to the veterans' group as an expression of gratitude and contrition to regain their standing within the group. The dancer and his family exit the powwow circle.

Ricky emphasizes during his interview that not all contest powwows stop when an eagle feather has fallen:

I've been up to some powwows where they just pick it up. They just pick it up because, in their belief, the eagle drops feathers all the time. He'll sit there and he'll be on a tree and flutter his wings or his tail and he'll drop a feather. And there are no veterans around there. It's a bird. It's an animal. It's a feather.

Ricky also recounts how fallen eagle feathers are handled differently at other powwows, "Sometimes they'll just have an elder go out, offer some tobacco and pick it right up."

Stan explains that at the NPCP, the "Feather Pick-Up Dance" is no longer performed when eagle feathers fall. In the Feather Pick-Up Dance, a song is played as four veterans dance around the eagle feather. When asked why the Feather Pick-Up Dance is not performed any more, Stan states:

It takes time for it to be done and it already takes time to have the veterans come and serve as they do during the ceremony we have. We have to stay on schedule, so we cannot include the Feather Pick-Up Dance. As we are talking about it, it makes me sad that we can't include it any longer.

How fallen eagle feathers are viewed and addressed is testament to the fact that powwows have different protocols depending upon the host group's traditions and values. In the interest of commercialization and grandness of the NPCP, specific ceremonies and traditions have been changed or eliminated.

CONCLUSIONS

Neither religion nor Native American spirituality was mentioned by any of the participants as a goal for the NPCP. Participants articulated that many people they have spoken with in their efforts to promote the North Plains Contest Powwow likened powwows to a Native American church service. Out of fidelity to their religion, those refusing to attend the powwow would never attend a church that was not theirs. Because the contest powwow is a celebration of song and dance that has nothing to do with Native American religion or spirituality, the refusal to attend the powwow frustrated our participants and they attribute the negative attitude to ignorance.

The participants wish that more in the community would come to their contest powwow to experience the positive feelings and uplifting of spirit Native American song and dance can evoke. In their view, by refusing to come to the contest powwow, people also forfeit a wonderful opportunity to learn more about Native Americans and their culture.

Because the Powwow Association's president and others participating in the current study want people to understand that the NPCP is not a religious event, they provide an educational program they call "Powwow 101" to community leaders in conjunction with the annual dinner and Blessing Ceremony, and for thousands of students each year during the Youth Day Symposium. Powwow 101 lets people see for themselves that the powwow is a celebration of Native American song, dance, traditions, and values, and that it is not a religious or spiritual gathering.

In events ancillary to the contest powwow, a traditional Lakota Four Directions song was performed, Christian-focused prayer was offered, and request was made for those attending the Youth Day Symposium to offer prayer. Anyone choosing to attend the powwow would not have been aware that these religious and spiritually focused events took place.

At the North Plains Contest Powwow, eight brief prayers were offered, two prayers at each of the powwow's four sessions. Some prayers were offered in English and others in Lakota; to God in some prayers and to Creator in others. As such, spiritual or religious behavior took place in each session of the powwow.

Two minutes of prayer in a four-hour-long session would not seem to make the powwow a religious service. And if the prayers did make the session's religious or spiritual services, it could be argued that some sessions were Christian gatherings and others were Native American spiritual gatherings. Can it be argued that the prayers were directed toward two different entities?

Native Americans prefer not to argue about such things. The Nez Perce Tribe banned Christian evangelists from mining souls on their lands in the late 1800s. In explaining the rationale for the decision, Chief Joseph stated:

They will teach us to quarrel about God, as Catholics and Protestants do. . . .
We do not want that. We may quarrel with men sometimes about things on Earth, but we never quarrel about the Great Spirit. We do not want to learn that. (Bates, 1971, p. 95)

Sporadically, dancers engaged in meditation or silent prayers of thanks. Occasionally, individual dancers pointed to the heavens as if to give God or Creator the glory for their performance. At times, dancers made the sign of the cross across their chest. The incidents were few and they were silent. They were individual acts and not something requisite to the powwow, pointed out by the announcers, or encouraged by the powwow's organizers. The rituals would not alarm Christians or adherents of Native spiritual traditions.

Though the ceremony performed in conjunction with the fallen eagle feather may appear to be a Native American religious ceremony to some spectators. The Powwow Association's president explained that the eagle feather is sacred because it symbolizes warriors. When the eagle feather falls from the regalia of a dancer, it is to be treated with respect. The same type of respect is to be demonstrated for a sacred symbol that represents the United States: The American flag. According to the Department of Defense (Lange, 2020), "the flag represents a living country and is, itself considered a living thing" (para. 4). When flags have become torn or tattered, a color guard is to present the flag to a chaplain, prayers are offered for the flag on behalf of a grateful nation and then, the flag is to be burned. The reverence given to the American flag and the eagle feather both spring from the secular meaning afforded each symbol.

During twelve sessions of the Gathering of Nations powwow, Aicinena never witnessed a ceremony used to respond to a dropped eagle feather. Ricky made it clear in the current study that at many powwows, activities are not stopped when eagle feathers are dropped. At many contest powwows, spectators would never see a ceremony used to address fallen eagle feathers. With 3,500 Native Americans dancing into the arena in full regalia over a period of thirty-five minutes, eagle feathers would certainly have fallen. Ceremonies were not held. What is done at individual contest powwows is up to the event's organizers.

Although eight prayers were made publicly during the North Plains Contest Powwow, it is unreasonable to claim that the North Plains Contest Powwow is a Native American spiritual or religious gathering. We conclude that the contest powwow is not a crucible in which religion or Native American spirituality is celebrated or tested. The North Plains Contest Powwow is a secular event.

NOTE

1. Most Native American languages do not have a word that equates to religion. As we explain in the review of literature, "spirituality" is a better term for Native American socioreligious activity. At this point in the chapter, we use the term "religion."

Chapter 6

The Contest Powwow

A Ceremony Fostering Tradition and Change

Culture includes institutions central to identity, including language, religious practices and objects, traditional practices, and forms of expression (Woolford, 2009). Powwows teach and strengthen a sense of identity, pride, and community in Native Americans (Andrews & Olney, 2007; Ellis et al., 2005; Hsiu-Yen Yeh, 2006; Lassiter, 1997, 1998). Living culture is observable at powwows.

Throughout the history of North America's Indigenous peoples, powwows have undergone change as individuals from various tribal groups encountered one another. Tribal groups shared, adopted, and adapted the ceremonial practices of others in alignment with their values and cultural beliefs (DesJarlait, 1997; Kracht, 1994). In doing so, ceremonial powwow traditions were modified over time.

Contest powwows came to being as dancers, government leaders, tribal leaders, and entrepreneurs saw that income and interest in Native American culture could be generated through public performance of culture (Clough, 2005; DesJarlait, 1997; Herle, 1994; Oxendine, 2011; Warren, 2009). Ceremonial aspects of traditional powwows were retained and transmitted through commercialized contest powwow spectacles (Albers & Medicine, 2005). As public commercialized events, contest powwows will continue to change as the strength of change factors including the need to be entertaining, the need to incorporate technology, and the need to become bigger and better intensify.

Horse (2005) explained that being Native American 200 years ago would not have been the same 100 years ago and change has continued since then. Change has impacted powwow cultures over time and two forms of the powwow have resulted. Observable differences exist within and between traditional and contest powwow environments (Albers & Medicine, 2005).

Native Americans living on the great plains of the United States in the early 1900s would have considerable familiarity with the sights and sounds of traditional powwows conducted by contemporary descendants of their tribes on reservations. Some of the dances, spiritual ceremonies, the styles of music, regalia, and other ceremonial activities would be quite recognizable.

Our mythical time travelers would undoubtedly recognize aspects of a large contemporary intertribal contest powwow including some songs styles, dance styles, and aspects of modern regalia. However, the participation of individuals from numerous tribal groups, the idea of competing for prize money, recognition of shared powwow culture, the existence of a competitive powwow circuit, the involvement of 3,500+ dancers, high-volume public-address systems, the participation of large numbers of competing drum groups, the presence of ticket-purchasing spectators, giant arenas, boisterous announcers, giant video screens, delayed replays of dances, time schedules, and other modern modifications to the traditional powwow would be quite foreign.

As noted by Albers and Medicine (2005), the Native American powwow and dance culture has been used by Native Americans to negotiate new social and cultural realities as it has protected tribal and community values. Contest powwows have served to maintain and transmit Pan-Indian traditions and values as they have become more widespread, entertaining, and commercially viable. In this chapter, we seek to determine how the contest powwow and traditional powwow differ, how the contest powwow has changed, and how the contest powwow functions to preserve Native American culture in the experience of contemporary contest powwow dancers.

LITERATURE REVIEW

As is true with all social institutions, the powwow sprang forth from culture. The powwow has long been impacted by change forces originating from within and outside of Native America. Titanic change in the lives of Native Americans led to the creation of the contest powwow. The contest powwow serves as a Native American institution which channels behavior in culturally prescribed ways.

To appreciate the importance of the contest powwow in the continuation of Native American culture, it is necessary to understand the vital relationship existent between culture and Native American identity, Native American values, Pan-Indianism, and the relationship of Pan-Indianism and the contest powwow. Finally, it is important to understand that the contest powwow functions as a crucible of culture. Each of these topics is explored in our review of literature.

Culture and Native American Identity

Culture consists of the norms, behaviors, beliefs, and ideas common to peoples living within a specific geographic area (Varnum & Grossman, 2017). Powerful components of culture include religion and language. Differences in cultures are due to variations in the location and experiences of cultural groups over time (Appiah, 1994; Scheffler, 2007). Cultures do not remain static. Cultural evolution is inevitable through the course of time as change is initiated in any culture from within and from without (Horse, 2005; Varnum & Grossman, 2017). Native American cultures evolved over the millennia as tribal groups interacted with one another and as worldviews and traditions of Indigenous peoples, colonists, and expansionists collided.

Cultural identity is an individual's, "sense of self derived from formal or informal membership in groups that transmit and inculcate knowledge, beliefs, values, attitudes, traditions, and ways of life" (Jameson, 2007, p. 200). Cultural identity is a self-perceived internal state comprised of history, transmitted wisdom, and values shared across generations.

Numerous factors impact upon individuals as they establish Native American cultural identities. Relationships with family, the tribe, and all of creation are vitally important in traditional American Indian life and formulation of a Native American identity (Lucero, 2014). Cultural knowledge is important in establishing Native identity. Cultural knowledge includes knowledge of tribal history, traditions, and practices.

Belonging to a larger group of Native Americans including tribal groups and ancestors is also important in the establishment of Native identity (Blanchard et al., 2019; Evans-Campbell, 2008; Lucero, 2014). The Bureau of Indian Affairs (2021) acknowledges that knowledge of language, history, religion, and kinship are important in the establishment of Native American identity. Further, participation in tribal-specific cultural activities is important in formulation of tribal identity (Blanchard et al., 2019; Brown, et al., 2007; Hendry, 2003; Weaver, 2012). Native identity is dependent in part, upon understanding and behaving in ways that reflect traditional values (Lucero, 2014).

DNA testing is currently a popular means for individuals to determine their genetic background. Through genetic testing, individuals may learn they are of Native American ancestry. The discovery is nothing more than anecdotal information when cultural knowledge is absent and the individual has not participated in culture (Blanchard et al., 2019). An Indigenous college student expressed disdain for those claiming to be Native American in the absence of cultural knowledge and involvement (Beijsens, 2015):

David isn't a true Native. Megan either. David can't prove his ancestry and both of them don't know anything about their cultures. Almost none of the members of [the Native American Student Association] know how to define their ancestors. One of the first questions I ask is: who are your elders? And they can't seem to even answer that. . . . They don't even know what is happening in their tribe. They never go to their governments' meetings or elections. So, when they want to come and talk about culture, they can't talk. (p. 42)

Ancestry can be determined through DNA testing, however, one's cultural identity is dependent upon involvement in culture and the value one places upon group affinity (Perez & Hirschman, 2009).

Native American and American Cultural Values

As a component of culture, values can be thought of as the standard of what is important within the culture. Values can differ from culture to culture and within any society's subcultures. Native American tribal groups share core beliefs and philosophies that are remarkably similar (Rhodes, 1991). Commonly shared Native American collectivist values come into sharp conflict with those of the dominant individualistic American culture.

Garrett et al. (2014) compiled a list of values and expectations identified by various researchers as common within traditional Native and non-Native cultures. In the following pages, commonly shared *Native American values appear first* and *dominant American values* follow. The list reflects that of Garrett et al. (2014) includes some minor variations in wording: *harmony with nature* vs power over nature, *cooperation* vs competition, *group needs are most important* vs personal goals are most important, *one should not interfere with others* vs one should try to control others, *self-discipline* vs expression of self, *observe then act* vs learn by trial and error, *things are explained through nature* vs science explains everything, *rely on family* vs rely on experts, *emotional relationships are valued* vs facts are valued, *patience* vs aggressive and competitive behavior, *humility* vs fame and recognition, *win and let others win also* vs win all the time, *adhere to old ways* vs importance of progress and change, *present time focus* vs plan for the future and how to get ahead, *share what you have freely* vs private property, and *speak softly and slowly* vs speak louder and faster (p.43).

Elders are often revered in Native American culture and they serve as purveyors of cultural knowledge inclusive of values, history, tradition, protocol, and sacred ways (Garrett et al., 2014). Extended family and tribal kinship are highly valued in traditional Native American culture. Family and tribal elders, extended family, and others within the community teach, model, and reinforce values and expected behavior.

Because of the differences in values, expected behavior in the Native American cultures can be much different than that which is expected within dominant American culture. For example, Native Americans emphasize non-verbal communication that is devoid of direct eye contact and moderation in speech. Looking into a speaker's eyes is a sign of disrespect. Contrarily, verbal communication is preferred within the dominant culture, expression through inflection and direct eye contact is expected. Failure to give eye contact is a sign of disrespect (Garrett et al., 2014).

Female urban Indians interviewed by Lucero (2014) expressed that traditional Native values were important to their identification as Natives. One participant explained:

The general Lakota values, that's always in the back of my head. Am I following my ways? . . . And for us that means living by the Lakota values—humility, gratitude, fortitude, bravery. That really defines us as a person. (p. 13)

Several of Lucero's participants shared that their values are challenged when walking in the white world. They must do what is expected in the dominant culture to keep a job, for example being aggressive and confrontational, but it was important for them to "be Indian" when the job was done.

Pan-Indianism

Core beliefs and philosophies of tribal groups throughout North America are remarkably similar (Bender, 2003; Rhodes, 1991). Pan-Indianism is the advancement and celebration of shared Native American values and traditions, including powwow traditions. Acknowledgment of Pan-Indian culture unites individuals from disparate tribal groups in shared regional and national identities (Garrett & Carroll, 2000).

Indication of the importance of Pan-Indian identification is provided by the fact that approximately 30 percent of all Native Americans no longer identify as members of specific tribes (Perez & Hirschman, 2009). Intertribal activities, such as contest powwows, are of special interest to younger Natives. Traditional powwow activity is valued more highly by older generations of tribal members (Bender, 2003).

Pan-Indianism and the Contest Powwow

An emphasis upon traditions is common in Indigenous cultures. For example, in any Amazonian society, there exist traditionalist who cling to traditional ways while modernist actively seek and advocate for cultural change (Rubio et al., 2009). Native American traditionalists argue that contest powwows are an inauthentic form of the powwow because they lack much of the ceremonial activity characteristic of traditional powwows, because members of numerous tribes compete in the contest powwow, and because local tribal rituals, history, song, and dance are not emphasized (Dell'Angela, 2003; Howard, 1983). Public powwows such as the contest powwow became secular events following World War II (Gamble, 1952; Howard, 1983; Lurie, 1971). The events are said to be devoid of overtly religious activity. However, Browner (2002) suggests that contest powwow dancers can still experience the spiritual while dancing and view their participation as belonging within the realm of the sacred. Lerch and Bullers (1996) noted that traditional powwows serve to inculcate independent tribal identity, while large contest powwows are more likely to promote Pan-Indianism.

Contest powwows are Pan-Indian celebrations that bring together competitors and spectators from multiple tribal backgrounds, and people of all ages, levels of cultural knowledge, and tribal involvement (Bender, 2003). While competing in contest powwows, dancers can represent their tribes by incorporating tribal symbols into their regalia (Kavanaugh, 1982). They may compete in dances like those performed by their ancestors, and dance to songs their ancestors may have danced to (Ellis & Lassiter, 2005). Within the contest powwow milieu, there is ample opportunity for competitors to express tribal identity, to feel connected with their tribe, and to feel close to their ancestors. They are not, however, required to focus upon tribal-specific beliefs and traditions.

The Contest Powwow as a Crucible of Culture

The contest powwow is a cultural institution that celebrates Pan-Indian cultural values, traditions, ceremonies, song, and dance. Howard (1983) acknowledged that traditionalists may view the contest powwow and Pan-Indianism as the end of Native America's beautiful songs and dances. However, change is inevitable, and he concludes, "Better Pan Indianism than no Indianism" (p. 81).

Hill (1996) asserts that the intertribal contest powwows have assisted in spreading a Pan-Indian identity throughout North America. The events function as dynamic agents of cultural renewal (Hughes, 2001). Contest powwows encompass how Native American dress, how they dance, how they sing, and unifies them by serving as a source of collective identity. The contest powwow is an indispensable site within which Native Americans express themselves, connect with their ancestors, and participate in culture (Lucero, 2014). In the current chapter, we seek to determine how the contest powwow and traditional powwow differ, how the contest powwow has changed, and how the contest powwow functions to preserve Native American culture in the lives of contemporary contest powwow dancers.

METHOD

We utilize the grounded theory technique to assemble qualitative data through semi-structured interviews to ascertain how large intertribal contest powwows differ from traditional forms of the powwow, how contest powwows have changed, and how the contest powwow functions to preserve Native American culture in the lives of contemporary contest powwow dancers. We select participants from the New Mexico state fairgrounds during the 2018 Gathering of Nations (GON) Powwow in Albuquerque, New Mexico.

Institutional Review Board (IRB) approval was obtained from University of Texas of Permian Basin. In addition, we received approval from the GON administration to conduct interviews with powwow dancers. Dancer participants represent a wide range of ages and all were over the age of nineteen at the time interviews were conducted. We confirm that their participation in this study is anonymous and confidential. Pseudonyms are assigned to each of the fourteen participants.

We also include a number of photographs in our assessments which illustrated Native American art, ceremonial dress, dance, and symbols. The rationale for using these photographs was to discover additional crucial evidence with respect to Native American powwow. Aicinena is a professional photographer. Professional grade cameras and lenses were allowed into the powwow facility in 2016 and 2017. As the event was public, photographs could be taken. In 2017, Aicinena received a media pass from the event organizers, which provided access to the floor of the arena. Some of the photographs from the 2017 powwow were published in the *Odessa American*. Aicinena holds the copyright for all photos included in this book. None of the participants interviewed for the current study are included in the accompanying photographs. Additional photographs can be found at https://zenfolio.page .link/LDFt. Photographs were not taken during the 2018 powwow at which interviews were conducted. Permission was granted by the GON to include the photographs appearing in this chapter.

This participatory study allows the researchers to characterize the dancers' perspectives and experiences regarding Native American collective identity. Our main goal is to reach a complete understanding of the participants' sense of the powwow, the meanings of the ceremony in the Native American community, and the overall powwow context in which Native America culture including art, identity, dance, spirituality, religion, and dancers exist.

In order to conduct in depth and semi-structured interviews to understand powwows dancers' lived experiences and to evaluate the meaning, identity, and transformation of the powwow, we ask primary questions such as, what does powwow mean to you? What aspects of the powwow have changed in the observation of the dancers? What differences have the participants observed in the traditional and contest forms of the powwow? What caused any perceived difference in the behavior of participants at traditional and contest powwows?

We began to evaluate the composite data with open coding to code the findings of this study. In this phase, our focus is upon field notes, photographs, transcribed interviews, and participant observations (Soyer & Ziyanak, 2018). During axial coding, we generate key concepts such as the role of the powwow in Native American culture, powwow drama, evolution of the powwow, regalia, symbol of the cross in Native American dress and art, observed changes regarding sacred and religious aspects of powwow, traditional powwows and contest powwows, and acknowledgment of culture. We examine and reorganize our findings and confirmations concerning each theme and subtheme. In our data analysis, the selective coding stage concludes the coding process. We organize the data though the mapping step enabling us to place all collected information into a coherent form (Corbin & Strauss, 2007).

FINDINGS AND DISCUSSION

Participants described differences between traditional and contest powwows, noted that changes have occurred in contest powwows during their lifetimes, acknowledged that cultural norms and symbols are components of the contest powwow, explicated the existence and genesis of powwow drama occurring in conjunction with contest powwows, and indicated that contest powwows are not overtly religious celebrations. Most notably, participants clearly articulated that contest powwows are vital in maintaining the shared culture of Native Americans.

Respondent's Characteristics

The average age of the participants is 37.71. Male and female participants average 37.85 and 37.57 years of age, respectively. Participants represent eighteen Indigenous tribal groups including Cheyenne, Chippewa, Cochiti Tewa, Colorado River Indian Tribes, Cree, Crow, Dakota Sioux, Hidatsa, Lakota Sioux, Mandau, Navajo, Ojibwe, Potawatomi, Pueblo, Shoshone, Sioux, Tututni, and Zuni. Seven participants claim more than one tribal affiliation. Female participants compete in nine different dance styles: Fancy Shawl, Fancy Southern, Jingle, Northern Buckskin, Northern Cloth, Northern Traditional, Southern Cloth, Victory Dance, and Zuni Traditional. Males participate in three dance styles: Grass Dance, Prairie Chicken Dance, and Men's Traditional Northern.

Observed Differences between Traditional and Contest Powwows

We address the following question: What differences have the participants observed in the traditional and contest forms of the powwow? Dee believes that both versions of the powwow share similarities, "but there are differences." Our findings demonstrate that the great majority of the participants note differences between contest and traditional powwows.

At traditional powwows, participants are more sociable. Amy notices that, "people are more outgoing and happy at traditional powwows." Abe describes dancers as being, "a lot nicer." Freda shares that during traditional powwows, "the elders are more involved. They are there teaching all of us." According to Eric, schedules are not tightly adhered to at traditional powwows, people are, "more laid back. [There is] no hustle and bustle." Gill professes, "At community powwows, dancers are humble."

Participants perceive significant antisocial behavior at contest powwows. Bill's observes that, "people are more aloof and they stay away from each other. They don't get as close. The feeling is different." Frank echoes the contention, "People ignore one another at contest powwows." Geneva declares that "people are not as friendly at contest powwows." Carla is often disturbed at contest powwows, "I have seen cattiness and I have seen fights at contest powwows. I have not seen these things at traditional powwows." Freda notes that elders teach at traditional powwows but, "they do not teach at contest powwows." Eric observes that, "at competition powwows, people are out to impress. They wear new regalia, bead-work, make-up and such." Consequently, Gill concludes, "Some [contestants] are big-headed and prideful."

In highlighting the differences between traditional and competition powwows, participants emphasize how competitors treat one another. Traditional powwows are characterized by family, friendships, community, learning from elders, and relaxation. At times, contest powwow dancers exhibit selfishness, prideful behavior, edginess, and envy that is absent in the traditional environment. However, the findings show that the antisocial behavior was not always visible in all or most contest powwows. Generalizability is not one of the features of qualitative study. Nevertheless, it would appear based upon the observations made by our participants that antisocial behavior would be observed more often in the contest powwow setting.

Powwow Drama

What causes the perceived difference in the behavior of dancers at traditional and contest powwows? Participants explain that large numbers of dancers in competitions leads to aggravation and stress. Further, as time schedules are tight at contest powwows, competitors do not have the same opportunities to create friendships and socialize.

Participants also attribute the difference in observed behavior between traditional and contest powwows to the impact of competition and a resulting overemphasis upon winning by some competitors. In the eyes of our participants, competition brings out behavior proscribed by traditional Native culture that which is self-centered, individualistic, and prideful in the pursuit of victory. In essence, competition results in antisocial behavior that creates "powwow drama."

Observed Changes in Powwows

The majority of the participants indicate that contest powwows have changed in the course of their lifetime. We address the following question: What aspects of the contest powwow have changed in the observation of the dancers?

Abe has seen crowds grow larger, particularly at contest powwows, "There are starting to be a lot more spectators." He believes that the large crowds serve to "bring more energy" to his performances. He also notes that the pace of the dances has increased. Crowds enjoy watching the fast-paced dances as characterized by increased levels of cheering and clapping during and after performances.

Dance moves have evolved to be more eye-catching to judges and crowds. Bill explains how social media has accelerated the change, "Facebook and social media have accelerated change. People see new things and adopt them."

Chuck notes that technology has influenced powwow judging, "Scoring systems are digital now. It saves time and makes it easier for judges. In the past, judges hand-picked the winners." Chuck believed that digital scoring serves to decrease the influence of subjectivity in the selection of winners.

Changes in the traditional form of the powwow were necessary in order to conduct powwow spectacles involving thousands of performers and spectators. Standardization of activities and judging in addition to tight scheduling became necessary. Frank observes that contest powwows have become more highly organized and standardized, "When I started, things were not scheduled. Now, most are held in arenas and coliseums. Everything is tightly scheduled."

Betty observes that the wide availability of powwow prize money is a, "recent thing." In Dave's lifetime, the opportunity to win money in dance contests has increased dramatically, "In the old days, we did not have [contest powwows]. Several participants noted that some powwow dancers and their families earn their annual income on the "powwow highway."

Carla believes that powwows, especially contest powwows, will continue to evolve over time, "We are modernists. We evolve as well." Change will likely be slower in traditional powwows as there is less focus placed upon competition and profit and more emphasis is placed upon local and regional traditions. Dance steps have evolved as a consequence of dancers' efforts to impress judges. Technology has been employed to share changes in dance performances and to improve the perceived fairness of scoring performances. Contest powwows have become standardized in terms of order of activities and general structure. Contest powwows are being held more often. Finally, it was acknowledged that components of the powwow will continue to evolve as participants are confronted with changes within the broader society.

Powwow Regalia

Regalia have become more colorful as designs and materials have changed, though some traditional components have remained. Geneva explains,

Figure 6.1 The Meaning of Symbols. The swastika is often associated with Nazi Germany; however, the symbol has long been used by Native Americans to represent the four directions, the whirling log of the Navajo, and more. *Source:* Steven Aicinena.

Figure 6.2 Symbolism of the Cross. Symbols such as the cross should not be assumed to have a relationship to Christianity. The cross has traditional significance in Native American cultures unrelated to Christianity. Often it represented the four directions. *Source:* Steven Aicinena.

"Beadwork and designs have become more elaborate and brighter. This was not so in the past, and it was not acceptable." Eric adds support for Geneva's contention, "In the old days, regalia were plain . . . People beaded and quilted their own regalia. They used to be given to us by family." Today, it is not uncommon for dancers to purchase their regalia. Abe, Amy, Betty, Bill, and Carla also identify changes in regalia as a remarkable transformation in the powwow.

Regalia have cultural significance to dancers (figure 6.1). For example, the cross, often associated with Christianity, is frequently displayed upon dancers' regalia. In Native American cultures, the cross has traditionally represented the four cardinal directions, the four basic elements, the four winds, male and female energy, or the four phases of life (Owusu, 1997) (figure 6.2). Tribally meaningful symbols can be seen on regalia and this may include symbols significant to specific familial groups. Eric explains, "I wear my family on my [regalia's] sleeve. I dance for my family and my nation."

Current cultural symbols important to male dancers such as NFL, NBA, or NCAA team logos can be seen on their regalia. The regalia of children, particularly the "Tiny Tots," include popular cartoon superheroes and Disney characters. Though some dancers wear their family on their sleeves, others wear symbols of importance in modern life on theirs. In doing so, some traditions are set aside as the present is celebrated within the context of the contest powwow.

Numerous changes have taken place in regalia during the lives of this study's participants. Regalia have evolved as new materials have become popular in mainstream society. The regalia of many competitors is flashier than it was traditionally. Some competitors purchase regalia, though traditionally it was made by dancers or given to them by family members. Designs appearing on regalia may include modern logos, designs, or cartoon characters, however, traditional symbols such as the cross continue to be used by dancers. Further, symbols appearing on regalia can have significant personal meaning to dancers (figure 6.3).

Figure 6.3 A Competitive Dancer's Regalia Has Personal Meaning. Regalia may combine a combination of the traditional and the new. Regalia has personal meaning and significance to contest powwow dancers. This Native American veteran was a proud member of the Marines. An American flag can be seen with the Eagle Staff on his medallion. *Source:* Steven Aicinena.

Competitive Dancing and Native American Spirituality

On the Tuesday preceding the powwow, the powwow organizers conduct a brief blessing ceremony over the arena. Each session of the powwow begins with a prayer in English or a Native American language. Christian ministers in English and/or Native languages offer prayers. Prayers are offered by elders who may or may not have been Christian. The prayers are a means to publically give thanks to Creator for safety in travel and for the opportunity to join together at the powwow as one. One prayer includes the following observation, "There is no other site like this in the whole world. We should be grateful." The prayers are quite similar to those given before sporting events and civic events at which prayers are offered. No intent is made to attract those in attendance to become a part of any formal religion.

Through our coding, we find that five participants discussed aspects of the supernatural or the sacred during interviews. Two of the five share the belief that some traditional dances, not performed at the contest powwow, are sacred and that they are not to be performed in public gatherings. Geneva states, "We have to keep some things sacred. We can't share everything." Eva who is a member of a Pueblo tribe, avows, "I am in a group that performs our [tribe's] public dances, but there are dances that are sacred to us. We don't perform them in public."

Traditionally, some tribes refused to perform their sacred dances in public. For example, the Iroquois prohibited outsiders, even members of other tribal groups, from participating in or observing their powwows. Pueblo tribes still refrain from performing some of their dances in public (Herle, 1994). Eva and Geneva note there is a sacred component to some culturally significant dances. In doing so, participants convey that tribal groups continue to maintain control of important cultural traditions.

Religion is directly mentioned by Eric, "I prefer traditional powwows because there are religious ceremonies there." When explaining the purpose of dancing, Eva addresses traditional spirituality, "We dance for good spirits." Chuck shares, "I feel spiritual when I win." Betty describes powwows as being all-encompassing and, "something spiritual." As she prepares to compete, Geneva says prayers, completes a smudging ceremony, and gives thanks to Creator. She observes that the sacred and spiritual aspects of powwows have waned in her lifetime, "In the old days, powwows helped us learn to conduct ourselves. When we were upset, we were taught to pray and find peace." Her spiritually related activity comes from her upbringing and she laments that youth are not receiving the same training (figure 6.4).

Figure 6.4 Entering the Circle at a Young Age. A mother is preparing her very young daughter to participate in the Tiny Tots dance at the Gathering of Nations. *Source:* Steven Aicinena.

The vast majority of participants do not mention anything related to the supernatural or the sacred. The relatively limited mention of symbols or rituals related to the sacred and supernatural during the interviews offers support for the contention that powwows have been primarily secular events since World War II (Gamble, 1952; Howard, 1983; Lurie, 1971).

Acknowledgment of the Contest Powwow's Relationship to Native American Culture

We ask participants how dancing in the contest powwow relates to their culture. Freda notes that through contest powwow dancing, "Culture is shared and reproduced." Contest powwows are described as being, a "big" part, and a "key" to tribal culture by Dee and Geneva respectively. Participants emphasize that contest powwows provide a means of "sharing," "learning about,"

"participating in," "maintaining," and "passing on" the traditions of ancestors. According to Chuck, the contest powwow is a place to "meet with and
learn from elders." Freda explains that contest powwows are "very important
because they provide a sense of history."

According to Amy, Dave, Bill, Chuck, and Frank, contest powwows are
sites where "traditions" and "traditional styles of dance" are passed on to
others. Frank cites traditional dance performed in the contest powwow as a,
"way to get back to how we were before. My dance goes back to how it was
when we were hunting and going to war."

Abe states, "I was brought into the powwow circle for dances during my
first year of life. I started dancing when my tribal groups allowed it, at the age
of two." He explains that in some tribes, children are literally carried into the
powwow circle before they can walk. With other tribes, convention requires
that children must be able to walk on their own before they can enter the
powwow circle. Clearly, it is important for powwow dancers to socialize their
children into the culture of the powwow at very early ages. In observing interactions between parents, extended family, and children we note that teaching
them the right way to dance, to dress, and how to comport themselves within
the powwow circle is important. The observed interactions demonstrate the
familial and cultural importance placed upon the contest powwow, its philosophy, and protocols.

CONCLUSIONS

The current sample of contest powwow dancers clearly articulates that the
contest powwow continues to serve an important role in celebration, maintenance, and transmission of Native American history and culture. Dance is an
activity through which this study's participants participate in Native culture
and it serves as an opportunity for them to pass traditions on to younger generations. Finally, participants in this project consider dance as a means to stay
connected with their ancestors.

Our participants have observed changes in contest powwows over the
span of their lives. Changes identified included technology, regalia, the
impact of social media, and commercialization leading to increases in the
size of crowds and prize money. However, tribal affiliation is maintained and
reflected through dances and regalia worn by competitors.

Thousands of Native Americans participate in contest powwows and
hundreds of thousands of people enjoy watching them compete each year.
Within its social and cultural context, contest powwow dancing develops a
reciprocated connection between the audience, dancers, and spectators. All

are considered participants in the celebration of Native culture which is the contest powwow.

As of 2018 the contest powwow functions as an important institution in the lives of Native American people. The philosophy of the contest powwow is observed, learned, and internalized by participants and it fashions a sense of collective identity among members of the Native American community through celebration of shared traditions, values, and history. Native American culture lives on and it can be experienced by all at the contest powwow.

Chapter 7

Cultural Tethering Theory

Millions of people have immigrated to the Unites States to escape poverty, war, persecution, political turmoil, and for a myriad of other reasons. Over fifteen million immigrated to the United States between 1900 and 1915 alone (Library of Congress, n.d.). As immigrants spend more time in America, their sense of separateness weakens, and the assimilation process is enhanced (Abramitzky, 2017; Abramitzky et al., 2020).

According to Ziyanak and Sert (2018), the desire to effectively function in American society helped many families fully assimilate within a few generations. Brown and Bean (2006) reported that in the 1900s, European immigrants to the United States fully assimilated within three to four generations. Immigration and assimilation patterns for immigrants from Asia, Latin America, and the Caribbean have been like those of the early 1900s European immigrants. Between the 1960s through the early 2000s, second-generation immigrants demonstrated increased levels of American citizenship, home-ownership, English language proficiency, job status, and income compared to their parents (Waters & Jimenez, 2005).

The road to assimilation for Native Americans has not been as positive as it has been for immigrants. One in three Native Americans lives in poverty (Bureau of Labor Statistics, 2019). Fifty-six percent of Native Americans sleep in locations not meant for human habitation and sixty-seven out of 10,000 are homeless (Moses, 2020). Only 19 percent of Native Americans attend college compared to 41 percent of the overall American population (PNPI, 2019). Indigenous women are murdered at a rate ten times higher than other ethnic or racial groups (Native Women's Wilderness, n.d.). 56.1 percent of Native American women experience sexual violence and 81.6 percent experience some form of violence in their lifetime (Rosay, 2016).

Fifty-eight of every one thousand Native American homes do not have plumbing (Morales, 2019). Native Americans are 50 percent more likely than non-Hispanic white adults to be obese (HHS.Gov, 2020). Obesity is related to serious health problems including diabetes, high blood pressure, and heart disease. Substance abuse and suicide rates are higher for Native Americans than for any other population in the United States (Kaliszewski, 2021; National Indian Council on Aging, 2019).

Native Americans were not immigrants to North America and governmental efforts to force assimilation into the dominant culture have not been fully effective, even after a period of centuries. To a significant degree, Native Americans have maintained collectivist cultural values and traditions despite deafening calls from the dominant American society to assimilate.

Native Americans are a proud people who have had to fight the American government and ever-present agents of cultural change to maintain their unique cultural identity. "The frost of racist and assimilative federal Indian policies has settled deeply into the Indian country, yet our memories have not withered and our roots yet retain their strength" (Rice, 1996, p. 189).

We both hold a personal and professional interest in culture. As we completed the research included within this book, our interest in assimilation and Native American resistance to assimilation remained high. Based upon our research findings and information gleaned from our literature reviews, we developed a theory of assimilation that explains why some individuals and groups assimilate into a dominant society while others resist. In this chapter, we introduce *The Cultural Tethering Theory*.

REVIEW OF LITERATURE

Before turning our attention to *The Cultural Tethering Theory*, we will address a series of topics that were foundational to its conception. First, we discuss the concepts of culture, cultural change, acculturation, and assimilation. We then explain how and why modern Native American cultures are experiencing an erosion of traditional values, a rapid loss of traditional languages, changes in social organization, limited opportunity to learn culturally valued knowledge, reduced opportunity to observe culturally appropriate behavior, and the influence of technology. We then examine Native American identity and seek to determine who can legitimately claim to be a Native American. Topics addressed include blood quantum, cultural knowledge, cultural participation, being Indian and playing Indian. Finally, we describe the difference between being Native American and playing Indian in powwow and pseudocultural powwow environments.

Culture

Societies consist of the people who share common beliefs. According to Varnum and Grossman (2017), culture consists of the norms, values, behaviors, beliefs, and ideas common to peoples living within a specific geographic area. Components of culture are passed down through multiple generations (Maguire, 2018). Effectively, culture is the product of a people's history for all cultures result from human activity over time (Appiah, 1994; Scheffler, 2007). Communities are held together by a shared culture.

The impact of culture upon individuals was well-articulated by Ziyanak and Jordan (2018):

> Culture has a prominent power on every single individual and contributes to who he or she is, what they believe, what certain rituals are performed, how they behave, how they eat, and why they act in definite ways. (p. 92)

Culture matters to all human beings whether they choose to ignore it, embrace it, or replace it. It is impossible to understand individuals if their culture is not taken into consideration (House et al., 2006; Varnum & Grossman, 2017).

We align with the symbolic interactionism model of socialization which holds that individuals through thought and construction of meaning are active in shaping their social worlds (Herman & Reynolds, 1994). All human beings choose to align their behaviors and beliefs with convention or choose to depart from it. People are not puppets or pawns blindly manipulated by genetic and social forces.[1] Each of us has the capacity to challenge conventions and initiate change within our culture (Giddens, 2004). However, each of us is impacted in important ways through the process of socialization.

"Socialization is a process of learning and social development, which occurs as we interact with one another and become familiar with our social environments" (Coakley, 2017, p. 52). Through the process of socialization, individual members of a culture learn norms and values as they interact with others. Culture is reflected in individual personalities; however, symbolic interactionism holds that the behavior of individuals is influenced by their personality traits as well as specific situational variables (Fleeson, 2004). Not all individuals, therefore, respond the same to all situations within any culture.

Cultural and Social Change

Human cultures are dynamic, not static (Varnum & Grossman, 2017). The malleability of a culture is impacted by the strength of social norms, ethnic homogeneity, and the degree of isolation from the influence of others.

Because the strength of each of these factors differs from cultural group to cultural group, cultural change is non-linear. Change can occur rapidly or slowly.

Varnum and Grossman (2017) employ a biological evolutionary approach to explain how and why cultures change. Cultural change occurs through the process of cultural evolution or in response to alterations of a group's cultural ecology.

Cultural evolution occurs in response to the introduction of novel ideas or technologies. The process is likened to changes in genes, which are important in passing on genetic information within individuals (Campbell, 1965; Dawkins, 1976). Genetic information is passed on in living organisms from generation to generation and alteration in the genetic code of an organism results in change. In a similar fashion, culture is passed on from generation to generation. The introduction of something novel to members of a culture has the potential to initiate cultural change.

Creativity, discoveries, and new visions can also serve to instigate cultural change. According to Varnum and Grossman (2017), whether or not a novel value, behavior, or technological innovation takes hold and effects change in individuals or cultures depends upon the interaction between four forms of cultural bias, including conformity bias (the tendency to copy the behavior of others), prestige bias (the tendency to copy the behavior of important people), self-similarity bias (the desire to act like others in the group), and innovation bias (the tendency to adopt new technologies or behaviors considered beneficial to the culture's members).

Ecological evolution is initiated when components of the social group's environment are changed. For example, changes in population density, the availability of resources, and the introduction of external threats can result in alteration of established beliefs and behaviors. Chaotic events such as those caused by natural disasters disrupt established social systems can also initiate ecological evolution (Cajete, 2004). Ecological evolution can occur rapidly if it is necessary to ensure cultural survival. Ecological evolution occurred in Native American history when the government forced tribes to relocate from their ancestral lands to reservations.

Acculturation and Assimilation

Acculturation is the process through which individuals or groups replace traditional cultural values and behaviors for those held by another social group (Garrett & Pichette, 2000; Rubio et al., 2009; Suinn et al., 1987). It is, more specifically, "the process of change that happens at the individual and group levels as a result of being in a dominant culture and adopting the behavior patterns, attitudes, and norms of that surrounding culture" (Garrett

& Pichette, 2014, p. 478). Acculturation occurs more readily at the microcultural level than it does at the macrocultural level.

Based upon the work of Herring (1996) and LaFramboise et al. (1990), Garrett and Prichette (2000) conceptualized individual Native Americans as fitting into one of five levels of acculturation as they moved from the traditional end of the acculturation continuum to the assimilated end and back. Those at the *Traditional Level* often speak and think in tribal languages. They adhere to traditional customs, values, and forms of worship. Individuals in the *Marginal Level* may be bilingual but do not fully accept tribal customs and values. Native Americans in the *Bicultural Level* understand, accept, and practice mainstream values and behaviors as well as those of their tribal group. Those in the *Assimilated Level* have adopted the values and behaviors of the dominant society and no longer accept or practice the values or behaviors of their tribal group. Individuals in the *Pantraditional Level* have been assimilated but strive to return to the traditional language, values, beliefs, and practices of their people.

The Arapaho viewed Euro-American culture as being so averse to theirs that they referred to is as "Crazy" or *hohookeenizi* (Anderson, 2011). Of course, non-Natives often viewed Native American culture to be crazy as well. In his paper, *Remarks Concerning the Savages of North America*, Benjamin Franklin (1784) observed that both the Indians and colonists believed their culture was superior to that of the others, "Savages we call them, because their manners are different from ours, which we think the Perfection of Civility, they think the same of theirs" (para. 1).

People do not become fully comfortable in foreign cultures overnight, but in time and through the impact of acculturation, they can become comfortable, but at a cost. The Kiowa grandmother of Horse (2005) lamented, "Someday we're all going to be like white people" (p. 61). Horse's grandmother had observed that Kiowa children seldom used their native language, and they ate prepackaged food instead of traditional foods. Popular American culture had run rampant among her people. The Kiowa often intermarried with other races and members of other tribes and as they did, tribal culture was lost. Horse confessed, "Fifty-four years later, I look around and think we may not be white people but indeed we are more like them" (p. 61).

Full assimilation is achieved when individuals or cultural groups embrace the dominant culture's expectations, behaviors, and values to the exclusion of those traditionally held (Garrett & Pinchette, 2000). Cultures die when the young assimilate, and the group's elders die out. When cultures vanish, the people cease to exist as a unique cultural entity (Maguire, 2018).

Amnesty International (2021) estimates that there are approximately 5,000 different Indigenous people groups in the world today. Countless Indigenous cultures have disappeared because of the impact of disease, cultural evolution, and changes in social ecology. Most often, Indigenous collectivist cultures have vanished as the people assimilated in response to the forces of industrialization and other socioeconomic factors. As they did, their traditional cultures passed on into oblivion.

At this point it is important to share the musings of Maffesoli (2016). Postmodern times have created social situations in which individuals are free to choose the cultural environments within which they prefer to spend time. All are empowered to join social groups or "tribes" based upon individual tastes and interests.[2]

The physical and virtual areas in which postmodern tribal groups meet to celebrate and participate in shared interests are referred to as "hotspots." Hotspots serve as "social cement" that binds the fleetingly faithful together. Within hotspots, individuals are free to let tastes and passions reign supreme.

In the past, according to Maffesoli, "There was once a domestication of social manners and a civilization of the passions which prevailed throughout the times of modernity, there is now a return to the wild taking place in this world" (p. 746). By "return to the wild," Maffesoli posits that human are with ever-increasing frequency NOT socialized to, nor are they required to, conform to the archaic and illogical expectations of cultures and their institutions. If Maffesoli is correct, ALL the world's established cultures are in peril of being radically transformed.

NATIVE AMERICAN IDENTITY:
WHO ARE "REAL INDIANS?"

Determination of who can rightfully claim Native American identity has been argued by historians, governments, legal scholars, anthropologists, and Indigenous peoples themselves (Schmidt, 2011). There is no consensus. If someone is referred to as Native American, the designation is based upon personal attitudes, preferences, and concepts including culture, race, and legal status (Rice, 1996).

If typical Americans were asked to describe what a Native American looks like, they would likely provide descriptors based upon phenotypes: they have black hair, brown eyes, and dark skin (Jacobs & Merolla, 2016). But does possession of the genes responsible for expression of physical "Indianness" make someone Native American? How can a Native American have white skin, light hair, and green eyes? Could individuals of 100 percent Native American ancestry be classified as Native American if they were adopted and raised by Martians? What if they have never set foot on a reservation? What if they have no knowledge of their tribal culture? Who is Native American?

A great increase in the number of Americans identifying as Native American occurred between the 1970 and 2010 U.S. Census when the population rose from 800,000 to 5.2 million. Most "New Indians" were typically multiracial and had identified in previous censuses as a member of a different racial group (Jacobs & Merolla, 2016). New Indians are often referred to as "reclaimers" as they seek to reclaim an identity that was lost to them through full familial assimilation, ancestral intent, or accidents of history. Today it is common for Native Americans to have parents with genetic and cultural ties to multiple tribes and other races (Haozous et al., 2014).

Reclaimers, often have very little Native American blood, so to speak, running through their veins. Rarely are reclaimers "full bloods," those whose genetic make-up is completely American Indian. Reclaimers can be saddled with the moniker, "Wannabe Indian." "Wannabes" are often held in contempt by Native Americans residing on reservations. Although the "wannabes" claim Native American identity, they have not experienced the hardships associated with the contemporary Native Americans experience (Douglas, 2018).

Typically, Native American identity is determined by blood quantum, cultural knowledge and participation, or some combination of the two. In the following sections, we address each method of determining Native American identity.

Blood Quantum

Native Americans are the only minority group in the United States that must prove racial identity (Garrett et al., 2014). The U.S. government instituted the concept of blood quantum, the percentage of Native American DNA one possesses, to delineate where its responsibilities ended for those claiming Native American ancestry. The Bureau of Indian Affairs ceased tracking tribal memberships in the 1980s (U.S. Department of the Interior, n.d.).

Currently, a Certificate of Degree of Indian Blood (CDIB) is required to prove Native American ancestry. A CDIB can be obtained from tribal governments if ancestry can be proven through provision of maternal and paternal documents demonstrating family lineage such as birth or death certificates. Those who hold a CDIB are commonly known in Native American communities as "carded" or "card-carrying" Indians (Estes, 2013). A Tribal Roll Number is assigned to everyone receiving a CDIB.

Tribal regulations set blood quantum standards required for membership and they differ between tribes (Bureau of Indian Affairs, 2021c; Garroutte, 2001). About 66 percent of the tribes recognized by the U.S. government require a minimum blood quantum of 25 percent for tribal enrollment (Garroutte, 2001). The federal government requires a blood quantum of 25 percent or higher before individuals qualify for federal benefits.

The Dawes Rolls were generated by the U.S. government to establish who was to be legally considered a member of the Cherokee, Chickasaw, Choctaw, Creek, and Seminole tribes residing in Oklahoma territory between 1898 and 1907. Tribal members registered with the government and were provided with Indian census numbers. Additions were made to the rolls up to 1914 (Oklahoma Historical Society, n.d.). Any blood quantum level based upon the Dawes Rolls of 1906 allows one to be enrolled as a member of the Cherokee Nation (Cherokee Nation, 2021).

Few reclaimers possess enough Indian DNA to meet federal or tribal requirements needed to be considered a politically authenticated Native American (Jacobs & Merolla, 2016). These reclaimers can be referred to as "thindians" or "delusional Indians" (Parades, 1995). Reclaimers emphasize cultural participation and minimize the importance of blood quantum when discussion concerning identity are held (Jacobs & Merolla, 2016).

In summary, ancestral connection to Native American tribes must be proven through blood quantum to be considered Native American by tribes and the U.S. government. Tribal membership is determined by tribal governments and blood quantum levels differ from tribe to tribe. Is the receipt of a CDIB all that a person needs to establish a legitimate claim to Native American identity?

Cultural Knowledge and Participation

A sample of urban Native American women interviewed by Lucero (2013) identified three important requisites for creating and maintaining an authentic Native American identity. First, the individual must be genetically Native American to some degree and interact with other Native people. Second, the individual must be involved in Native culture. Finally, the individual must possess knowledge of Native culture.

Family, tribal affiliation, and culture, rather than specific blood quantum levels, serve as the source of identity for most Native Americans (Garrett et al., 2014). Although ancestral origin is a fact determined by DNA, one's identity is the product of group membership and affinity. For many Native Americans, culture is more important in determining identity than genetic profiles (Jacobs & Merolla, 2016; Perez & Hirschman, 2009). According to a Native American college student interviewed by Beijsens (2015), "Knowing the culture is the essential thing to being a Native" (p. 33).

According to the participants in a study conducted by Blanchard et al. (2019), legitimate Native American identity flows from experiences and relationships with Indigenous culture. Identity is not, according to the study's participants, the consequence of genetics alone. They considered genetic testing to discover one's indigeneity as something offensive. Though individuals may learn they are of Native American ancestry through DNA analysis, the knowledge becomes nothing more than anecdotal information in the absence of cultural participation. When people know nothing about Native American culture, they cannot legitimately claim Native American identity.

Being Indian and Playing Indian: Narrative and Emotivist Powwows

Emotivism is a philosophical product of our postmodern times and through it, personal preferences have replaced cultural imperatives advocated and reinforced through cultural institutions such as nation, church, and family (Roberts, 2011). Individuals can be who and what they believe themselves to be. They are free do as they please. To emotivists, the only legitimate judges of individual choices and behaviors are the individuals themselves. Emotivists appropriate signs and identities from groups, "to which they have no 'legitimate' connection other than their own feelings and attitudes of affinity" (Roberts, 2011, p. 196). Identity is something emotivists can choose (Gonzalez, 2002). If I believe that I am a Native American, who are you to disagree?

Emotive powwows are pseudocultural powwows often organized by non-Indians. Through participation in pseudocultural powwows, the personal identity of "wannabe" or "hobbyist" Indians is expressed. They play Indian to claim an identity to which they are not entitled (Gonzalez, 2002). For example, Caucasian American and German hobbyists with no genetic or cultural ties to Indigenous people groups organize and participate in powwows because they appreciate and have a great respect for Native American culture (Roberts, 2011; Watchman, 2005).

Emotivists believe it is okay to wear regalia, dance in powwows, and even organize powwows though they possess not a smidgen of Indian blood and may have never spent significant time in Native American culture (Roberts, 2011). Persons with authentic ties to Native America tell a narrative through participation in powwows and other aspects of Indigenous culture. Narrative powwows are conducted by and for Native Americans out of a collective identity and a common understanding of what it means to be Indigenous (Roberts, 2011).

CHANGE IN NATIVE AMERICAN CULTURE

According to the United Nations (2021), collectivist Indigenous cultures have been viewed as primitive, inferior, and irrelevant by members of technologically advanced individualistic cultures. In their hubris, interlopers from

Western cultures harbored the belief that Indigenous cultures were, and are, something to be transformed or eradicated. Currently, the Indigenous cultures of the world are in danger of extinction due to loss of traditional lands, loss of languages, the inability of elders to pass on culture to children, consumption of nontraditional foods, and loss of traditional knowledge. Western influences threaten the survival of Indigenous cultures (Luu, 2019).

A history of persecution, suffering, and loss is a legacy shared by all Native American tribal groups (House et al., 2006). Native Americans suffered persecution because interlopers viewed them as socially and technologically inferior peoples who worshiped ineffective pagan Gods. In the interest of assimilating Native Americans and cleaving them from their debased "savage" ways, the American government implemented and enforced policies that would "ideally" eradicate Native American cultures from the face of the earth (see chapters 1 and 5). Today, the explicit war upon Native American culture seems to have ended and efforts to maintain and revitalize traditional culture are legion. However, more insidious factors are acting implicitly to disunite Native Americans from their culture.

Cultures are complex, and components of cultures interact in impactful and meaningful ways. Change in one institution yields change in others, for each is interconnected. Changes in one aspect of the culture, religious practices, for example, can impact language, family structure, values, ceremonial activity, and identity.

Cultural anthropologists equate the culture of people groups with shared values, language, social organization, shared knowledge, observed behavior, and technology (Maguire, 2018). In the following pages, we examine how erosion of traditional Native American values, loss of traditional languages, changes in social organization, reduced opportunity to observe and learn traditional cultural knowledge and culturally valued behavior, and technology have functioned to impact change in Native Americas and their cultures.

Erosion of Traditional Native American Values

Studies of specific cultures often involve the assessment of existent levels of collectivism and individualism (Beckstein, 2014). Traditional and contemporary Native American cultures are classified as collectivist cultures and social scientists have identified core collectivist values and behaviors that are shared by various tribal nations throughout North America (Beckstein, 2014; Goodluck, 2002; House et al., 2006; LaFromboise & Dizon, 2003).

Commonly shared Native American values and related behaviors include a deep respect for elders, sharing, acceptance, the importance of community, cooperation, harmony, balance, noninterference, extended family, attention to nature, and immediacy of time (Garrett et al., 2014). Traditional collectivist Native American values are a natural product of the people's cosmology. Indigenous peoples practicing traditional forms of spirituality believe Creator, also known as the Great Spirit, called into being all physical and spiritual components of the universe. As human beings and all animate and inanimate creations were fashioned by Creator, all that exists within the universe is related and interdependent. This worldview impacted Native American economics, religious expression, politics, morality, and ethics.

In the dominant American culture, acquired possessions, personal achievements, financial status, and social status are monikers of worth, status, and identity. It is important to plan for the future, be responsible for yourself, impose your will upon others, change what you do not like, and utilize nature to achieve personal goals. Human beings are second in importance only to God. To the secularist, nothing is paramount to the human being. The difference in competing worldviews makes living in the dominant society a challenge for many Native Americans. One of Thornton's (2009) participants explained:

> But we also have to exist in the non-Native world. A place where we have to dress in a certain way, go by clock time, and always are serious at work. . . . It is a place where money is all that counts along with how much we earn and how we earn it. . . . Seeing all of this makes me feel sorry for non-Native people. I walk a fine line and keep one foot in each world. That is how it is for me. (p. 36)

Significant changes in the world's cultures occurred as socioeconomic development associated with the transition from agricultural-based to industrial-based societies proliferated (Fukuyama, 1999). The Industrial Revolution led to greater intensity and frequency of contact with non-kin and others outside of established cultural groups. Frequent exposure to the values and norms of others assisted in adoption of individualistic norms and behaviors.

Change continues today at a rapid rate. Santos et al. (2017) found that individualism increased by 12 percent in the seventy-eight developed and developing countries examined between 1960 and 2011. Socioeconomic development accounted for 35–58 percent of the variance in change over time. Increases in the availability of white-collar jobs, income, and education were powerful factors in the changes observed.

As societies have begun to transition from the industrial age to the information era, noteworthy cultural shifts have taken place. Between the 1960s and 1990s, social conditions in the industrialized world deteriorated. Individualism flourished as collectivism waned. Social disorder and crime increased as kinship declined. Divorce rates climbed and birthrates fell as increases in the number of single-family households were observed.

These social ills have increasingly plagued Native American communities as individualism has spread and collectivism has waned. For example, as the Arapaho culture has adopted individualistic practices aligned with increasing consumerism and socioeconomic change, there have been increases in violence, substance abuse, crime, suicide, and other forms of social malady (Anderson, 2009).

Native Americans understood the impact of individualism and capitalism, upon relations long ago. The words of Canassetego, a Mohawk, were told to Benjamin Franklin (1784) through a translator:

> You know our Practice. If a white Man in travelling thro' our Country, enters one of our Cabins, we all treat him as I treat you; we dry him if he is wet, we warm him if he is cold, and give him Meat & Drink that he may allay his Thirst and Hunger, & we spread soft Furs for him to rest & sleep on: We demand nothing in return. But if I go into a white Man's House at Albany, and ask for Victuals & Drink, they say, where is your Money? and if I have none, they say, Get out, you Indian Dog. You see they have not yet learnt those little good things . . . our Mothers taught them to us when we were Children. (para. 10)

The U.S. government required Native American children to attend Indian Boarding Schools as a part of its forced assimilation efforts (Harding, 2001; Pratt, 1892). An explicit goal of the Boarding School System was to replace traditional collectivist values with those of individualism deemed necessary to function effectively within the dominant culture. Native Americans held a negative opinion of the American educational system's effectiveness well before the institution of the Boarding School System in 1879.

In the late 1700s, commissioners for the State of Virginia offered to educate half a dozen Native American boys for free. After taking some time to duly consider the offer overnight as was tradition, a representative of the Six Nations replied:

> Several of our young people were formerly brought up at the Colleges of the Northern Provinces; they were instructed in all your Sciences; but, when they came back to us, they were bad Runners, ignorant of every means of living in the Woods, unable to bear either Cold or Hunger, knew neither how to build a Cabin, take a Deer, or kill an Enemy, spoke our Language imperfectly, were therefore neither fit for Hunters, Warriors, nor Counsellors; they were totally good for nothing. We are however not the less obliged by your kind Offer, tho' we decline accepting it; and to show our grateful Sense of it, if the Gentlemen of Virginia will send us a dozen of their Sons, we will take great Care of their Education, instruct them in all we know, and make *Men* of them. (Franklin, 1784, p. 3)

Clearly, the education of youths in the American educational system did not prepare them to function within the Native American's world. The knowledge, values, and behaviors important to effectively navigate and succeed within the dominant culture were not functional in the world of the Mohawks or other Native American tribal groups.

Within modern educational institutions, children are taught explicitly and implicitly that objectivity is important and that the "old ways" of the elders are silly superstitions which were the product of ignorance. The old ways have no place in the contemporary world (Bowers et al., 2000). Science is foundational to modern ideologies that have resulted in the extinction of many traditional collectivist cultures. And science tells us that since only the strongest and fittest survive, the vanquished deserved their fate. A preoccupation with advancement and individual success threatens retention of collectivist values in all remaining human cultures.

We have been told by Hillary Clinton, Oprah Winfrey, Michelle Obama, and others that it "takes a village to raise a child." Some have speculated that the collectivist friendly saying is perhaps a mix of African tradition, a feel-good Hallmark movie culture, and folk sentiments (Goldberg, 2016). The village which is contemporary America teaches its children that they are alone responsible to themselves, accountable to themselves, and can make themselves whatever they wish to be.

Loss of Traditional Languages

Luu (2019) lamented that forceful and homogenizing influences of Western colonialism threaten the survival of the world's remaining Indigenous languages. Ninety percent of the world's 6,000–7,000 remaining languages are expected to fall from use within the next 100 years (United Nations, 2021). All languages contain wisdom and culture amassed over the collective experience of untold generations (Reyhner, 1996). Languages carry and convey cultural values that shape identity. Use of a culture's language is vital for the culture's integrity. When languages are lost so is the wisdom and culture resonating within them. When languages die, the integrity of cultures weakens (United Nations, 2021).

Distinct language separates Native Americans from other cultural groups in the United States (House et al., 2006; Kipp, 2007). Over 300 native languages were once spoken in North America. Historically, one goal of Government-run and Christian-run Indian Boarding Schools was replacement of native languages with English. Because Indian children were removed from their homes and because use of their native languages was prohibited, fluency in use of their Native languages was impeded, leading to a decrease in their usage within their communities.

According to the Bureau of Indian Affairs (2021a), 200 Native American languages are still in use. Throughout North America, tribal languages are falling into disuse. In 1878 all eight hundred remaining members of the Northern Arapaho tribe spoke their native language fluently. In 2005, fewer that 7 percent of the tribe's six thousand members spoke Arapaho fluently (Anderson, 2009). As of 2021, the Salish tribe had fewer than fifty fluent speakers, none under the age of fifty. The Kootenai tribe has fewer than twelve who can speak their language fluently (Keck, 2021). According to Krauss (1992), the Eyak language had two fluent speakers, the Mandan had six, the Abenaki-Penobscot had twenty, and the Iowa had five.

Crawford (1995) provided additional disturbing information concerning the paltry number of individuals who can speak Native American languages fluently:

> Out of 20 native languages still spoken in Alaska, only Central Yupik and St. Lawrence Island Yupik are being transmitted to the next generation. Similarly, in Oklahoma only 2 of 23 are being learned by children. All of California's 31 Indian languages are moribund; of these, 22 are spoken only by small groups of elders. Among the 16 indigenous tongues still spoken in Washington State, few if any have fluent speakers under the age of 60. (p. 18)

For the vast majority of contemporary Native Americans, English is the predominant language in schools, workplaces, and homes (Bureau of Indian Affairs, 2021a). It is projected that most Native languages will have no fluent speakers within one or two generations (Lutz, 2007).

In the Northern Arapaho tradition, there is always a good/correct way for things to be done (Anderson, 2009). Language was an important aspect of performing traditional spiritual rituals in the correct way. Today, cultural-specific rituals are conducted by individuals who do not speak Arapaho. Modern ceremonies, therefore, depart from tradition and some of their meaning is lost in translation.

It is worth noting that in the 1880s native languages were used by missionaries and educators to achieve specific goals. At reservation schools, use of Native languages was prohibited in the Holy name of forced assimilation. On Sundays, however, Christian ministers spoke to congregations in native languages to achieve evangelistic goals (Anderson, 2009). Use of languages in homes, between family members, and within the context of cultural activities helped to maintain language use contrary to externally imposed restrictions meant to eradicate them. Sharing of native languages in homes and community interactions helped Native Americans retain their identity as tribal members.

Today, most Indian children do not learn their native language at home and English is their first language (Lutz, 2007; Reyhner, 1996). In an attempt to quell the loss of traditional languages, programs have been incorporated within reservation schools that include instruction in tribal languages (Bureau of Indian Affairs, 2021a; Keck, 2021; Spicer et al., 2012). Language revitalization programs instituted within the schools have not been highly effective in creating fluent speakers (Anderson, 2011). Illustratively, language programs on the Northern Arapaho reservation have not produced a single fluent speaker.

Native American children receive competing messages concerning the superiority of English over Native languages at schools (Lee, 2009). Though, the importance of the Native languages in tribal and Pan-Indian cultures is acknowledged, it becomes clear to students that the English language is required for personal and financial success in life. Young Arapaho, for example, do not view their tribal language as important to their future employment or security and do not see a need to learn it (Anderson, 2009). So, many don't.

In traditional reservation communities, some Native children are surrounded by strong extended kin networks. Children interact with members of their extended kin network and peers as they learn their native language through informal means (Reyhner, 1996; Sarche & Whitesell, 2012). As family members move to cities, and those living in cities are separated physically from one another, it becomes difficult to use tribal languages regularly and children are exposed to them with decreasing frequency. If you are not around your grandmother a lot, why would you feel the need to learn her language? If she were with you daily and the whole family spoke her tribal language, how could you not?

During an interview with Beijsens (2015), a Native American college student living in a large American city confessed an inability to speak his tribal language and expressed that he lacks motivation to do so, "My grandmother sometimes sends me texts with some mambo jumbo I don't understand from her Native language. But I don't really do much with that part of my background" (p. 23).

The impact and acceptance of American values and popular culture has also contributed to the decrease in use of Native American languages. A Native student interviewed by Lee (2009) explains:

> The most obvious cause for our lack of knowledge in our language and culture points to the fact that we are no longer spending time at home learning traditional aspects of our culture from our grandparents and elders, instead we are off learning things about the modern, English-dominated world around us. The scary thing is that the BIA schools are no longer the obvious threat to our survival as a culture, now the danger is internal; it is within us as a community. (316)

Changes in Native American Social Organization

Tribal groups are characterized, in part, by their social organization (House et al., 2006). How, where, and when contact and interactions took place was, and is, important in transmission and maintenance of traditional culture. Tribal social organization has been impacted greatly by the relegation of Native American tribal groups to reservations historically, and migration to cities in recent times.

Before the arrival of European colonialists, individual tribal groups inhabited or moved within specific geographic areas. Some tribes such as the Abenaki of the American Northeast resided in permanent villages (Waldman, 2006). Other tribes such as the Sioux tribes (Dakota, Lakota, & Nakota) were highly mobile and traveled through large geographic areas. The introduction of the horse into Plains Indian culture led to shifts in culture including how the people hunted, how and when they should travel, the number of possessions they could accumulate, decision-making required of elders, ceremonial life, and in many other ways (Anderson, 2011; Waldman, 2006).

As Native lands were purloined by colonists and expansionists, Native Americans were displaced from traditional lands and relocated to reservations (Anderson, 2016; Cave, 2003; Everett, 2009). Today there are 326 land areas in the United States that serve as reservations (Bureau of Indian Affairs, 2021d).

Native American spiritual and cultural practices are tied to homelands and living away from homelands makes developing and maintaining cultural identification difficult (Hendry, 2003; Weaver, 2012). The Arapaho and other Native American tribes experienced an exile from traditional concepts of time as they were exiled from their lands (Anderson, 2011). In response, they began to structure cultural practices, ceremonies, and movements with distribution of goods and services offered by federal authorities.

Relocation of Native Americans from reservations has also resulted in reconfiguration of social organization. Approximately 40,000 Native Americans moved from reservations to cities to secure gainful employment during and following the World War II. In the 1950s, an additional 30,000 moved to cities because of federally supported Indian relocation programs (Lucero, 2013; Weaver, 2012). Today, young Native Americans choose to move to cities from reservations as they seek jobs and personal fulfillment. Approximately 72 percent of all Native Americans now reside in cities (Norris et al., 2012).

The exodus of Native Americans from reservation communities to cities has led to a generalized decrease in the strength of tribal identity and familiarity with tribal-specific traditions and ceremonies. An urban Indian interviewed by Lucero (2013) observed, "It's harder to do your culture or live your culture here in the city, so then it's also easier to get away from it and eventually lose it" (p. 15). A Native American high school student provides another reason for traditional culture becoming irrelevant, "I'm sure if I lived in Tahlequah [a reservation community] my heritage would be more a part of my life. But being here in the city it's not as much a part of your life" (Felder, 2017, p. 15).

Historically, identification with a specific tribe was more important that identifying as a Native American. To identify as Navajo or as Native American conveys different meanings. Identification with a tribe associates individuals with a specific cultural group that has a unique history, resides on specific sacred lands, holds specific beliefs, engages in its own forms of spiritual practice and ceremony, and speaks its own language.

The exodus of Native Americans to cities has increased the prevalence of Pan-Indianism, the adoption, and celebration of supra-tribal values and activities, and has led to individuals identifying as a Native American rather than claiming identity through tribal membership (Lucero, 2013; Powers, 1980; Weaver, 2012). About 30 percent of all self-identified Native Americans no longer identify as members of specific tribes (Perez & Hirschman, 2009).

It was traditionally important for Native Americans to be connected to extended family and community (House et al., 2006). Connections are vital in the living, celebration, and continuation of Native American cultures. A participant in a study undertaken by House, Stiffman, and Brown (2006) explained how extended family and elders taught him his tribe's traditional culture:

> I learned from my uncles and my grandfather, a little bit from my grandmother, but mainly from my uncles and grandfather. My uncles are in charge of teaching me. They know all the things that happened in our clan. (p. 400)

As families were fragmented through exodus to cities, Native Americans often lost direct access to extended family networks that traditionally assisted with child-rearing, provision of social support, and transmission of culture (Evans-Campbell, 2008; Lucero, 2013; Sarche & Whitesell 2012; Weaver, 2012).

Shared Knowledge and Observed Behavior

Human beings learn culturally relevant information formally and informally. Typically, formal education takes place in institutions such as schools. Time is set aside for instructors to share knowledge through employment of a variety of instructional methods. Curricular goals are set and serve as the basis of instructional activities on a daily and annual basis.

In developed countries, formal education serves to prepare students to function effectively within modern society as they learn to read, write, and compute. Schools are also sites in which values important to the dominant culture are inculcated as course readings are completed and classroom activities are conducted (Guthrie, 1983). Books have been written in which authors tout the need to teach values in schools and explain how teachers can go about doing so (Cairns et al., 2003). Values important to success in industrialized society are also reputedly taught, adopted, and reinforced through participation in extracurricular activities such as interscholastic athletics (Aicinena & Ziyanak, 2021; Coakley, 2017; Sage et al., 2019).

Informal education takes place as individuals interact with members of the nuclear family, extended family, community members, and friends outside of formal educational settings (Informal Education, 2013). By spending time with one another, speaking and listening to one another, and doing things together, informal education results in transmission of history, family stories, cultural wisdom, traditions, legends, language, values, and norms. Much of what is important in a culture is "caught" during informal education rather than being formally "taught" in schools.

In traditional Native American cultures, teaching was done informally by family and community members through oral transmission (Anderson, 2009). Formal education attendance requirements have lessened the opportunities available for informal instruction in valued traditions, activities, language and other areas of cultural value and importance.

During the school year, if children spend eight hours a day at school and eight hours a day sleeping, only eight hours remain for them to spend with family, elders, and community members five days a week. They have an additional thirty-two hours available each weekend. The youth have a maximum of seventy-two hours a week available for informal tribally specific education during the school year. And that is without interference from television, the Internet, social media, and other distractions that draws them away from participation in traditional activities.

Before formal instruction was offered in schools, youths spent sixteen waking hours a day in informal learning environments, a total of 112 hours per week was available for informal education every week of the year. In the past, much more time was available for children to receive extensive informal education as they matured.

Cultural activities including ceremonies, rituals, gathering food, preparing and eating traditional foods, and other activities are important in the formation of a tribal identity (Brown et al., 2007). For tribally specific cultural activities to have personal meaning, "teachers" such as elders, extended family members, and powwow announcers serve as mediators who explain the meaning of the activities. "Teachers" encourage participation in cultural activities, share oral histories, teach language and songs, and much more. Informal tribal teachers have a direct impact upon an individual's tribal identification. Knowledge of culture-centric stories and legends and possession of other forms of tribal knowledge are also important in the formation of a Native American identity (House et al., 2006).

In Native American cultures, family elders and elders of the tribe have a special responsibility to informally teach important aspects of culture. Today, grandparents do their best to actively support their grandchildren's participation in traditional cultural activities (Robbins et al., 2005). However, where families are separated by great distances, when parents work outside of the home, and when children spend large amounts of time away from the home, this responsibility cannot be met and much of the information concerning how one should believe and behave is not effectively transmitted to or reinforced in youths.

Changes in home construction from single space structures to multiroom houses have also lessened opportunities for informal traditional educational opportunities within the home (Rhodes, 1993):

> The [traditional] Arapahoe cultural home was happy because of the respect for one another generated by living in this communal space; it was further enhanced by the cultural and spiritual teaching of the tribe. Even in times of sadness related to the death of a family member, we would gather in this communal home, and we would feel as if we were wrapped in the arms of someone who loved, respected, and cared for us. The communal environment felt alive with a ritual, cultural, and spiritual essence. . . . The typical house that a young Indian child now encounters is full of compartments and dividers, and it has a minimum of communal space. This arrangement separates the younger children from the moderating influence of their elders, and it breaks the chain of learning cultural values, norms, language, and life survival skills that once took place in the communal space of traditional extended-family units. (p. 42)

Elders were once the purveyors of ideologies, language, religion, and other markers of Native American culture (Anderson, 2009). For contemporary Native youth, the wisdom of elders is challenged by the prevailing culture, and it leads many to an indifference toward "old ways." In their view, things no longer need to be done in the traditional way. A quick trip to town and the quick flip of a switch can address most needs. The impact of dismissive attitudes toward tradition was well-illustrated by a college student interviewed by Beijsens (2015):

> Traditions are being lost along the way due to modern ways and notions, but also because the youth simply doesn't care. For example, back in the day

everyone knew how to find plants and to cure them, and that while cutting the plant and while curing it one must say a specific prayer for each action in order to transform it into some medicine or food. These simple things are being lost. (p. 24)

Young Native Americans no longer exhibit the patience called for by tradition. In a modern "get it in a minute" culture driven by consumerism and technology; children do not often learn to be patient. Patience is counterintuitive in a culture emphasizing entitlement, speed, efficiency, and productivity. Moving quickly up within a social hierarchy without regard to tradition and time for maturation is viewed as crazy (*hohookeenizi*) by the Arapaho but is considered desirable in the dominant culture (Anderson, 2011).

Things moved much slower in the past and the pace of life was functional in the development and sustaining of social relationships and cultural norms:

Elders today recall traveling in horse and wagon on and beyond the reservation at a pace of perhaps ten miles a day. Such travel included visiting friends along the way for overnight rest, food, and conversation. With automobiles and telephones, elders note that people do not stop and visit each other as much in the traditional way. (Anderson, 2011, p. 251)

The speed of transportation and the frenzy of modern life have conspired to limit contact between youth, elders, family, and their Native American community. Limitations in the amount of direct contact yields infrequent and inadequate opportunity for youths to observe and learn culturally treasured knowledge, values, traditions, and behaviors.

Technology

Technological development is linked to our evolution as a species and to social change (McLain et al., 2019). Technology sparked the transition from the preindustrial age to the current information age and continues to serve as a catalyst for change in individuals and their cultures (Laszlo, 1992). The Industrial Revolution was made possible by advances in science and technology, and it led to the movement of populations from rural areas to cities as new forms and patterns of employment were instituted.

The development of technological innovations and their use is not free of cultural perspective, context, or interest. They are the product and embodiment of experimentation and learning taking place as a culture evolved over countless generations (Caporael, 1997). In traditional Micronesian sailing techniques, the stars and their movements were used to navigate the open seas for days at a time. As their navigational techniques were developed, the people assumed that the sun, stars, and planets revolved around the earth. What the stars are and how they came into existences was part of cultural history, religion, traditions, and knowledge. Nautical navigation in Micronesia sprang forth from the Micronesian culture, belief systems, and practices. It was effective and still is. But it has fallen from disuse.

Today GPS systems make traversing the seas more accurate, dependable, and faster. Adoption and implementation of GPS location technologies require acceptance of postmodern culture which values efficiency and productivity as it deems myths and religion to be impediments to progress. Modern navigators would view the Micronesian sailors as inferior and ignorant.

In the world of art and other segments of culture, "technical innovations have frequently been interpreted as conscious challenges to established conventions" (Marontate, 2005, p. 288). Technology and the spread of information have continued and continue to significantly alter the lives and cultures of Indigenous peoples around the world through cultural hegemony (Biel, 1999).

Guns and militarization of conquering colonizers were impactful upon traditional cultures as they were used by the government to defeat and sequester Native tribal groups. America's Native peoples were impacted by the advent and proliferation of railroads. Printed media, radio, television, and other forms of technology have led Native Americans to internalize the importance of pop culture and consumerism which cleaves youth from their traditional culture (Anderson, 2009).

Linear time is based upon seconds, minutes, days, weeks, months, and years and has been studied for approximately 2,500 years. In Western thought, linear time is considered "objective" or "scientific time" (Dowden, 2021). Some modern philosophers, however, believe that Western conceptions of time do exist not in the real world but only in the minds of mathematicians.

Native Americans viewed Euro-American linear concepts of time to be radical, forgetful of the past, tyrannically cyclical, incomplete, and erratic (Anderson, 2011). Western characterizations of time are not part of the perceptible world for they lack grounding in lived experiences. Time is not something requisite in the lives of human beings. The sun, moon, and stars traverse the skies whether we use standardized measures of time to measure their movements or not. 7:00 a.m. means something only because human beings attribute meaning to the hour of the day and that meaning has much to do with work and productivity in modern culture.

The concept of linear time was used by colonizers to control, segregate, assimilate, and govern Native Americans. Linear time has been imposed upon Native Americans through, "formal education, Christian doctrine, federal agencies, the legal system, mass popular culture, and various forms of technology from cars to computers" (Anderson, 2011, p. 233). Native Americans were and are taught that there is a time for everything, and that time should not be wasted.

Euro-American concepts of time have served as a source of conflict between Native Americans and Euro-Americans, and adoption of Euro-American concepts of time in part or in whole have had a significant impact upon Native American cultures and the people living within them (Anderson, 2011). Those who do not adopt linear views are deemed primitive, inferior, and lazy.

In traditional Native culture, time is allocated for activities deemed non-productive by Euro-Americans, such as socializing, caring for relatives, assisting others when needed, spending time contemplating in nature, and participating in ceremonial activities not held on a regular and precise time schedule. Natives are often labeled as uncommitted to success because of the value placed upon their "unproductive" allocation of time. Traditionally, Arapaho time was based upon nature and the interaction of the people with the environment (Anderson, 2011).

Gell (1992) discounts cultural variances in the function of time. To Gell, time as viewed and experienced in industrialized societies is the only legitimate way to conceptualize time. Any other concepts of time are not worthy of study. The stance exemplifies the ubiquitous Western view of "proper culture" and the place of time within it.

Computers pose a special problem for those who believe traditional Native American cultures should be maintained. The use of computers in classrooms reinforces culture-transforming patterns toward individualism, consumerism, globalism, and dependence upon technology (Bowers et al., 2000). As dependency upon computers and Internet accessible cell phones grows, youths come to be controlled by marketplace forces.

The transformation in life instigated by computer technology belies traditional tribal knowledge, traditions, and spiritual connectedness. Computer technology impacts patterns of thinking, experiencing, and communicating that are contrary to Native American tradition. Instead of learning from elders, kin, and tribal members, youths are taught to create their own truths and that they are responsible to and for themselves.

In Native American communities, computer devices and the Internet are perceived as a necessity, but they are Trojan Horses that promote Western individualism and produce a meaningless, physically disconnected existence (Howe, 1988). The Internet is no place for tribalism for its lessons are individualistic and contrary to the existence of collectivist tribal traditions and values. Fleming (2019) claims that Americans have become wandering pagans because they lack grounding in anything eternal and true due to the encroachment of technology upon daily life.

Cultural life depends upon human interaction for its creation and continuance. Computer-based learning cannot save cultures existing on life support.

Learning a few words of Navajo or reading a story about coyote stealing fire is a poor substitution for being immersed within environments where tribal languages are spoken, legends are shared, and traditions are lived. But perhaps, as they say in Mexico, *"Es mejor que nada."*

THE CULTURAL TETHERING THEORY

Wilson et al. (2018) investigated why students from the Appalachian area of the United States did not seem to participate as extensively in the university community as did students from other areas of the country. They concluded that familial tethering, externalized tethering, ecological tethering, and social tethering served to prevent Appalachian students from full participation and immersion into the primary culture of the university and acted as impediments to academic achievement. The concept of grounding the culture of a group or one's cultural identity by way of specific tethers seemed promising as a means of explaining how individuals and cultures do or do not assimilate fully into foreign cultures. We propose here, *The Cultural Tethering Theory of Assimilation and Identity*.

The following definition and description of the term "institution" was developed from the work of Miller (2019). Institutions are complex social forms created and endorsed by established social groups that transcend individuals and function to transmit and reinforce the group's common interests, values, and behaviors. Institutions are commonly said to include language, family, education, government, media, religion, business organizations, political systems, and more. They are not social norms on the micro-level, nor are they societies on the macro-level. Institutions are complex, yet there is a limited role that each institution alone plays in society.

General properties of social institutions include structure, function, culture, and sanctions (Miller, 2019). *Structure* is demonstrated through the interdependence and successful fulfillment of the roles by individuals within the institution. Institutions implicitly *function* to transmit to the cultural group's members what is valued, how one is to behave, and how one is to think. *Culture* is the informal aspect of an institution, yet culture permeates each institution. For example, because American culture emphasizes directness, effective use of time, and assertiveness, Americans tend to adopt these characteristics in their personal and professional interactions. However, people from collectivist cultures often consider Americans rude because indirect communication is often preferred, unassuming rather than assertive behavior is valued, and doing things quickly is not necessarily considered important. *Sanctions* are important is maintaining appropriate behavior in the group's membership. Negative sanctions may be as minimal as a disapproving glance, or as severe as banishing someone from the institution. Positive sanctions may include an approving smile or the issuance of a reward.

Institutions are important in a society's continued development. The United Nations (2015) identified the presence of weak social institutions and limited access to justice as threats to the effectiveness of global sustainability initiatives. Positive progress cannot occur in a country plagued by unscrupulous institutions such as a corrupt government, or a rogue military.

Institutions are also a key to effecting social change. Andreski (1972) speculated that efforts to overthrow the American political system would require the involvement of or change in several established American institutions, including higher education, the American military, police forces, the economic system, social class structure, and the media. Finally, the constitution of the United States and legal system would need to be altered. Andreski's essay demonstrates how the American political system is dependent upon numerous institutions and that the political system impacts the country's other institutions.

We hold a holistic view of institutions and believe each of a society's institutions is interrelated (Miller, 2019). In holistic terms, an institution can be equated to a living organism (Spencer, 1971). Living things are comprised of many independently operating parts, but for the organism to thrive, all parts must effectively function interdependently. If one part fails to function effectively, the organism becomes unhealthy, or dies. Strong and vibrant societies, as collections of people, are supported by numerous, firmly established, and effectively functioning institutions. When institutions die, the culture's viability is threatened.

Today, there are 574 Native American tribes recognized by the U.S. government (Bureau of Indian Affairs, 2021). Each tribe is an independent society possessing distinct cultural characteristics. Historically, institutions functioned within each tribe to transmit culture to its members. As we explained in chapter 1 and earlier in this chapter, traditional Native American social institutions including those of education, religion, language, family, economy, and others have been and continue to be assaulted. In response to the continuing assaults, much of Native American culture has been altered or lost.

Today, the powwow as an institution is a symbol of Native American culture and identity (Arndt, 2005; Ellis, 2005; Gilley, 2005). The stomp dance as conducted by tribal groups in Oklahoma, for example, is a complex social institution through which specific cultural differences of tribes including values, customs, and beliefs are made visible to others (Jackson, 2005). Kavanagh (1982) described the Comanche powwow as a social institution. Cornelius and O'Grady (1987) described the Soaring Eagles Drum as an institution of the Oneida Tribe. Mid-Atlantic tribes have adopted the plains powwow culture to replace their weakened and ineffective institutions, for all that had remained were their churches and schools (Cook et al., 2005). Adoption of the plains-style powwow provided them with an institution that could provide a Native American identity.

With ever-increasing frequency, traditional tribal-specific powwow cultures have been supplanted by Pan-Indian powwow culture (Howard, 1955). The modern intertribal contest powwow is a cross-cultural institution that binds together people from diverse tribes and traditions. It, "enforces cultural codes and relationships that are connected to tribally specific practices" (Ellis, 2005, p. 9). With ever-increasing frequency, contest powwows will serve as sites in which Native American culture and identity are celebrated, transmitted, and reinforced. With the passage of time, the contest powwow will become the only remaining institution that will tether Native Americans to their traditional culture.

Cultural Threads

Cultural threads are individual components of any significant aspect of a culture. Religion, for example, is a prominent aspect of many cultures. Religion is characterized by music, song, prayer ritual, scriptures, worship rituals, social organization, values, norms, and so on. Each of a religion's many components is an individual cultural thread.

Cultural threads deemed highly important to any individual are thick and resistant to change, while those of low importance are thin and readily severed by social change agents such as secularism, politics, media, socioeconomics, family, technology, and others. Any cultural thread such as that of a specific codified prayer ritual may be extremely important to an individual who prays several times a day, not applicable at all to another individual who does not pray under any circumstances, and of some importance to those praying occasionally. The more important a cultural thread is to an individual, the more difficult it is to sever and remove from the individual's life.

Let us consider sport, and several of its numerous cultural threads. The importance and therefore the thickness of the following threads can be greater or lesser for sport participants and sport fans: racism (the degree to which racism is celebrated or challenged), economics (income or expense is important to my participation or non-participation as an athlete or spectator), gender (the importance of sport as a site in which gender is demonstrated, reinforced, or challenged), values (the importance of sport as an environment in which my values are exhibited, reinforced, or challenged), religion (the importance of sport as a site where my religious beliefs and practices are exhibited, reinforced, or challenged), tradition (the historical emphasis my community or family places upon sport participation or spectatorship), family (the importance of participation or spectatorship to family members), art (the degree to which sport and skilled performance is viewed as beautiful), education (the degree to which learning and teaching occur in sport), and competition (the degree to which I enjoy or detest competition as a spectator or participant). At any given time of life, the thickness of each of the threads identified may range between extremely thick to nonexistent for any individual.

Individual holding no regard for any of the cultural threads comprising sport will not participate in sport or be a fan of sport. If some of the threads are significant to individuals, they may be casual sport participants or sport fans. On the other hand, if all of sport's cultural threads are very important to individuals, they will be committed participants or fans. Experiences and changes in life's circumstances result in adjustments in the importance attributed to specific cultural threads and change impacts the thread's thickness.

The contest powwow as an important aspect of contemporary Pan-Indian culture, also consists of many cultural threads. Each cultural thread may have greater or lesser importance to any individual powwow dancer, singer, spectator, or official. The contest powwow's cultural threads would include but are not limited to song lyrics, music, language, dance, food, family, art, tradition, education, values, race, regalia, ceremonial tradition, norms, humor, and competition.

Cultural Tethers

Cultural threads function together much like individual threads of hemp that, when bound together, constitute an industrial grade rope that can be used to tether hot air balloons to the ground. We refer to collections of cultural threads as *cultural tethers*. If, for example, an important aspect of culture was characterized by ten components, the thickness of the tether and its ability to resist change forces is dependent upon the overall thickness of the ten cultural threads combined. Thicker tethers are more resistant to severing and more effectively ground individuals to their traditional culture. Thinner tethers are more readily severed due to the influence of agents of social change. When completely severed, cultural tethers can no longer ground individuals to their traditional culture.

Not all cultural tethers are composed of the same number of cultural threads. The more important an aspect of a culture and the more influential it is in other aspects of society, the greater the number of cultural threads the tether contains. For example, the cultural tether of Native American spirituality would consist of a potentially greater number of cultural threads than contemporary hunting activity. Hunting as an aspect of contemporary Native American culture may be comprised of cultural threads including food, recreation, challenge, and family. In the history of the Plains Indians, hunting was an essential part of tribal cultures. Buffalo hunts involved cultural threads of survival, spirituality, worship, gender, family, tribe, song, dance, clothing, medicine, tradition, family, bedding, housing, food, tools, and more. The variance in the importance of hunting in historic and contemporary Native American life demonstrates how the thickness of cultural tethers may change due to the influence of history and circumstance.

Cultural tethers act to ground individuals to their culture, just as tethers connect a hot air balloon to the ground. Where cultural tethers are grounded, the identity of individuals is found. Cultural tethers act to restrain the influence of cultural change agents (figure 7.1).

Model 1—Severing of Cultural Tethers and Assimilation: The Progression

For the process of acculturation to begin, one or more of a cultural tether's cultural threads must be severed. As cultural threads are severed, they are disconnected from the cultural tether grounded in the traditional culture and

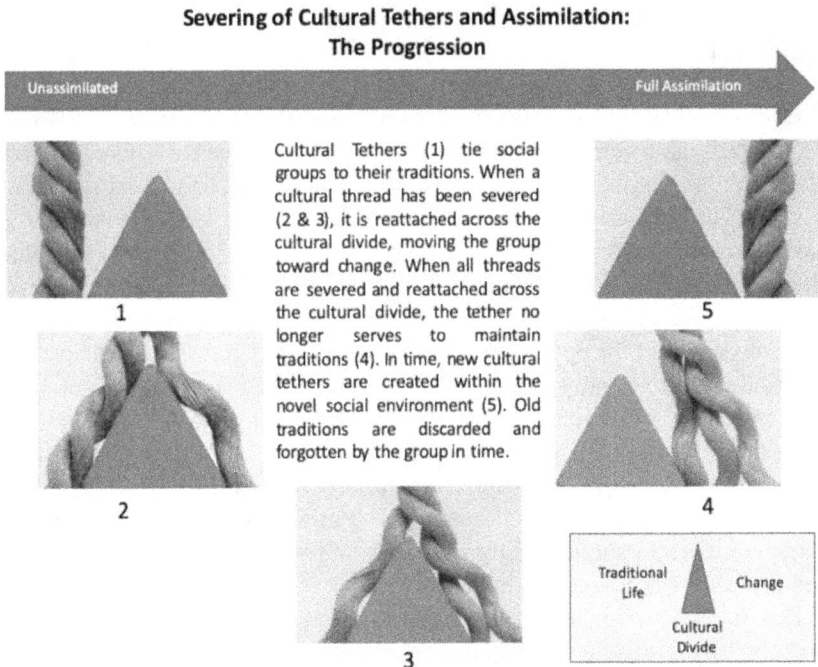

Figure 7.1 Severing of Cultural Tethers and Assimilation: The Progression.

"regrounded" within the new culture. "Regrounding" is the recoupling of a severed cultural thread or cultural tether within another culture's cultural milieu. When a cultural thread, collection of cultural threads, or a cultural tether is regrounded, it again functions to resist the various forces of cultural change. Small numbers of threads and thin tethers offer little resistance to change.

In the following pages, we provide an example of the function of cultural threads and tethers as religious acculturation and assimilation occur in members of a fictitious Native American tribe. We employ the Native American acculturation model proposed by Garrett and Prichette (2000) in conjunction with our cultural tethering theory in the following example.

All members of the tribal group are initially full participants and devoted believers of the tribe's spiritual practices and beliefs. All tribal members employ the tradition's spiritual mandates in their daily lives. Each of the spiritual tradition's cultural threads holds great importance because of the importance of spiritual beliefs and practices in cultural life. As such, the cultural tether of traditional spirituality is thick and resistant to change from within the tribe and from without. The members of the group are all in the Traditional Level of acculturation as described by Garrett and Prichette.

A Christian missionary comes to the village in hopes of saving souls by converting the savages to the one true religion. The power of God and Jesus Christ is shared with the tribe's members. The power of the Christian God has been witnessed by the tribe since his arrival. Great illness has taken the lives of numerous tribal members, but the missionaries are not infected, and they do not die when caring the stricken members of the tribe. Great power is magic observed in the possessions of the missionary, and he attributes all power in his possessions to the greatness of his God. He conveys that all his God's greatness and power is found in the Book given to his people by this all-powerful God.

A small group of tribal members considers adopting Christianity as a belief system because of the power it seems to possess. They refuse to participate in their culture's spiritually significant ceremonies, and instead attend sermons and participate in communion, and responsive reading rituals. When they do, several threads of their spiritual tether are severed and regrounded within Christianity. The initial severing and regrounding of cultural threads initiate the process of religious acculturation and partial religious assimilation has taken place. The members of the group are in the Marginal Level of Garrett and Prichette's acculturation model.

Due to the missionary's further proselytizing, the small group of tribal members adopts more of Christianity's beliefs and practices. As they do, additional cultural threads are severed and regrounded within Christianity.

The members of the group are fully aware of the differences between their traditional spiritual beliefs and practices, yet they continue to employ both in their lives. They then are in the Bicultural Level of Garrett and Prichette's assimilation model. Syncretism observed at this level of religious acculturation was characteristic of the Native Americans' Ghost Dance and is currently observed within the Native American Church. Historically, Christian missionaries expressed frustration when new Native American converts clung to some of their traditional religion's beliefs and practices.

As the process of religious acculturation continues, additional cultural threads are severed and regrounded within the Christian belief system. When all the cultural threads that once grounded the individuals to their traditional spiritual belief system have been severed and regrounded within Christianity, religious assimilation has occurred. Not a single cultural thread grounds them to the tribe's traditional belief system and the individuals fully identify as Christian. They are in the Assimilated Level of Garrett and Prichette's acculturation model regarding their religious belief system.

For complete cultural assimilation to occur in any individual, all tethers grounding them to their culture must be severed and regrounded within another culture. If or when full assimilation ever occurs is dependent upon the individual. Some Native Americans, for example, have become fully assimilated, some have become partially assimilated and others have not.

To this point, our discussion has focused upon acculturation, assimilation, and identity on the micro or individual level. On the macro or group level, the Cultural Tethering Theory can also account for acculturation, assimilation, and identity. Native American tribes have lost much of their culture and some, such as the Monacan have lost all of their traditional culture (Cook et al., 2005). In the case of the Monacans, all cultural threads and cultural tethers were severed and regrounded within the dominant cultural milieu.

Model 2—History of Native American Resistance to Assimilation

Cultural tethers once serving to provide stability to Native American tribal cultures have been under attack since the arrival of Europeans to the North American continent. Attempts by the American government to assimilate Native Americans through war, implementation of the Indian Boarding School System, implementation of the reservation system, and prohibition of traditional religious activities have severed, either partially or fully, cultural tethers including language, religion, values, geographic ecology, and others (figure 7.2).

Historical Native American Resistance to Assimilation

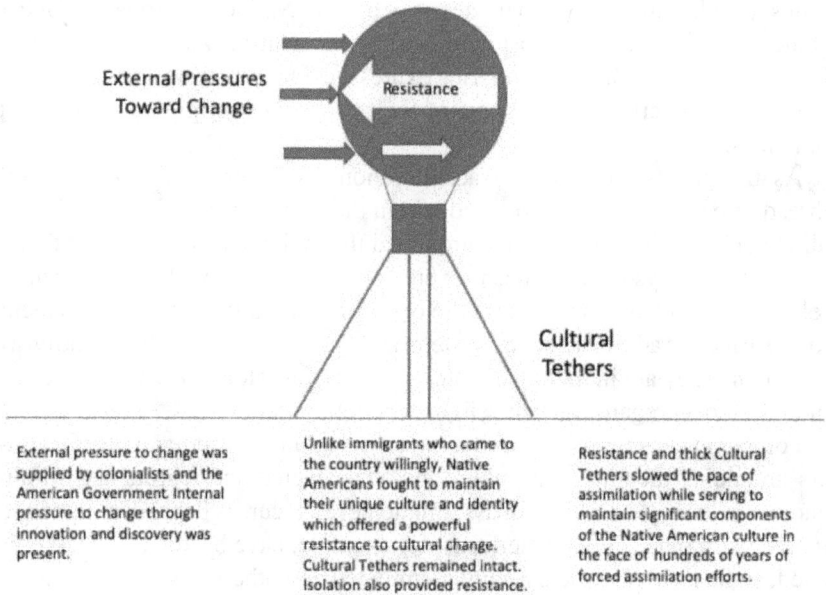

| External pressure to change was supplied by colonialists and the American Government. Internal pressure to change through innovation and discovery was present. | Unlike immigrants who came to the country willingly, Native Americans fought to maintain their unique culture and identity which offered a powerful resistance to cultural change. Cultural Tethers remained intact. Isolation also provided resistance. | Resistance and thick Cultural Tethers slowed the pace of assimilation while serving to maintain significant components of the Native American culture in the face of hundreds of years of forced assimilation efforts. |

Figure 7.2   Historical Native American Resistance to Assimilation.

CONCLUSION

According to the United Nations (2021), Indigenous cultures have been considered primitive, inferior, and irrelevant since the age of exploration began. Explorers, missionaries, colonists, and expansionists often sought, and seek, to eradicate Indigenous peoples and their cultures, in the name of progress, God, and greed.

Amnesty International (2021) estimates that today there are more than five thousand different Indigenous people groups in the world. Remaining Indigenous cultures are in danger of extinction due to loss of traditional lands, loss of languages, the inability of elders to pass on culture to children, consumption of nontraditional foods, and loss of traditional knowledge as it is replaced in importance by that of foreign cultures. In South American Amazonian cultures, people groups have avoided assimilation by avoiding contact with foreigners (Rubio et al., 2009). Avoidance was accomplished as they moved deeper into the expansive Amazon Forest.

Model 3—Modern Native American Culture: Hanging by a Cultural Tether

In the United States, Native Americans were and are unable to retreat from the American culture. Their traditional homelands have been taken and most tribal languages are moribund. Elders infrequently pass on culture to youths and the people consume nontraditional foods. Traditional knowledge is being replaced by science, technology, and popular culture. A college student interviewed by Beijsens (2015) noted, "I feel that the culture we once had as Native people is slowly eroding, and it is only a matter of time until most Natives have [assimilated] into Western society. It's inevitable in my opinion" (p. 23). Why? We believe it is because long-term and ever-increasing exposure to American culture has resulted in severing and regrounding of cultural threads and cultural tethers that once grounded Native Americans to their traditional cultures.

Here, we have listed some Native American cultural tethers that have been severely frayed. Technology will accelerate the pace with which intact cultural threads and tethers are severed and the speed with which further acculturation occurs.

Tether 1: Language

Hundreds of Native American languages have fallen into disuse and most that are still in use are on life support.

Tether 2: Social Organization

Members of various tribal groups continue moving to cities from reservations. The exodus has resulted in alteration of traditional social organization including living arrangements and access to extended family, tribal elders, and an available network of tribal members.

Tether 3: Traditions and Traditional Knowledge

Fragmentation of Native American communities has lessened opportunities to observe valued cultural activity and opportunities to learn culturally valued knowledge, ceremonies, and rituals.

Tether 4: Traditional Spiritual Practices and Beliefs

In reservation communities and in urban Indian communities, Christianity, belief in modern medicine, and belief in science and technology have replaced traditional spirituality. In the 2010 census, only 3 percent of Native Americans identified with traditional Native American religion, while 37 percent identified as Christians (Kosmin et al., 2001). The ability of Native American spirituality to assist in maintenance of traditional culture will continue to wane.

Tether 5: Traditional Collectivist Values

Traditional Native American values will face continued erosion as individualism and consumerism continue it spread within Native American communities. Tribal-specific knowledge and traditions will be ever-increasingly forgotten because they are deemed unimportant by contemporary Native American youths, and because elders are not provided the opportunity to pass them on to succeeding generations. With ever-increasing frequency, we are likely to hear comments like the following, "My mom is the last generation of full bloods [in her tribe]. There's really not many traditional people left" (Lucero, 2013, p. 15).

Core Native American values and traditions are celebrated and transmitted through Pan-Indianism. Pan-Indian values, history, and traditions will live on within the institution which is the intertribal contest powwow. Native American traditionalists discount the contest powwow's ability to transmit culture because it is not tribally specific, because it is a competitive event, and because spiritual ceremonies and practices are excluded (Dell'Angela, 2003). Perhaps the traditionalist's stance is myopic and not unlike traditional Christians who maintain that "true worship" is to be conducted in the structure and form brought by European missionaries. To them, inclusion of Native symbols, the use of the drum in musical portions of a worship service, and the burning of sage makes the worship activity syncretistic and, therefore, inauthentic (Twiss, 2015).

What the contest powwow does and does not supply to participants is individually determined and assessed. Competitive powwow dancers and singers do not leave their tribal culture at the arena door (Ellis & Lassiter, 2005). Native American culture is brought into the contest powwow's circle and Native American culture exudes from within it.

The vast majority of Native Americans are "urban Indians." They are often isolated from extended family, reservation communities, and traditional culture. The opportunity to participate in traditional powwows and other culturally significant ceremonies is limited. To a meaningful degree, contest powwows offer non-Natives and Native Americans residing within and outside the boundaries of reservations an opportunity to learn what it means to be Native American and to celebrate it.

Contest powwows will continue to be held because they are of value to Native Americans as a source of cultural identity and because non-Natives view attending the powwow as a valuable cultural experience. Finally, because sponsors, including major corporations, are willing to provide money

Modern Native American Culture: Hanging by a Cultural Tether

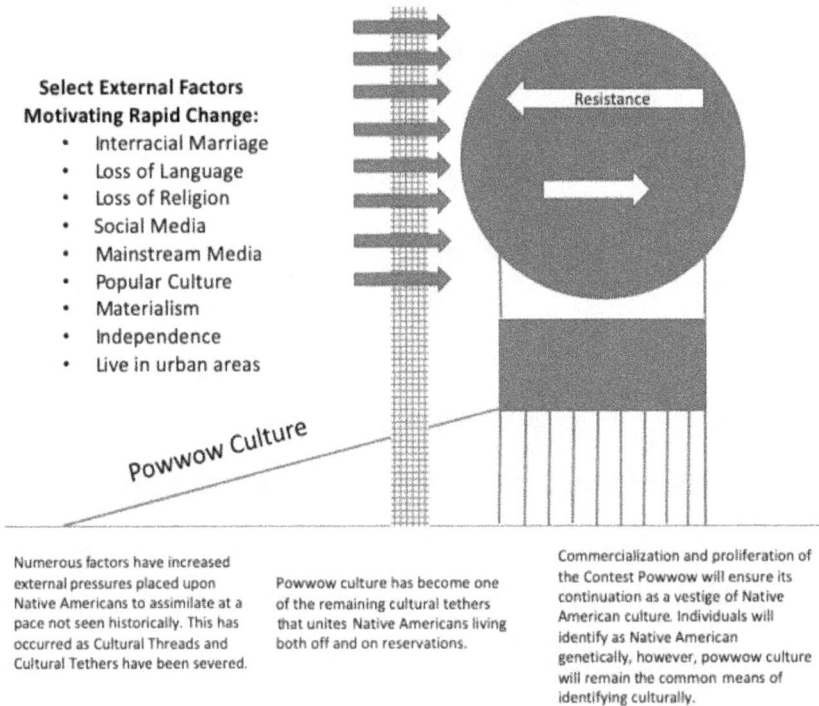

Select External Factors Motivating Rapid Change:
- Interracial Marriage
- Loss of Language
- Loss of Religion
- Social Media
- Mainstream Media
- Popular Culture
- Materialism
- Independence
- Live in urban areas

Resistance

Powwow Culture

Numerous factors have increased external pressures placed upon Native Americans to assimilate at a pace not seen historically. This has occurred as Cultural Threads and Cultural Tethers have been severed.

Powwow culture has become one of the remaining cultural tethers that unites Native Americans living both off and on reservations.

Commercialization and proliferation of the Contest Powwow will ensure its continuation as a vestige of Native American culture. Individuals will identify as Native American genetically, however, powwow culture will remain the common means of identifying culturally.

Figure 7.3   Modern Native American Culture: Hanging by a Cultural Tether.

to support contest powwows, and because vendors and others generate income during the spectacles, intertribal contest powwows will remain both viable and relatively widespread within the United States and Canada well into the future.

During contest powwows, all who are present are enveloped within Native American culture. The joy associated Native American traditions and culture is available to both competitors and spectators. Accordingly, the contest powwow will continue to serve as a cultural tether, grounding Native Americans to their past as they continue to evolve as a people. Generations from now, intertribal contest powwow emcees will proclaim, "We're still here!" (figure 7.3).

NOTES

1. Reece McGee's Statement (1975) was similar to the one made here, but an original source could not be located for proper citation.

2. Tribe in Maffesoli's use of the term has nothing to do with Native American tribal groups.

References

116th Congress (2019). House resolution 83. https://www.congress.gov/116/bills/
hres83/BILLS-116hres83ih.xml#:~:text=feathers,represent%20tribal%20communi
ties%2C%20Native%20American

Abdul-Karim, A. (2015). Annual powwow to be held in New Haven's East Rock
Park. *New Haven Register (CT)*. https://www.nhregister.com/lifestyle/article/
Annual-powwow-to-be-held-in-New-Haven-s-East-11356312.php

Abourezk, J. (1978). S. J. Res.102—Joint resolution American Indians Religious
Freedom. *Government Printing Office*, pp. 86–87. https://play.google.com/books/
reader?id=G129PnhHtlsC&hl=en&pg=GBS.PA86

Abramitzky, R. (2017). What history tells us about assimilation of immigrants?
Stanford Institute for Economic Policy Research. https://siepr.stanford.edu/res
earch/publications/immigrants-assimilate

Abramitzky, R., Boustan, L., & Eriksson, K. (2020). Do immigrants assimilate
more slowly today than in the past? *American Economic Review: Insights*, 2(1),
125–141. DOI: 10.1257/aeri.20190079

Adams, D. W. (1995). *Education for extinction: American Indians and the boarding
school experience, 1875–1928*. University Press of Kansas.

Addis, C. (2005). The Whitman Massacre: Religion and manifest destiny on the
Columbia Plateau, 1809–1858. *Journal of the Early Republic*, 25(2), 221–258.

Addis, C. (2018). 23 Great Plains Indian wars. *History Hub*. http://sites.austincc.edu
/caddis/great-plains-wars/

Aicinena, S. (2017). Implicit religion and the use of prayer in sport. *American Journal
of Sociological Research*, 7(1), 56–65. DOI:10.5923/j.sociology.20170701.08

Aicinena, S. J., & Ziyanak, S. (2019). Examining the gathering of nations powwow
and a NCAA Division I basketball game. *Journal of Human Sciences*, 16(3),
875–884. DOI: 10.14687/jhs.v16i3.5742

Aicinena, S. J., & Ziyanak, S. (2021). Contest powwow: Sport and Native American
culture. *The Qualitative Report*, 26(1), 27–51. DOI: 10.46743/2160-3715/2021.4517

189

Akhavan P. (2017). Cultural genocide: Legal label or mourning metaphor? *McGill Law Journal*, 62(1), 243–270. https://www.canlii.org/en/commentary/doc/2017 CanLIIDocs356#!fragment//BQCwhgziBcwMYgK4DsDWszIQewE4BUBTAD wBdoByCgSgBpltTCIBFRQ3AT0otokLC4EbDtyp8BQkAGU8pAELcASgF EAMioBqAQQByAYRW1SYAEbRS2ONWpA

Akoth, S. O. (2017). Positioning and making citizenship through Obama K'Ogelo cultural festivals in Siaya County, Kenya. *Journal of African Cultural Studies*, 29(2), 194–210. DOI: 10.1080/13696815.2017.1297698

Albers, P. C., & Medicine, B. (2005). The sound of the drum will revive them and make them happy. In C. Ellis, L. E. Lassiter, & G. H. Dunham (Eds.) *Powwow* (pp. 1–23). University of Nebraska Press.

Allison, M. (1980). *A structural analysis of Navajo basketball*. Doctoral dissertation, University of Illinois. *IDEALS*. http://hdl.handle.net/2142/68689

Allison, M. (1982). Sport, ethnicity and assimilation. *Quest*, 34(2), 165–175. DOI: 10.1080/00336297.1982.10483775

Allison, M., & Lueschen, G. (1979). A comparative analysis of Navaho and Anglo basketball systems. *International Review of Sport Sociology*, 14, 76–86. DOI: 10.1177%2F101269027901400304

Amnesty International (2021). Indigenous peoples. *Amnesty International*. https://ww w.amnesty.org/en/what-we-do/indigenous-peoples/#:~:text=There%20are%20370 %20million%20Indigenous,70%25%20%E2%80%93%20live%20in%20Asia

Anderson, G. (2016). The native peoples of the American west: Genocide or ethnic cleansing? *Western Historical Quarterly*, 4(1), 407–434. DOI: 10.1093/whq/ whw126.

Anderson, J. D. (2009). Contradictions of space-time and knowledge in Northern Arapaho language shift, In P. V. Kroskrity & M. C. Field (Eds.) *Native American Language ideologies: Beliefs, practices, and struggles in Indian country* (pp. 48–76). University of Arizona Press.

Anderson, J. D. (2011). The history of time in the Northern Arapaho tribe. *Ethnohistory*, 58(2), 229–261. DOI: 10.1215/00141801-1163028

Andrews, T., & Olney, J. (2007). Potlatch and powwows: Dynamics of culture through lives lived dancing. *American Indian Culture and Research Journal*, 31(1), 63–108. DOI: 10.17953/aicr.31.1.f7n87533224174g7

Appiah, K. A. (1994). Race, culture, identity: Misunderstood connections. The tanner lectures on human values. *University of California at San Diego*. https://philpapers .org/rec/APPRCI

Armstrong, K., Walsh, P., and Dees, W. (2019). Sport marketing. In P. Pedersen & L. Thibault (Eds.) *Contemporary Sport Management* (6th edition, pp. 247–271). Human Kinetics.

Arndt, G. (2005). Ho-Chunk Indian powwows during the early twentieth century. In C. Ellis, L. E. Lassiter, & G. H. Dunham (Eds.) *Powwow* (pp. 46–67). University of Nebraska Press.

Baird-Olson, K. (2005). Retraditionalism and revitalization movements, plains. In S. J. Crawford & K. F. Dennis (Eds.) *American Indian religious traditions: An ency-clopedia* (Vol. 3, pp. 917–24). ABC Clio.

Baker, W. (1988). *Sports in the Western world.* University of Illinois Press.

Barker, J. (2010, November 7). Heartbeat of the people. *Northwest Florida Daily News.* https://login.ezproxy.utpb.edu/login?url=http://search.ebscohost.com/login. aspx?direct=true&db=n5h&AN=2W63743096603&site=ehost-live

Banjo, A. (2011). Hosting mega-sport events, expectations, and perceptions: A review. *African Journal for Physical, Health Education, Recreation & Dance,* 17(3), 416–428.

Barker, J. (2010, November 7). Heartbeat of the people. *Northwest Florida Daily News.* https://login.ezproxy.utpb.edu/login?url=http://search.ebscohost.com/login. aspx?direct=true&db=n5h&AN=2W63743096603&site=ehost-live.

Bates, E. M. (1971). *I have spoken: American history through the voice of Indians.* Swallow Press.

Baumann, J. (2019). The Denver march pow wow tells the story of dance and tradition, prayer and perseverance. *CPR News.*https://www.cpr.org/2019/03/21/the-denver -march-pow-wow-tells-the-story-of-dance-and-tradition-prayer-and-perseverance/

Baumgardner, F. (2006). *Killing for land in early California: Indian blood at round valley, founding the Nome cult Indian farm.* Algora Publishing.

Beatty, W. (1961). History of Navajo education. *America Indigena,* 21, 7–31.

Beckman, K. (2009). *Bullets, bugles & cannonfire. An Irish prince goes to war.* Lulu Publishing Company.

Beckstein, B. (2014). Native American subjective happiness: An overview. *Indigenous Policy Journal,* 25(2), 1–6. http://www.indigenouspolicy.org/index.php/ipj/article /view/251/256

Beth, S. (2005). Taking to the streets: Dalit mela and the public performance of Dalit cultural identity. *Contemporary South Asia,* 14(4), 397–410. https://doi-org.ezpr oxy.utpb.edu/10.1080/09584930600839081

Beyers, J. (2017). Religion and culture: Revisiting a close relative. *HTS Teologiese Studies/Theological Studies,* 73(1), 1–9. DOI: 10.4102/hts.v72i1.3864

Biel, E. R. (1999). The impact of technological change on developing countries. *Canada-United States Law Journal,* 25, 257.

Black Hills and Badlands (n.d.). Lakota. *Black Hills and Badlands South Dakota.* https://www.blackhillsbadlands.com/lakota

Blanchard, J. W., Outram, S., Tallbull, G., Royal, C. D. M., Leroux, D., Lund, D. N. J., & Watkins, J. E. (2019). We don't need a swab in our mouth to prove who we are: Identity, resistance, and adaptation of genetic ancestry testing among Native American communities. *Current Anthropology,* 60(5), 637–655. https://doi-org .ezproxy.utpb.edu/10.1086/705483

Bloom, J. (1996). Show what an Indian can do: Sports, memory, and ethnic identity at federal Indian boarding schools. *Journal of American Indian Education,* 35(3), 33–48.

Bloom, J. (2000). *To show what an Indian can do: Sports at Native American board-ing schools.* University of Minnesota Press.

Blumer, H. (1969). *Symbolic interaction.* Prentice-Hall.

Booth, T. (2010). Cheaper than bullets: American Indian boarding schools and assimilation policy, 1890–1930. In M. B. Spencer (Ed.) *Images, Imagination and*

Beyond (pp. 46–56). Durant: Southeastern Oklahoma State University. http://www
.se.edu/nas/files/2013/03/NAS-2009-Proceedings-Introductory.pdf

Bowannie, M. (2006, April 6). Albuquerque Indian School only a memory. *Indian
Country.* https://www.indiancountrynews.com/index.php/news/politcs-business/28
-albuquerque-indian-school-only-a-memory

Bowden, H. (1981). *American Indians and Christian missions: Studies in cultural
conflict.* The University of Chicago.

Bowers, C. A., Vasquez, M., & Roaf, M. (2000). Native people and the challenge of
computers: Reservation schools, individualism, and consumerism. *The American
Indian Quarterly,* 24(2), 182–199. https://www.jstor.org/stable/1185870

Brigham, W. (1836). *The compact with the charter and laws of the colony of new
Plymouth: Together with the charter of the Council at Plymouth, and an appendix,
containing the articles of confederation of the United Colonies of New England,
and other valuable documents.* Dutton and Wentworth. https://play.google.com/b
ooks/reader?id=SeGwAAAAMAAJ&printsec=frontcover&output=reader&hl=en
&pg=GBS.PP1

Brinson, P. (1985). Epilogue: Anthropology and the study of dance. In P. Spencer
(Ed.) *Society and the dance* (pp. 206–214). Cambridge University Press.

Broadman, M. (2016). The Camp Grant massacre: Arizona's terrible day. *True West:
History of the American Frontier.* https://truewestmagazine.com/the-camp-grant
-massacre/

Brown, C. M., Gibbons, J. L., & Smirles, K. E. (2007). Tribal teachers are important
to American Indian adolescents' tribal identity development. *American Indian
Culture & Research Journal,* 31(2), 103–111. https://doi-org.ezproxy.utpb.edu/10
.17953/aicr.31.2.4787x72422853788

Brown, S., & Bean, F. D. (2006). Assimilation models, old and new: Explaining a
long-term process. *Migration Policy Institute.* https://www.migrationpolicy.org/art
icle/assimilation-models-old-and-new-explaining-long-term-process

Browner, T. (2004). *Heartbeat of the people: Music and dance of the northern powwow.* University of Illinois Press.

Bruce, S. (2011). Defining religion: A practical response. *International Review of
Sociology—Revue Internationale De Sociologie,* 21(1), 107–120.

Bryant, A., & Charmaz, K. (Eds.). (2007). *The Sage handbook of grounded theory.*
Sage.

Buford, K. (2012). *Native American son: The life and sporting legend of Jim Thorpe.*
University of Nebraska Press.

Bullhead, E. (2018). *Tate Uyetopa O'lawa* (English translation). Lyrics Translate.
https://lyricstranslate.com/en/tate-uyetopa-olawa-four-winds-songfour-directions
-song.html

Burbridge, O. (2018). Gathering of Nations 2018. *Oteil.* https://oteilburbridge.com/
gathering-nations-2018/

Bureau of Indian Affairs (2020). About us. U.S. Department of the Interior Indian
Affairs. https://www.bia.gov/about-us

Bureau of Indian Affairs (2021a). Do all American Indians and Alaska Natives speak
a single traditional language? Our Nation's American Indian and Alaskan Citizens.
https://www.bia.gov/frequently-asked-questions

Bureau of Indian Affairs (2021c). Who is an American Indian or Alaska Native? Our Nation's American Indian and Alaskan Citizens. https://www.bia.gov/frequently -asked-questions

Bureau of Indain Affairs (2021d). What is a federal reservation? Our Nation's American Indian and Alaskan Citizens. https://www.bia.gov/frequently-asked-questions

Bureau of Indian Education (2019). Schools. *Bureau of Indian Education.* https://bie .edu/Schools/

Bureau of Labor Statistics (2019). American Indian and Alaska Natives in the U.S. labor force. *Monthly Labor Review*, November. https://www.bls.gov/opub/mlr/2 019/article/american-indians-and-alaska-natives-in-the-u-s-labor-force.htm#:~:te xt=The%20unemployment%20rate%20of%20AIANs,percent%20for%20the%20t otal%20population

Burke, M. (2000). Powwow a healing experience. *Windspeaker*, 18(2). https://ammsa. com/publications/windspeaker/powwow-healing-experience-0.

Cairns, J., Gardner, R., & Lawton, D. (2003). *Education for values : Morals, ethics and citizenship in contemporary teaching.* Routledge.

Cajete, G. (2004). Philosophy of native science. In A. Waters (Ed.) *American Indian thought: Philosophical Essays* (pp. 45–57). Blackwell.

Callahan, A. (1993). *The Osage ceremonial dance I'n-Lon-Sschka.* University of Oklahoma Press.

Callenbach, E. (1996). *Bring back the buffalo: A sustainable future for America's Great Plains.* University of California Press.

Campbell, D. T. (1965). Variation and selective retention insocio-cultural evolution. In H. R. Barringer, G. I. Blanksten, & R. W. Mack (Eds.) *Social change in develop-ing areas: A reinterpretation of evolutionary theory* (Vol. 19, pp. 26–27).

Campbell, D. T. (1997). From evolutionary epistemology via selection theory to a sociology of scientific validity. *Evolution and Cognition*, 3(1), 5–38. https://kli.ac. at/webroot/files/file/Evolution%20%26%20Cognition/1997%203-1.pdf

Caporael, L. R. (1997). Vehicles of knowledge: Artifacts and social groups. *Evolution and Cognition*, 3(1), 39–43. https://kli.ac.at/webroot/files/file/Evolution%20%26 %20Cognition/1997%203-1.pdf

Carus, P. (1880). The cross among the North American Indians. *The Open Court*, 296–312. https://opensiuc.lib.siu.edu/cgi/viewcontent.cgi?referer=https://www.g oogle.com/&httpsredir=1&article=1041&context=ocj

Cave, A. (2003). Abuse of power: Andrew Jackson and the Indian removal act of 1830. *Historian*, 65(6), 1330–1353.

Chang, K., & Hsieh, T. (2017). From having fun to applause: The study of relation-ships among festival benefits, festival identity and festival support by viewpoints of the hosts and guests. *Sustainability*, 9, 2240. DOI: 10.3390/su9122240

Charmaz, K. C. (2006). *Constructing grounded theory: A practical guide through qualitative analysis.* Sage.

Cheek, L. (2004). *The Navajo long walk. Look west series.* Rio Nuevo Publishers.

Cherokee Nation (2021). Tribal Registration. *Cherokee Nation.* https://www.che rokee.org/all-services/tribal-registration/

Clough, J. (2005). Vanishing Indians? Cultural persistence on display at the Omaha world's fair. *Great Plains Quarterly*, 25(2), 67–86.

Coakley, J. (2017). *Sports in society: Issues and controversies* (12th edition). McGraw-Hill.

Cogley, R. (1995). Two approaches to Indian conversion in Puritan New England: The missions of Thomas Mahew Jr. and John Eliot. *Historical Journal of Massachusetts*, 23(1), 44–60. http://www.wsc.mass.edu/mhj/pdfs/Cogley%20co mbined.pdf

Cogley, R. (1999). *John Eliot's mission to the Indians before King Philip's war.* Harvard University Press.

Contreras, D., & Bernstein, D. (1996). *We dance because we can: The people of the powwow.* Longstreet Press.

Cook, S. R., Johns, J. L., & Wood, K. (2005). The Monacan nation powwow: Symbol of indigenous survival and resistance in the Tobacco Row Mountains. In C. Ellis, L. E. Lassiter & G. H. Dunham (Eds.) *Powwow* (pp. 199–221). University of Nebraska Press.

Corbin, J., & Strauss, A. L. (2015). *Basics of qualitative research techniques and procedures for developing grounded theory* (4th edition). Sage.

Costa, D. J. (2003). *The Miami-Illinois language.* Nebraska Press.

Coyne, T. (1990). Group attacks non-Indian pow-wows. *Tulsa World*, April 10. https ://tulsaworld.com/archive/group-attacks-non-indian-pow-wows/article_6309ca09 -6209-5791-b4c5-7e206425b847.html

Crawford, J. (1995). Endangered Native American languages: What is to be done and why? *The Bilingual Research Journal*, 19(1), 17–38.

Crespi-Vakkbona, M., & Richards, G. (2007). The meaning of cultural festivals: Stakeholder perspectives in Catalunya. *International Journal of Cultural Policy*, 13(1), 103–122. DOI: 10.1080/10286630701201830

Csikszentmihalyi, M. (1975a). *Beyond boredom and anxiety: Experiencing flow in work and play.* Jossey-Bass.

Csikszentmihalyi, M. (1975b). Play and intrinsic rewards. *Journal of Humanistic Psychology*, 15(3), 41–63.

Csikszentmihalyi, M., & Csikszentmihalyi, I. S. (Eds.). (1992). *Optimal experience: Psychological studies of flow in consciousness.* Cambridge University Press.

Csordas, T. (1999). Ritual healing and the politics of identity in contemporary Navajo society. *American Ethnologist*, 26(1), 3–23.

Cushing, C. (1856). Relation of Indians to citizenship. *Official Opinions of the Attorneys General of the United States* (Vol. 7). Robert Farnham.

Crawford, S., & Kelley, D. (2005). *American Indian Religious Traditions: An Encyclopedia.* ABC-Clio.

Creswell, J. (2015). *30 essential skills for the qualitative researcher.* Sage.

Creswell, J., & Plano, C. (2011). *Designing and conducting mixed method research.* Sage.

Czech, D., Wrisberg, C., Fisher, L., Thompson, C., & Hayes, G. (2004). The experience of Christian prayer in sport: An existential phenomenological investigation. *Journal of Psychology and Christianity*, 23(1), 3–11.

Davidson, M. (2009). United States v. friday. *Denver University Law Review*, 86(3), 1133–1153.

Dawkins, R. (1976). *The selfish gene*. Oxford University Press.

Dell'Angela, T. (2003, June 17). Impresario creates controversy with powwow success. *Chicago Tribune*. http://articles.chicagotribune.com/2003-06-25/features/0306240407_1_first-powwow-tribes-american-indian

Deloria, V. (1994). *A sender of words: Essays in memory of John G. Neihardt*. Howe Brothers.

Deloria, V. (1999). *For this land: Writings on religion in America*. Routledge.

Deloria, V. (2003). *God is red: A Native view of religion* (3rd edition). Fulcrum

Devine, J. W., & Frias, F. J. L. (2020). Philosophy of sport. In E. N. Zalta (Ed.) *The Stanford encyclopedia of philosophy* (Fall 2020 edition). https://plato.stanford.edu/archives/fall2020/entries/sport/

DesJarlait, R. (1997). The contest powwow versus the traditional and the role of the Native American community. *Wicazo Sa Review*, 12(1), 115–127. DOI: 10.2307/1409165

Douglas (2018, September 10). The perplexing nature of "Wannabe" Indians. *American Indian Republic*. https://americanindianrepublic.com/the-perplexing-nature-of-wannabe-indians/

Dowden, B. (n.d.). Time. *Internet Encyclopedia of Philosophy—A Peer Reviewed Academic Resource*. https://iep.utm.edu/time/#H1

Dufrene, P. (1990). Exploring Native American symbolism. *Journal of Multi-Cultural and Cross-Cultural Research in Art Education*, 8(1), 38–50. DOI: 10.2307/1320676

Durkheim, E. (1915). The elementary forms of the religious life. *Hollen Street Press LTD*. https://www.gutenberg.org/files/41360/41360-h/41360-h.htm

Dyerson, M. (1993). The playing fields of progress: American athletic nationalism and the 1904 St. Louis Olympics. *Gateway Heritage*, 14(2), 11–13.

Eisen, G. (1978). Games and sporting diversions of the North American Indians as reflected in American historical writings of the sixteenth and seventeenth centuries. *Canadian Journal of History of Sport and Physical Education*, 9(1), 58–85.

Eitzen, D. S. (2009). American sport in the new millennium. In D. S. Eitzen (Ed.) *Sport in Contemporary Society* (8th edition, pp. 10–15). Paradigm.

Eitzen, D. S. (2015). The Super Bowl as a microcosm of society. In D. S. Eitzen (Ed.) *Sport in Contemporary Society* (10th edition, pp. 15–19). Oxford.

Eldridge, T. (2019, December 16). Why so many empty seats? *The Wichita Eagle*. https://www.kansas.com/sports/college/wichita-state/article238297693.html

Elliott, V. (2018). Thinking about the coding process in qualitative data analysis. *The Qualitative Report*, 23(11), 2850–2861. https://nsuworks.nova.edu/tqr/vol23/iss11/14

Ellis, C. (1999). We don't want your rations; we want this dance: The changing use of song and dance on the southern plains. *The Western Historical Quarterly*, 30(2), 133–154. DOI: 10.2307/970489

Ellis, C. (2003). *A dancing people: Powwow culture on the southern plains*. University Press of Kansas.

Ellis, C. (2005). The sound of the drum will revive them and make them happy. In C. Ellis, L. E. Lassiter, & G. H. Dunham (Eds.) *Powwow* (pp. 3–25). University of Nebraska Press

Ellis, C., & Lassiter, L. E. (2005). Introduction. In C. Ellis, L. E. Lassiter, & G. H. Dunham (Eds.) *Powwow* (vii–xv). University of Nebraska Press.

Eschbach, K., & Applbaum, K. (2000). Who goes to powwows? Evidence from the survey of American Indians and Alaska Natives. *American Indian Culture and Research Journal*, 24(2), 65–83. DOI: 10.17953/aicr.24.2.d3363512g776l31h

ESPN (1999, July 10). Top N. American athletes of the century. http://www.espn .com/sportscentury/athletes.html

Estes, R. (2013, April 6). Card carrying Indians vs those who don't. *Native Heritage Project*. https://nativeheritageproject.com/2013/04/06/card-carrying-indians-vs-those-who-dont/

Evans-Campbell, T. (2008). Perceptions of child neglect among urban American Indian/Alaska Native parents. *Child Welfare*, 87(3), 115–142. DOI: 10.1177/1077559504266800

Everett, D. (2009). Indian Territory. *The Encyclopedia of Oklahoma History and Culture*. www.okhistory.org

Fallasi, A. (1987) Festival: Definition and morphology. In A. Falassi (Ed.) *Time out of time* (pp. 1–10). University of New Mexico Press.

Fast, R. (2007). The land is full of stories: Navajo histories in the work of Luci Tapahonso. *Women's Studies*, 36(3), 185–211. DOI: 10.1080/00497870701255388.

Faulkner, T. (1903). *From the ballroom to hell*. The Henry Publishing CO.

Felder, B. (2017). Cultural identity a challenge for urban Native American students. *The Oklahoman*. December 26, 2017. https://oklahoman.com/article/5577155/cu ltural-identity-a-challenge-for-urban-native-american-students

Fewkes, J. (1925). The Osage tribe. *Thirty-ninth report of the Bureau of American Ethnology to the secretary of the Smithsonian Institution*. Government Printing Office. https://archive.org/stream/annualreportofbu39smithso/annualreportofbu3 9smithso_djvu.txt

Fitzgerald, H. (1992, July 3). *Sun Sentinel*. https://www.sun-sentinel.com/news/fl -xpm-1992-07-03-9202170666-story.html

Fleeson, W. (2004). Moving personality beyond the person-situation debate: The challenge and the opportunity of within-person variability. *Current Directions in Psychological Science*, 13(2), 83–87. https://doi-org.ezproxy.utpb.edu/10.1111/j .0963-7214.2004.00280.x

Fleming, P. (2019). The spiritual case against the mobile office. *America*, 220(4), 48–50.

Flynn, N. (2016). The sacred tradition of the eagle staff. *Canadian Army*. http://www .army-armee.forces.gc.ca/en/news-publications/national-news-details-no-menu .page?doc=the-sacred-tradition-of-the-eagle-staff/iaiir9qg

Folkestad, G. (2002). National identity and music. In R. A. Macdonald, D. J. Hargreaves & D. Meill (Eds.) *Musical identities* (pp. 151–162). Oxford University Press.

Foster, M. (1991). *Being Camanche: A social history of an American Indian community*. University of Arizona Press.

Fowler, L. 2005. Local contexts of powwow ritual. In C. Ellis, L. Lassiter & G. Dunham (Eds.) *Powwow* (pp. 68–82). University of Nebraska Press.

Franklin, B. (1784). Remarks concerning the savages of North America. *National Archives*. https://founders.archives.gov/documents/Franklin/01-41-02-0280

Fukuyama, F. (1999). The great disruption. *Atlantic*, 283(5), 55–80.

Fuller, M. (2021, March 19). Richard Pitino's six-year New Mexico deal worth $5 million; Gophers buyout impact unclear. *Star Tribune*. https://www.startribune .com/richard-pitino-s-six-year-new-mexico-deal-worth-5-million-gophers-buyout -impact-unclear/600035990/#:~:text=Pitino%2C%20who%20was%20hired%20by ,obtained%20by%20the%20Star%20Tribune

Gagnon, B. O. (2013). Territorializing indigeneity and powwow markets. *Anthropologica*, 55(1), 197–209.

Gamble, J. (1952). *Changing patterns in Kiowa dances*. In S. Tax (Ed.) *Selected Papers of the 29th International Congress of Americanists* (pp. 94–104). University of Chicago Press.

Garrett, M. T., & Carroll, J. J. (2000). Mending the broken circle: Treatment of substance dependence among Native Americans. *Journal of Counseling & Development*, 78, 379–388. DOI: 10.1002/j .1556-6676.2000.tb01921.x

Garrett, M. T., Parrish, M., Williams, C. Grayshield, L. Portman, T. A., Rivera, et al. (2014). Invited commentary: Fostering resilience among Native American youth through therapeutic intervention. *Journal of Youth and Adolescence*, 43(3), 470–490. DOI: 10.1007/s10964-013-0020-8

Garrett, M. T., & Prichette, E. F. (2000). Red as an apple: Native American acculturation and counseling with or without the reservation. *Journal of Counseling and Development*, 78(1), 3–13. DOI: 10.1002/j.1556-6676.2000.tb02554.x

Garroutte, E. M. (2001). The racial formation of American Indians: Negotiating legitimate identities within tribal and federal law. *American Indian Quarterly*, 25(2), 224–239. DOI: 10.1353/aiq.2001.0020

Garroutte, E., Beals, J., Keane, E., Kaufman, C., Spicer, P., Henderson, J., Henderson, P., Mitchell, C., Manson, S., & The AI-SUPERPFP Team (2009). Religiosity and spiritual engagement in two American Indian populations. *Journal for the Scientific Study of Religion*, 48(3), 480–500. https://www.ncbi.nlm.nih.gov/pmc/articles/ PMC4645987/

Garroutte, E. M., Anderson, O. A., Nez-Henderson, P., Croy, C., Beals, J., Henderson, J. A., Thomas, J., Manson, S. M, and the AI-SUPERPFP Team (2015). Religio-spiritual participation in two American Indian populations. *Journal for the Scientific Study of Religion*, 53(1), 17–37. DOI: 10.1111/ jssr.12084

Gathering of Nations (2018a). *Gathering of nations powwow: Official program*. Gathering of Nations.

Gathering of Nations (2018b). *Gathering of nations powwow program*. Albuquerque: Gathering of Nations. Retrieved from http://www.gatheringofnations.com/pow wow.aspx

Gell, A. (1992). The anthropology of time: Cultural constructions of temporal maps and images. *Berg*. https://monoskop.org/images/a/aa/Gell_Alfred_The_Anthro

pology_of_Time_Cultural_Constructions_of_Temporal_Maps_and_Images_1992 .pdf

Giddens, A. (1984). *The constitution of society: Outline of the theory of structuration.* University of California Press.

Gill, H. (2004). Colonial germ warfare. *Colonial Williamsburg*, Spring, 2004. http:// www.history.org/foundation/journal/spring04/warfare.cfm.

Gilley, B. (2006). *Becoming two-spirit: Gay identity and social acceptance in Indian Country.* University of Nebraska Press.

Goertzen, C. (2005). Purposes of North Carolina powwows. In C. Ellis, L. E. Lassiter, & G. H. Dunham (Eds.) *Powwow* (pp. 275–302). University of Nebraska Press.

Goldberg, J. (2016, July 30). It takes a village to determine the origin of an African proverb. *National Public Radio.* https://www.npr.org/sections/goatsandsoda/2016 /07/30/487925796/it-takes-a-village-to-determine-the-origins-of-an-african-proverb

Goldschmidt, W. (1951). Nomlaki ethnography. *University of California Publications in American Archeology and Ethnography*, 42(4). University of California Press.

Golobos.com (2020, January 16). Athletics releases fan survey results. *University of New Mexico Athletics.* https://golobos.com/news/2020/01/16/mens-basketball-ath letics-releases-fan-survey-results.

Golobos.com (2021). University of New Mexico lobos athletic website. https://go lobos.com/index.aspx?path=mbball.

Gonzalez, M. C. (2002). Painting the white face red: Intercultural contact presented through poetic ethnography. In J. N. Martin, T. K. Nakayama, & L. Flores (Eds.) *Readings in intercultural communication: Experiences and contexts* (pp. 485–494). McGraw-Hill.

Goodluck, C. (2002). First Nations' children and youth well-being indicators: A strengths perspective. *Casey Family Programs and the National Indian Child Welfare Association.* https://www.yumpu.com/en/document/read/41169999/na tive-american-children-and-youth-well-being-indicators

Gover, K. (2015, May 22). American Indians serve in the U.S. military in greater numbers than any ethnic group and have since the revolution. *Huffington Post.* https://www.huffingtonpost.com/national-museum-of-the-american-indian/ameri can-indians-serve-in-the-us-military_b_7417854.html.

Gowen, B. (2011). God's power in the powwow. *Devotionals.* https://resources.fo ursquare.org/gods_power_in_powwow/

Greenstein, N. (2014). Why the U.S. flag is red, white and blue. *TIME Magazine.* https://swampland.time.com/2013/07/04/why-the-u-s-flag-is-red-white-and-blue/

Guthrie, J. T. (1983). Values from textbooks. *Journal of Reading*, 26(6), 574–576. https://www.jstor.org/stable/40031775

Hackett, C., & McClendon, D. (2017). Christians remain world's largest religious group, but they are declining in Europe. *Pew Research Center.* https://www.pew research.org/fact-tank/2017/04/05/christians-remain-worlds-largest-religious-gro up-but-they-are-declining-in-europe/

Haozous, E. A., Strickland, C. J., Palacios, J. F., & Solomon, T. G. A. (2014). Blood politics, ethnic identity, and racial misclassification among American Indians and

Alaska Natives. *Journal of Environmental and Public Health*, 2014, 321604. https ://doi-org.ezproxy.utpb.edu/10.1155/2014/321604

Harding, L. (2001). The Carlisle Boarding School and its literary legacy: The war with the pen. In 2001 Monograph Series, Proceedings of the Annual Meeting of African American Studies, the National Association of Hispanic and Latino Studies, the National Association of Native American Studies, and the International Association of Asian Studies (pp. 205–240).

Havelock, E. (1914). The philosophy of dancing. *The Atlantic Monthly: The Making of America Project*, CXIII, 197–207.

Heidenreich, C. (2005). Missionization, northern plains. In J. Crawford Suzanne, & F. Kelley Dennis (Eds.) *American Indian religious traditions: An encyclopedia* (Vol. 2, pp. 534–43). ABC Clio.

Heine, S. J. (2008). *Cultural psychology*. Norton.

Hendry, J. (2003). Mining the sacred mountain: The clash between the Western dualistic framework and Native American religions. *Multicultural Perspectives*, 5(1), 3–10. DOI: 10.1207/S15327892MCP0501_2

Henry, R. (2010). Festivals. In S. Kleinert & M. Neale (Eds.) *The Oxford companion to aboriginal art and culture* (pp. 586–587). Oxford University Press.

Herle, A. (1994). Dancing community: Powwow and Pan-Indianism in North America. *Cambridge Anthropology*, 17(2), 57–83. https://www.jstor.org/stable/23820415

Herman, N., & Reynolds, L. T. (1994). *Symbolic Interactionism*: An Introduction to Social Psychology. General Hall, Inc.

Herring, R. D. (1996). Synergetic counseling and Native American Indian students. *Journal of Counseling & Development*, 74(6), 542–547. https://doi-org.ezproxy.u tpb.edu/10.1002/j.1556-6676.1996.tb02290.x

Heth, C., & Vennum, T. (1997). American warriors: Songs for veterans. *RYKO Records*. https://media.smithsonianfolkways.org/liner_notes/hart/HRT15014.pdf

HHS.Gov (2020). Obesity and American Indian/Alaska Natives. *U.S. Department of Health and Human Services*. https://minorityhealth.hhs.gov/omh/browse.aspx?lvl =4&lvlid=40

Hill, R. (1996). The light in the forest. In Ben Marra (ed.) *Powwow: Images along the red road* (p. 8). Abrams.

Hoefnagles, A. (2007 b). Prohibitions. *Native Dance*. http://native-dance.ca/en/rene wal/prohibitions/

Hoffmeyer, L. (2015). American Indian powwows: Multiplicity and authenticity. *Smithsonian Center for Folklife & Cultural Heritage*. https://folklife.si.edu/online -exhibitions/american-indian-powwows/history/smithsonian

Holy Bible (2011). *The Holy Bible*, new international version. Zondervan Publishing House.

Horse, P. G. (2005). Native American identity. *New Directions for Student Services*, 2005(109), 61–68. https://doi-org.ezproxy.utpb.edu/10.1002/ss.154

Hossain, Z., Skurky, T., Joe, J., & Hunt, T. (2011). The sense of collectivism and individualism among husbands and wives in traditional and bi-cultural Navajo families on the Navajo reservation. *Journal of Comparative Family Studies*, 42(4), 543–562. DOI: 10.3138/jcfs.42.4.543

House, L. E., Stiffman, A. R., & Brown E. (2006). Unraveling cultural threads: A qualitative study of culture and ethnic identity among urban Southwestern American Indian youth, parents and elders. *Journal of Child and Family Studies*, 15(4), 393–407. DOI: 10.1007/s10826-006-9038-9

Howard, J. (1983). Pan-Indianism in Native American music and dance. *Ethnomusicology*, 27(71), 71–82. DOI: 10.2307/850883

Howard, J. H. (1955). Pan-Indian culture of Oklahoma. *The Scientific Monthly*, 81(5), 215–220.

Howe, C. (1988). Cyberspace is no place for tribalism. *Wicazo sa Review*, 13(2), 19–28.

Hsiu-Yen Yeh, J. (2006). Singing and dancing matters: Performing "indigenousness" through Powwow. *European Review of Native American Studies*, 20(2), 1–7. https://www.academia.edu/1087195/Singing_and_Dancing_Matters_Performing _Indigenousness_through_Powwow; https://shapeamerica.tandfonline.com/doi/ full/10.1080/00336297.2015.1048373#.XmDqRJNKiF0

Hutch, R. (2012). Sport and spirituality: Mastery and failure in sporting lives. *Practical Theology*, 5(2), 131–152.

Hutchens, J. L. (2006). *Powwow calendar 2007*. Book Publishing Company.

Hutton, P. (1999). *Phil Sheridan and his army*. University of Oklahoma Press.

Hyer, S. (1990). *One house, one voice one heart: Native American education at Santa Fe Indian School*. Museum of New Mexico Press.

Ide, J. (1818). *The nature and tendency of balls, seriously and candidly considered in two sermons, preached in Medway*. H&W Mann.

IRS (n.d.). Getting ready for powwow season. *Internal Revenue Service*. https:// www.ncai.org/IRS_Office_of_Indian_Tribal_Governments_-_Getting_Ready_for _Pow_Wow_Season.pdf

Iyengar, S., & Durham, M. (2009). Live from your neighborhood: A national study of outdoor arts festivals. *National Endowment for the Arts Research Report #51*, https ://www.arts.gov/sites/default/files/Festivals-Executive-Summary.pdf

Jackson, J. B. (2005). East meets west: On stomp dance and powwow worlds in Oklahoma. In C. Ellis, L. E. Lassiter & G. H. Dunham (Eds.) *Powwow* (pp. 172–199). University of Nebraska Press.

Jacobs, M. (2016). Genocide or ethnic cleansing? Are these our only choices? *Western Historical Society Quarterly*, 47(4), 444–448. DOI: 10.1093/whq/whw104

Jacobs, M. R., & Merolla, D. M. (2016). Being authentically American Indian: Symbolic identity construction and social structure among urban new Indians. *Symbolic Interaction*, 40(1), 63–82. DOI: 10.1002/SYMB.266

Jenkins, S. (2012, July). Why are Jim Thorpe's Olympic records still not recognized? *Smithsonian Magazine*. https://www.smithsonianmag.com/history/why-are-jim -thorpes-olympic-records-still-not-recognized-130986336/

Jirasek, I. (2015). Religion, spirituality, and sport: From *religio athletae* toward *spiritus athletae*, *Quest Journal*, 67(3), 290–299.

Jocks, C. (2004). *Modernity, resistance, and the Iroquois longhouse people*. In J. Olupona (Ed.) *Beyond primitivism: Indigenous religions, traditions, and modernity* (pp. 139–148). Routledge.

Kachur, C. (2017). *The freedom and privacy of an Indian boarding school's sports field and student athletes' resistance to assimilation*, Master's thesis, Bowling Green State University. OhioLink Electronic Theses & Dissertations Center. https://etd.ohiolink .edu/!etd.send_file?accession=bgsu1510234437881951&disposition=inline

Kagitçibasi, C. (1997). Individualism and collectivism. In J. W. Berry, M. H. Segall, & C. Kagitçibasi (Eds.) *Handbook of cross-cultural psychology: Social behavior and applications* (pp. 1–49). Pearson.

Kanon, T. (2017). Brief history of Tennessee in the War of 1812. *Tennessee State Library Archives*. https://sos.tn.gov/products/tsla/brief-history-tennessee-war-1812

Kavanagh, T. W. (1982). The Comanche pow-wow: Pan-Indianism or tribalism. *Haliksa'I, University of New Mexico Contributions to Anthropology*, I, 12–13.

Keck, M. (2021). Indian education for all on Montana's Flathead reservation. *Academia Letters*, Article 619. DOI: 10.20935/AL619

Keene, A. (2010, May 11). When non-Native participation in powwows goes terribly wrong. *Native Appropriations*. https://nativeappropriations.com/2010/05/when -non-native-participation-in-powwows-goes-terribly-wrong.html

Kennett, P., Sneath, J., & Henson, S. (2001). Fan satisfaction and segmentation: A case study of minor league hockey spectators. *Journal of Targeting, Measurement and Analysis for Marketing*, 10(2), 132–142.

King James Bible (2021). King James Bible online. https://www.kingjamesbibleon-line.org/

Kipp, D. R. (2007). Observations on a tribal language revitalization program. In G. H. Capture, D. Champagne & C. C. Jackson (Eds.) *American Indian Nations: Yesterday, today, and tomorrow* (pp. 105–111). Altamira Press.

Kitayama, S., & Markus, H. R. (2000). The pursuit of happiness and the realization of sympathy: Cultural patterns of self, social relations, and well-being. In E. Diener & E. M. Suh (Eds.) *Culture and subjective well-being* (pp. 113–161). The MIT Press.

Korver, L. (2013). *The medicine game: Four brothers—One goal*. Lincoln, NE: Vision Maker Media.

Kosloski (2018). What to do when Holy Communion falls on the ground at mass. *Aleteia*. https://aleteia.org/2018/06/03/what-to-do-when-holy-communion-falls-on -the-ground-at-mass/

Kosmin, B. A., & Keysar, A. (2006). *Religion in a free market*. Paramount Market.

Kosmin, B., Mayer, E., & Keysar, A. (2001). *American religious identification survey: Key findings*. https://www.gc.cuny.edu/CUNY_GC/media/CUNY-Graduate -Center/PDF/ARIS/ARIS-PDF-version.pdf

Kracht, B. (1994). Kiowa powwows: Tribal identity through the continuity of the Gourd Dance. *Great Plains Research*, 4(2), 257–259. https://digitalcommons.unl .edu/greatplainsresearch/234/

Krauss, M. (1992). The world's languages in crisis. *Language*, 68, 6–10. https://doi -org.ezproxy.utpb.edu/10.2307/416368

Krech, S. (2006). Bringing linear time back in. *Ethnohistory*, 53, 567–93.

Krouse, S. (2001). Traditional Iroquois socials: Maintaining identity in the city. *American Indian Quarterly*, 25(3), 400–408.

Kyle, D. G. (2015). *Sport & spectacle in the ancient world* (2nd edition). Wiley Blackwell.

LaFromboise, T., Trimble, J. E., & Mohatt, G. V. (1990). Counseling intervention and American Indian tradition: An integrative approach. *The Counseling Psychologist*, 18, 628–654. DOI: 10.1177/0011000090184006

LaFrombroise, T., & Dizon, M. (2003). American Indian children and adolescents. In J. T. Gibbs & L. Huang (Eds.) *Children of color: Psychological interventions with culturally diverse youth* (pp. 45–90). Jossey-Bass.

Lange, K. (2020). How to properly dispose of worn-out U.S. flags. U.S. Department of Defense. https://www.defense.gov/Explore/Features/Story/article/2206946/how -to-properly-dispose-of-worn-out-us-flags/

Larse, S. (2018, April 13). Experience the world's largest Powwow. *National Geographic*. https://www.nationalgeographic.com/travel/destinations/north -america/united-states/new-mexico/things-to-do-albuquerque-gathering-of-nat ions-powwow/

Laszlo, E. (1992). Information technology and social change: An evolutionary systems analysis. *Behavioral Science*, 37(4), 237–249.

Lawrence, J. (2000). The Indian health service and the sterilization of Native American women. *American Indian Quarterly*, 24(3), 400–419. DOI: 10.1353/ aiq.2000.0008

Lee, T. (2009). Language, identity, and power: Navajo and Pueblo young adults' perspectives and experiences with competing language ideologies. *Journal of Language, Identity & Education*, 8(5), 307–320. https://doi-org.ezproxy.utpb.edu /10.1080/15348450903305106

Leeming, D. (2005). Wakan-Tanka. *The Oxford companion to world mythology*. https://www-oxfordreference-com.ezproxy.utpb.edu/view/10.1093/acref/9780195 156690.001.0001/acref-9780195156690-e-1669?rskey=ISEwCY&result=1

Lerch, P., & Bullers, S. (1996). Powwows as identity markers: Traditional or Pan-Indian? *Human Organization*, 559(4), 390–395. https://www.jstor.org/stable/44127856

Library of Congress (2018). Trail of tears: A local legacy. *Library of Congress*. http:// www.americaslibrary.gov/es/ky/es_ky_powwow_1.html?&loclr=reclnk

Library of Congress (n.d.). Indian Removal Act. *Primary Documents in American History*. http://memory.loc.gov/diglib/legacies/loc.afc.afc-legacies.200003267/

Library of Congress (n.d.). Immigrants in the progressive era. *U.S. History Primary Source Timeline*. https://www.loc.gov/classroom-materials/united-states-history -primary-source-timeline/progressive-era-to-new-era-1900-1929/immigrants-in -progressive-era/

Library of Congress (2020). Flag day. *Library of Congress*. https://www.loc.gov/ item/today-in-history/june-14/

Linck, M. (2004, August 28). Omaha Tribe celebrates 200th harvest festival. *Sioux City Journal*. https://siouxcityjournal.com/lifestyles/omaha-tribe-celebrates-200th -harvest-festival/article_3e9ae0fc-8569-5083-afe0-70f62c817ddf.html

Lockett, C. (2019, October 11). Organizers try to make Black Hills Powwow largest in nation. *SDPB Radio*. https://listen.sdpb.org/post/organizers-try-make-black-hills -pow-wow-largest-nation

Logan, L. (1993). Iroquois social dances: The life of dance in the dance of life. *Festival of American Folklife*, Document FESTBK1993_22, 74–76. https://festival. si.edu/articles/1993/iroquois-social-dances-the-life-of-dance-in-the-dance-of-life

Lottini, I. (2012). When Buffalo Bill crossed the ocean: Native American scenes in early twentieth century European culture. *European Journal of American Culture*, 31(3), 187–203. DOI:10.1386/ejac.31.3.187_1

Lucero, N. M. (2013). It's not about place, it's about what's inside: American Indian women negotiating cultural connectedness and identity in urban spaces. *Women's Studies International Forum*. 42, 9–18. DOI: 10.1016/j.wsif.2013.10.012

Lurie, N. (1971). The contemporary Indian scene. In E. Leacock & N. Lurie (Eds.) *North American Indians in Historic Perspective* (pp. 418–480). Random House.

Lutz, E. (2007, June, 2007). Saving America's endangered languages. *Cultural Survival Quarterly Magazine*. https://www.culturalsurvival.org/publications/cultural-survival-quarterly/saving-americas-endangered-languages

Luu, C. (2019, October 16. What we lose when we lose Indigenous knowledge. *JSTOR Daily*. https://daily.jstor.org/what-we-lose-when-we-lose-indigenous-knowledge/

Madley, B. (2016). Understanding genocide in California under United States rule, 1846–1873. *Western Historical Quarterly*, 47(4), 449–461. DOI: 10.1093/whq%2Fwhw176

Maffesoli, M. (2016). From society to tribal communities. *The Sociological Review*, 64, 739–747. DOI: 10.1111/1467-954X.12434

Maguire, G. J. (2018). A genocide by any other name: Cultural genocide in the context of Indigenous Peoples and the role of international law. *Journal of Human Rights*, 4(1), 1–24. https://www.strath.ac.uk/media/1newwebsite/department subject/law/documents/studentlawreview/fourthedition/Maguire_(1).pdf

Mails, T. (2012). *Fools Crow: Wisdom and Power*. Council Oaks Books.

Manning, F. (1992). Spectacle. In R. Bauman (Ed.) *Folklore, cultural performances, and popular entertainments* (pp. 291–299). Oxford University Press.

Marontate, J. (2005). Rethinking permanence and change in contemporary cultural preservation strategies. *The Journal of Arts Management, Law, and Society*, 34(4), 285–305. DOI:10.3200/JAML.34.4.285–305

Martin, J. (2001). *The land looks after us: A history of Native American religions*. Oxford University Press.

Masich, A. (2017). *Civil war in the southwest borderlands: 1861–1867*. University of Oklahoma Press.

Maslow, A. (1962). *Towards a psychology of being*. Van Nostrand.

Mather, I. (2010). *Arrow against profane and promiscuous dancing*. Kessinger Publishing.

Matulevičius, S. (2013). "Indianism" in Lithuania: Re-enchantment of the world through "playing Indians." Lietuvos etnologija/Lithuanian ethnology: *Socialinės Antropologijos Ir Etnologijos Studijos/Studies in Social Anthropology and Ethnology*, 13(22), 123–144.

Maurin, A., & Watson, P. (2019). Unearthing and analyzing data on festivals in the Caribbean. *Social & Economic Studies*, 68(1/2), 169–201.

McCluskey, M. (2009). *Your guide to understanding and enjoying pow wows*. Montana: opi.mt.gov Indian Education Division. https://opi.mt.gov/Portals/182/Page%20Files/Indian%20Education/Indian%20Education%20101/PowWows.pdf

McCoy, K. (2014). Manifesting destiny: A land education analysis of settler colonialism in Jamestown, Virginia, USA. *Environmental Education Research*, 20(1), 82–97. DOI: 10.1080/13504622.2013.865116

McDonald, F. W. (1972). *John Levi of Haskell*. World Co.

McDonnell, B. (2011, April 27). Red Earth Native American cultural festival gets ready for silver anniversary celebration. *The Oklahoman*. https://www.oklahoman.com/article/3562311/red-earth-native-american-cultural-festival-gets-ready-for-silver-anniversary-celebration#:~:text=Calvin%20Sharpe%2C%20Red%20Earth%20board,10%20powwows%20by%20USA%20Today

McLain, M., Irving-Bell, D., Wooff, D., & Morrison-Love, D. (2019). How technology makes us human: Cultural historical roots for design and technology education. *Curriculum Journal*, 30(4), 464–483. https://doi-org.ezproxy.utpb.edu/10.1080/09585176.2019.1649163

McLaren, B. (2016). *The great spiritual migration: How the world's largest religion is seeking a better way to be Christian*. Crown Publishing.

McMullen, A. (1996). Tribal historiography, Indian-white relations, and southeastern New England Powwows. *The Public Historian*, 18(4), 53–74. DOI:10.2307/3379787

McNally, M. D. (2000). The practice of Native American Christianity. *Church History*, 69(4), 834–859.

Megargee, S. (2019, March 3). College teams add more glitz in attempt to keep fans coming. *Chicago Tribune*. https://www.chicagotribune.com/sports/college/ct-spt-engage-college-fans-20190303-story.html

Meriam, L. (1928). *The problem of Indian administration*. The Johns Hopkins Press.

Michaelson, R. (1983). Red man's religion / White Man's religious history. *Journal of the American Academy of Religion*, 51(4), 667–684.

Miller, R. (2006). *Native America, discovered and conquered: Thomas Jefferson, Lewis & Clark, and manifest destiny*. Praeger Publishers.

Morales, L. (2019). Many Native Americans can't get clean water, report finds. *National Public Radio*. https://www.npr.org/2019/11/18/779821510/many-native-americans-cant-get-clean-water-report-finds

Morgan, T. J. (1892). Report of the Commissioner of Indian Affairs. In W. Michael (Ed.) *Message from the President of the United States to the two houses of congress at the beginning of the second session of the fifty-second congress, with the reports of the heads of departments and selections from accompanying documents (1893)* (pp. 687–751). Government Printing Office.

Moses, L. (1999). *Wild West shows and the images of American Indians, 1883–1933*. University of New Mexico Press.

Moses, J. (2020). State of homelessness: A look at race and ethnicity. *National Alliance to End Homelessness*. https://endhomelessness.org/state-of-homelessness-a-look-at-race-and-ethnicity/#:~:text=Native%20Americans%3A%20Unsheltered%20homelessness%20is,individuals%20overall%20(37%20percent)

Murphy, M., & White, R. (1995). *In the Zone: Transcendent experience in sports.* Penguin Books.

NAIA (2021). *NAIA presents the 40th annual Indian education Tennessee pow wow.* Native American Indian Association of Tennessee.

Nathanson, R. (2018, April 27). We feel at home. *Albuquerque Journal.* https://ww w.abqjournal.com/1164465/thousands-of-dancers-open-35th-gathering-of-nations .html

National Indian Council on Aging (2019). American Indian suicide rate increases. *National Indian Council on Aging.* https://www.nicoa.org/national-american-india n-and-alaska-native-hope-for-life-day/

Native Women's Wilderness (n.d.). Murdered and missing indigenous women. *National Womens Wilderness.* https://www.nativewomenswilderness.org/mmiw

Navajo-Hopi Observer (2021, February 17). Gathering of Nations powwow cancelled for 2md year in a row. *Navajo-Hopi Observer.* https://www.nhonews. com/news/2021/feb/17/gathering-nations-powwow-canceled-2nd-year-row/#:~: text=In%202019%2C%20the%20Gathering%20of,of%20%2422%20million% 20for%20Albuquerque

Naval History (2017). 20th century warriors: Native American participation in the U.S. Military. *Naval History.* https://www.history.navy.mil/research/library/online -reading-room/title-list-alphabetically/t/american-indians-us-military.html

NCAA (2018). NCAA men's basketball attendance: All divisions. *NCAA.org.* http:// fs.ncaa.org/Docs/stats/m_basketball_RB/Reports/attend/2017.pdf

NCAA (2020). Attendance Records. *National Collegiate Athletic Association.* http:// fs.ncaa.org/Docs/stats/m_basketball_RB/2021/Attend.pdf

Neihardt, J. (2008). *Black Elk speaks.* State University of New York Press.

Nerburn, K., & Mengelkoch, L. (1991). *Native American wisdom.* New World Library.

Nersessian, D. (2005). Rethinking cultural genocide under international law. *Carnegie Council for Ethics in International Affairs, Human Rights Dialogue.* https://www .carnegiecouncil.org/publications/archive/dialogue/2_12/section_1/5139

Nesper, L. (2003). Simulating culture: Being Indian for tourists in Lac du Flambeau's Wa-Swa-Gon Indian Bowl. *Ethnohistory,* 50(3), 447–472. DOI: 10.1215/00141801-50-3-447

New Mexico Nomad (2020). Gathering of Nations: Largest powwow in the world. *New Mexico Nomad.* https://newmexiconomad.com/gathering-of-nations/

Newcomb, S. (2008). *Pagans in the promised land: Decoding the doctrine of Christian discovery.* Fulcrum.

New Mexico Nomad (2020). Gathering of Nations. *New Mexico Nomad.* https://ne wmexiconomad.com/gathering-of-nations/#:~:text=Gathering%20of%20Nations %20(GON)%20is,to%20singers%20and%20dancers%20competing

Niezen, R. (2000). *Spirit wars. Native North American Religions in the age of nation building.* University of California Press.

Norris, T., Vines, P., & Hoeffel, E. (2012). The American Indian and Alaska Native population 2010: 2010 Census Brief. *United States Census Bureau.* https://www .census.gov/history/pdf/c2010br-10-112019.pdf

Nott, S., Gaston, K., & Fryberger, C. (2018). The lumbee Powwow: An economic impact analysis. *NC Growth*. https://ncgrowth.unc.edu/wp-content/uploads/2018/12/NCGrowth_LumbeeReport_07182018.pdf

Ohri, L. (2016). Political yields from cultural fields: Agency and ownership in a heritage festival in India. *Ethnos: Journal of Anthropology*, 81(4), 667–682. DOI: 10.1080/00141844.2014.989872

Oklahoman (1992). It's the year if the Indian in Oklahoma. *The Oklahoman*. https://oklahoman.com/article/2392646/its-the-year-of-the-indian-in-oklahoma

Oklahoma Historical Society (n.d.). Search the Dawes final rolls, 1894–1914. *Oklahoma Historical Society*. https://www.okhistory.org/research/dawes

O'Leary, Z. (2017). *Doing your research project* (3rd edition). Sage.

Olsen, L. (1998). Music and dance. In D. Walker (ed.) *Vol. 12 of Handbook of North American Indians: Plateau* (pp. 546–561). Smithsonian Institution Scholarly Press.

Olson, L. (2011). The essentiality of culture in the study of religion and politics. *Journal for the Scientific Study of Religion*, 50(4), 639–653. DOI: 10.1111/j.1468-5906.2011.01608.x

Ostler, J. (2015). Genocide and American Indian history. *Oxford Research Encyclopedia: American History*. http://americanhistory.oxfordre.com/view/10.1093/acrefore/9780199329175.001.0001/acrefore-9780199329175-e-3

Owen, S. (2008). The appropriation of Native American spirituality. *Continuum International Publishing Group*. http://web.b.ebscohost.com.ezproxy.utpb.edu/ehost/ebookviewer/ebook/bmxlYmtfXzM0NDM4M19fQU41?sid=479dce56-f947-4830-85a1-66cfcfbd876a@pdc-v-sessmgr01&vid=0&format=EB&rid=1

Oxendine, J. (2011). History of the powwow. *PowWows.com*. https://www.powwows.com/history-of-the-powwow/

Paraschak, V. (2000). Native Americans. In G. Kirsch, O. Harris & C. E. Nolte (Eds.) *Encyclopedia of Ethnicity and Sports in the United States* (pp. 329–335). Greenwood Publishing.

Paredes, J. A. (1995). Paradoxes of modernism and Indianness in the Southeast. *American Indian Quarterly*, 19(3), 341–360. https://www.jstor.org/stable/1185595

Pellerin, F. (2015). Festivals & Expositions France 2015. *Le Ministere de la Culture et de la Communication*. https://www.guides-culture.fr/fe15-flip/mobile/

Penwell, A. (2019). Lakota Nation invitational this weekend in Rapid City. *KOAT TV*. https://www.kotatv.com/content/news/Lakota-Nation-Invitational-this-weekend-in-Rapid-City-566294221.html

Perez, A. D., & Hirschman, C. (2009). The changing racial and ethnic composition of the US population: *Emerging American identities. Population and Development Review*, 35(1), 1–51. DOI: 10.1111/j.1728-4457.2009.00260.x

Peroff, N., & Wildcat, D. (2002). Who is an American Indian? *The Social Science Journal*, 39(3), 349–361. DOI: 10.1016/S0362-3319(02)00207-0

Peterson, L. (2018). The history of incense and why it is used at Mass. *Aleteia*. https://aleteia.org/2018/10/19/the-history-of-incense-and-why-its-used-at-mass/

Pew Research Center (2020). Religious landscape study. https://www.pewforum.org/religious-landscape-study/

PNPI (2019). Native American students in higher education. *The Postsecondary National Policy Institute.* https://pnpi.org/native-american-students/

Popescu, R., & Corbos, R. (2012). The role of festivals and cultural events in the strategic development of cities. Recommendations for urban areas in Romania. *Informatica Economică,* 16(4), 19–28. https://core.ac.uk/download/pdf/26749485.pdf

Portman, T., & Garrett, M. (2006). Native American healing traditions. *International Journal of Disability, Development and Education,* 53(4), 453–469.

Powers, W. (1980). Plains Indian music and dance. In W. R. Wood & M. Liberty (Eds.) *Anthropology on the Great Plains* (pp. 212–229). University of Nebraska Press.

Powwows.com (2015). Powwow taxes? *Powwows.com.*

Pow-Wow.org (2019a). *Rules for competition dancers.* https://www.pow-wow.org/rules-competition-dancers/

Pow-Wow.org (2019b). *Powwow judges.* https://www.pow-wow.org/pow-wow-judges/

Pratt, R. H. (1892). The advantages of mingling Indians with Whites. In I. Barrows (Ed.) *Official Report of The Nineteenth Annual Conference of Charities and Corrections at The Nineteenth Annual Session Held in Denver,* Colorado, June 23–29 (pp. 45–59).

Pratt, J., & Pride, B. (2020, February 9). An empty cathedral: Why aren't more students attending basketball games at the Palestra? *The Daily Pennsylvanian.* https://www.thedp.com/article/2020/02/palestra-penn-mens-basketball-attendance-student-culture-ivy-league

Price, S. L. (2010). Pride of a nation. *Sports Illustrated,* 113(2), 60–71. https://www.si.com/vault/2010/07/19/105961100/pride-of-a-nation

Pro football Hall of Fame (2019). Jim Thorpe: World's greatest athlete. *Pro Football Hall of Fame.* https://www.profootballhof.com/players/jim-thorpe/

ProPublica (n.d.). Gathering of Nations. *Nonprofit explorer.* https://projects.propublica.org/nonprofits/organizations/850369165

Quequesah, R. (2002, August 15). Reflections from the PowwowTrail. *Indian Country Toda.* http://www.indiancountry.com/content.cfm?id=1029416332

Rader, B. G. (2004). The greatest drama in Indian life: Experiments in Native American identity and resistance at the Haskell Institute homecoming of 1926. *Western Historical Quarterly,* 35, 429–450. DOI 10.2307/25443053

Rader, K. (2015). *Sport and spectacle in the ancient world* (2nd edition). Wiley.

Rahimi, S. (2005, June 18). Celebrating the powwow way of life. *New York Times.* https://www.nytimes.com/2005/06/18/nyregion/celebrating-the-powwow-way-of-life.html

Rappenglück, B. (2014). Cosmic dance: Correlations between dance and cosmos-related ideas across ancient cultures. *Mediterranean Archaeology and Archaeometry,* 14(3), 307–317.

Reid, H. (2011). *Athletics and philosophy in the ancient world.* Routledge.

Rendon, M., & Markusen, A. (2004). Native artists: Livelihoods, resources, space, gifts. *McKnight Foundation.* https://www.giarts.org/sites/default/files/NativeArtistsLivelihoodsResourcesSpaceGifts1209.pdf

Reyhner, J. (1996). Rationale and needs for stabilizing Indigenous languages. In G. Cantoni (Ed.) *Stabilizing indigenous languages* (pp. 3–14). Northern Arizona University.

Reyhner, J. (2018). American Indian boarding schools: What went wrong? What is going right? *American Journal of Indian Education*, 57(1), 58–78. DOI:10.5749/jamerindieduc.57.1.0058

Rhodes, J. (1991). An American tradition: The religious persecution of Native Americans. Montana Law Review, 52(1), 14–71. https://scholarship.law.umt.edu /mlr/vol52/iss1/4

Rhodes, D. S. (1993). My home: A communal American Indian home. Native peoples: The Arts and *Lifeways*, 6(3), 40–43.

Rice, G. W. (1996). There and back again—An Indian hobbit's holiday: Indians teaching Indian law. *New Mexico Law Review*, 26(2), 169–190. https://digital repository.unm.edu/nmlr/vol26/iss2/4/

Ridington, R., Hastings, D., & Attachie, T. (2005). The songs of our elders: Performance and cultural survival in Omaha and Dane-zaa traditions. In C. Ellis, L. Lassiter & G. Dunham (Eds.) *Powwow* (110–129). University of Nebraska Press.

Riggs, S. (1890). *Dakota-English dictionary*. Government Printing Office.

Roberts, K. (2002). Speech, gender, and the performance of culture: Native American "princesses". *Text and Performance Quarterly*, 22(4), 261–279.

Robinson, S. (2007). The spiritual journey. In J. Parry, S. Robinson, N. Watson & M. Nesti (Eds.) *Sport and Spirituality: An introduction* (pp. 38–59). Routledge.

Robbins, R., Scherman, A., Holeman, H., & Wilson, J. (2005). Roles of American Indian grandparents in times of cultural crisis. *Journal of Cultural Diversity*, 12(2), 62–68.

Roberts, K. G. (2011). Emotivism and pseudocultural identities. *The Howard Journal of Communications*, 14, 195–208. DOI: 10.1080/716100428

Robles, D. (2018, September 13). San Miguel Powwow has huge prize money, awesome singers & drums. *Indian Country Today*. https://indiancountrytoday.com/archive/san-manuel-pow-wow-has-huge-prize-money-awesome-singers-drums

Rosay, A. B. (2016). Violence against American Indian and Alaskan Native women and men. *National Institute of Justice*. https://www.ojp.gov/pdffiles1/nij/249736.pdf

Rubio, K. V., Undurraga, E., Magvanjav, O., Gravlee, C., Huanca, T., Leonard, W. R., McDade, T. W., Reyes-Garcia, V. Tanner, S., Godoy, R., & TAPS Bolivia Study Team (2009). Modernization and cultural loss: A natural experiment among Native Amazonians in Bolivia. *Tsimane' Amazonian Panel Study Working Paper*. https://he ller.brandeis.edu/sustainable-international-development/tsimane/wp/TAPS-WP-52.pdf

Ruegsegger, B. (2006, August 27) Nansemond tribal powwow: A spiritual gathering. *The Virginian-Pilot*. https://www.pilotonline.com/news/article_0847b8b5-947a-514c-ab3a-053be9f4d1e1.html

Ruehle, D. M. (2017). Relationship between promotions and attendance at Rochester Red Wings Games. Sport Management Undergraduate. Paper 129. https://fisherpub .sjfc.edu/cgi/viewcontent.cgi?article=1131&context=sport_undergrad

Sachs, C. (1937). *World history of the dance*. W. W. Norton Publishers.

Sage, H. G., Eitzen, D. S., & Beal, B. (2019). *Sociology of North American sport.* Oxford University Press.

Sampson, E. (2000). Reinterpreting individualism and collectivism: Their religious roots and roots and monologic versus dialogic person-other relationship. *American Psychologist*, 55(12), 1425–1432. DOI: 10.1037/0003-066X.55.12.1425

Santos, H. C., Varnum, M. E., & Grossmann, I. (2017). Global increases in individualism. *Psychological Science*, 28(9), 1228–1239. DOI: 10.1177/0956797617700622

Sarche, M. C., Croy, C. D., Big Crow, C., Mitchell, C. M., & Spicer, P. (2009). Maternal correlates of two-year-old children's social emotional development in a northern plains tribe. *Infant Mental Health Journal*, 30, 321–340.

Sarstedt, M., Ringle, C., Raithel, S., & Siegfried, G. (2014). In pursuit of what drives fan satisfaction. *Journal of Leisure Research*, 46(4), 419–447.

Scales, C. (2007). Powwows, intertribalism, and the value of competition. *Ethnomusicology*, 51(1), 1–29. https://www.jstor.org/stable/20174500

Scandale, M. (2018, September 13). The Winnebago Tribe's 145th annual homecoming celebration. *Indian Country Today.* https://indiancountrytoday.com/archive/the-winnebago-tribes-145th-annual-homecoming-celebration

Scheffler, S. (2007). Immigration and the significance of culture. *Philosophy & Public Affairs,* 35(2), 93–125. DOI:10.1111/j.1088-4963.2007.00101.x

Schmidt, R. W. (2011). American Indian identity and blood quantum in the 21st century: A critical review. *Journal of Anthropology.* DOI: 10.1155/2011/549521

Scott, H. (1911). Notes on the Kado, or sun dance of the Kiowas. *American Anthropologist*, 13(3), 345–379. https://www.jstor.org/stable/659914

Serrato, G. (2017). The Ghost dance and the Wounded Knee massacre of 1890. *StMU History Media.* http://www.stmuhistorymedia.org/the-ghost-dance-and-wounded-knee-massacre/

Sewell, S. (2005). Asserting Native American agency in an assimilationist institution. In C. Ellis, L. E. Lassiter, & G. H. Dunham (Eds.) *Powwow* (pp. 29–40). University of Nebraska Press.

Shea, J. (1857). *History of the Catholic missions among the Indian tribes of the United States, 1529–1854.* E. Dunigan and Brother.

Shepard, T. (1648). The clear sunshine of the Gospel breaking forth upon the Indians in New England. London: R. Cotes. (Reprinted in 1865 Joseph Sabin). https://archive.org/details/clearsunshineofg00sheprich

Shilling, C., & Mellor, P. A. (2014). Re-conceptualizing sport as a sacred phenomenon. *Sociology of Sport Journal*, 31(3), 349–376.

Shin, H., & Stevens, Q. (2013). Debates around cultural re-imagining and culture-led urban regeneration: The politics of two festivals in Gwangju and Glasgow. *Asian Journal of Social Science*, 41, 628–652. DOI:10.1163/15685314-12341325

Silverman, D. (2015). Native American religions. *Oxford bibliographies.* https://www.oxfordbibliographies.com/view/document/obo-9780199730414/obo-9780199730414-0156.xml

Simpson, K. (1987). Sporting dreams die on the rez. In D. S. Eitzen (Ed.) *Sport in contemporary society: An anthology* (pp. 217–224). Oxford University Press.

Slater, L. (2010). Calling our spirits home: Indigenous cultural festivals and the making of a good life. *Cultural Studies Review*, 16(1), 143–154. https://ro.uow.edu.au /artspapers/1391/

Smith, L. T. (2008). *Decolonizing methodologies: Research and Indigenous peoples*. Zed Books.

Soyer, M., & Ziyanak, S. (2018). The battle over fracking: The mobilization of local residents. *The Qualitative Report*, 23(9), 2222–2237. https://nsuworks.nova.edu/ tqr/vol23/iss9/13

Spack, R. (2000). English pedagogy and ideology: A Case study of the Hampton institute, 1878–1900. *American Indian Culture & Research Journal*, 24(1), 1–24. DOI: 10.17953/aicr.24.1.e240426137782120

Spicer, P., LaFramboise, T., Markstrom, C., Niles, M., West, A., Fehringer, K., et al. (2011). Toward an applied developmental science for Native children, families, and communities. *Child Development Perspectives*, 6(1), 49–54. DOI: 10.1111/j.1750-8606.2011.00212.x

Spores, R. (1993). Too small a place: The removal of the Willamette Valley Indians. *American Indian Quarterly*, 17(1), 171–191. DOI: 10.2307/1185526

Stannard, D. (1992). *American holocaust*. New York, NY: Oxford University Press.

Stuckey, S. (1995). Christian conversion and the challenge of dance. In S. L. Foster (Ed.) *Choreographing history* (pp. 54–68). Indiana University Press.

Sullivan, S. (2005). Federal boarding schools in New Mexico. In C. Ellis, L. E. Lassiter, & G. H. Dunham (Eds.) *Powwow* (pp. 57–89). Lincoln: University of Nebraska Press.

Suinn, R. M., Rickard-Figueroa, K., Lew, S., & Vigil, P. (1987). The Suinn-Lew Asian self-identity acculturation scale: An initial report. *Educational and Psychological Measurement*, 47(2), 401–407. https://doi-org.ezproxy.utpb.edu/10 .1177/0013164487472012

Suits, B. (1973). The elements of sport. In W. J. Morgan & K. V. Meyer (Eds.) *Philosophic inquiry in sport* (pp. 39–48). Human Kinetics.

Summers, L. (2014). *White soul/forbidden body: Dancing Christian from Ruth st. Denis to pole dancing for Jesus*. Peer reviewed thesis/dissertation, University of California Riverside. https://escholarship.org/uc/item/0jn9b19p

Swensen, J. (2019). Bound for the fair: Chief Joseph, Quanah Parker, and Geronimo and the 1904 St. Louis world's fair. *American Indian Quarterly*, 43(4), 439–470. DOI:10.5250/amerindiquar.43.4.0439

Swensen, J. R. (2019). Bound for the fair. *American Indian Quarterly*, 43(4), 439–470.

Talbot, S. (2006). Spiritual genocide: The denial of American Indian religious freedom, from conquest to 1934. *Wicazo SA Review*, 21(2), 7–39.

Taliaferro, C. (2019). Philosophy of religion. In Edward N. Zalta (Ed.) *The Stanford Encyclopedia of Philosophy*. https://plato.stanford.edu/archives/fall2019/entries/ philosophy-religion/

Tamari, D. (2017). Home court advantage: A case study of NCAA Division I basketball student sections. University of North Carolina, Masters Thesis.

Taylor, C. (1988). *The Indian hobbyist movement in Europe. History of Indian-White relations, Volume 4 of Handbook of North American Indians* (pp. 562–569). Smithsonian Institution.

Taylor, S. (2017, January). Seven ways to engage fans and drive ticket sales. *Athletic Business*. https://www.athleticbusiness.com/marketing/seven-ways-to-engage-fans -and-drive-ticket-sales.html

Theis, M. (2016, September 7). SXSW economic impact up slightly in 2016; hotel rates hit new high. *Austin Business Journal*. https://www.bizjournals.com/austin/ news/2016/09/07/sxsw-economic-impact-up-slightly-in-2016-hotel.html

The National Native American Boarding School Healing Coalition (2019). US boarding school history. *The National Native American Boarding School Healing Coalition* https://boardingschoolhealing.org/education/us-indian-boarding-school-history/

Thornton, R. (1987). *American Indian holocaust and survival: A population history since 1492*. University of Oklahoma Press.

Thornton, R. (2005). Native American demographic and tribal survival into the twenty-first century. *American Studies*, 46(3), 23–38.

Thorpe, J. (2020). Jim Thorpe website: The official website of Jim Thorpe. *CMG Worldwide*. https://www.cmgww.com/sports/thorpe/quotes/

Tinker, G. (1993). *Missionary conquest: The gospel and Native American cultural genocide*. Fortress Press.

Torres, C. R. (2014). *The Bloomsbury companion to the philosophy of sport*. Bloomsbury.

Triandis, H. C. (2018). *Individualism and collectivism: New directions in social psychology*. Routledge. DOI: 10.4324/9780429499845

Tucker, M., & Grim, J. (2009). Introduction: The emerging alliance of world religions and ecology. *Daedalus*, 130(4), 1–22.

Twiss, R. (2015). *Rescuing the gospel from the cowboys: A Native American expression of the Jesus way*. InterVarsity Press.

UNESCO (2001). Article 4—Human rights guarantees of cultural diversity. *UNESCO Universal Declaration on Cultural Diversity*. http://portal.unesco.org/en/ev.php-URL_ID=13179&URL_DO=DO_TOPIC&URL_SECTION=201.html

United Nations (1948). Convention on the prevention and punishment of the crime of genocide. *United Nations*. https://www.un.org/en/genocideprevention/documents /atrocity-crimes/Doc.1_Convention%20on%20the%20Prevention%20and%20 Punishment%20of%20the%20Crime%20of%20Genocide.pdf

United Nations (2021). Culture. *United Nations Department of Economic and Social Affairs: Indigenous Peoples*. https://www.un.org/development/desa/indigenous peoples/mandated-areas1/culture.html

United States Census Bureau (2012). 2010 census shows nearly half of American Indians and Alaska Natives report multiple races. *United States Census Bureau*. https://www.census.gov/newsroom/releases/archives/2010_census/cb12-cn06 .html

United States Forest Service (1993). *The principal laws relating to forest service activities*. United States Department of Agriculture.

UNM Lobos (2020, January 16). Athletics releases fan survey results. *GoLobos.com*. https://golobos.com/news/2020/01/16/mens-basketball-athletics-releases-fan-survey-results/

U.S. Code (1998). Chapter 1—The flag. *US Code.* https://uscode.house.gov/view.xhtml?req=granuleid%3AUSC-prelim-title4-chapter1&saved=%7CZ3JhbnVszWlkOlVTQy1wcmVsaW0tdGl0bGU0LXNlY3Rpb24tYnpb242%7C7C%7C7C%7C7C0%7Cfalse%7Cprelim&edition=prelim

USCCB (2020). Chapter IV: The different forms of celebrating mass. *United States conference of Catholic Bishops.* http://www.usccb.org/prayer-and-worship/the-mass/general-instruction-of-the-roman-missal/girm-chapter-4.cfm#footnote-10010-104

U.S. Department of Education (2021). Equity in athletics data analysis. *U.S. Department of Education.* https://ope.ed.gov/athletics/#/

U.S. Department of the Interior (n.d.). A guide to tracing American Indian & Alaska Native ancestry. *Office of Public Affairs-Indian Affairs.* https://www.bia.gov/sites/bia.gov/files/assets/public/pdf/idc-002619.pdf

Utter, J. (1993). *American Indians: Answers to today's questions* (2nd edition). University of Oklahoma Press.

Van Willigen, J. (1987). Serving at the Lord's table: Symbol and meaning in Christian communion ritual in a rural American community. *Indian Anthropologist,* 17(2), 49–62. www.jstor.org/stable/41919563

Varnum, M. E., & Grossmann, I. (2017). Cultural change: The how and why. *Perspectives on Psychological Science,* 12(6). 956–972. DOI: 10.1177/17456916176999

Vecsey, C. (1997). *The path of Kateri's kin.* University of Notre Dame Press.

Waldman, C. (2006). *Encyclopedia of Native American Tribes* (3rd edition). Infobase Publishing.

Ward, G., & D. Duncan (2001). New perspectives on the west. *The West Film Project, PBS.* http://www.pbs.org/weta/thewest/

Warren, S. (2009). To show the public that we were good Indians: Origins and meanings of the Meskwaki powwow. *American Indian Culture and Research Journal,* 33(4), 1–28.

Watchman, R. (2005). Powwow overseas. In C. Ellis, L. E. Lassiter, & G. H. Dunham (Eds.) Powwow (pp. 241–257). University of Nebraska Press.

Waterman, S. (1998). Carnivals for the Elites? The cultural politics of arts festivals. *Progress in Human Geography,* 22(1), 54–74.

Waters, M. C., & Jimenez, T. R. (2005). Assessing immigrant assimilation: New empirical and theoretical challenges. *Annual Review of Sociology,* 31, 105–125. https://scholar.harvard.edu/files/marywaters/files/waters_and_jimenez_2005.pdf

Wearn, D., & Lajimodiere, D. (2015). American Indian health disparities: Psychosocial influences. *Social and Personality Psychology Compass,* 9(10), 567–579. DOI: 10.1111/spc3.12198

Weaver, J. (1998). From I-Hermeneutics to We-Hermeneutics. In J. Weaver (Ed.) *Native American religious identity* (pp. 1–3). Orbis.

Weaver, H. (2012). Urban and Indigenous: The challenges of being a Native American in the city. Journal of Community Practice, 20, 470–488. DOI: 10.1080/10705422.2012.732001

Wenger, T. (2011). Indian dances and the politics of religious freedom, 1870–1930. *Journal of the American Academy of Religion,* 79(4), 850–878.

Wheeler, R. (1979). *Jim Thorpe: World's greatest athlete*. University of Oklahoma Press.

Wightman, A. (2012). Disappointing indigeneity. *Ethnology*, 51(1), 55–74.

Willis, C. (2017). *Walter Lingo, Jim Thorpe, and the Oorang Indians: How a dog kennel owner created the NFL's most famous traveling team*. Rowman & Littlefield.

Wilson, A. (1991). *World Scriptures: A comparative anthology of sacred texts*. Paragon House.

Wilson, S., Goer, J., Renfro, A., Blake, M., Muncie, E., & Tredway, J. (2018). The tether to home, university connectedness, and the Appalachian student. *Journal of College Retention: Research, Theory and Practice*, 20(1), 139–160. https://journal s.sagepub.com/doi/full/10.1177/1521025116652635

Winnebago Tribe of Nebraska (2021). History. *Winnebago Tribe of Nebraska*. http: //www.winnebagotribe.com/index.php/about-us/tribal-history#:~:text=The%20T ribe%20was%20moved%20from,treaties%20of%201865%20and%201874.&text =The%20tribe%20is%20federally%20recognized,the%201934%20Indian%20 Reorganization%20Act

Wittry, A. (2020, October 29). 25 men's college basketball team with the highest attendance in 2019–20. *NCAA.com*. https://wwwcache.ncaa.com/news/basketbal l-men/article/2020-10-27/25-mens-college-basketball-teams-highest-attendance -2019-20

Woolford, A. (2009). Ontological destruction: Genocide and Canadian aboriginal peoples. *Genocide Studies and Prevention*, 4(1), 81–97. https://scholarcommons .usf.edu/gsp/vol4/iss1/6

World Council of Churches (2012). Statement on the doctrine of discovery and its enduring impact on Indigenous Peoples. *World Council of Churches*. https://www .oikoumene.org/en/resources/documents/executive-committee/2012-02/statement -on-the-doctrine-of-discovery-and-its-enduring-impact-on-indigenous-peoples

Worthington, D. (2016). Biggest atrocity of the revolutionary war at Gnadenhutten. *New Historian*. https://www.newhistorian.com/6072-2/6072/.

WTOP (2017). In Indian country, honoring flag might mean different anthem. *Associated Press*. https://wtop.com/national/2017/11/in-indian-country-honoring -flag-might-mean-different-anthem/slide/1/

Zhou, X. (2015). Expectations of sport event tourism experiences. Master's Thesis, Lund University: Department of Service Management and Service Studies.

Zirin, D. (2005). Sports: An offer we can't refuse. In D. S. Eitzen (Ed.) *Sport in Contemporary Society* (9th edition, pp. 3–7). Paradigm Publishers.

Ziyanak, S. (2014). New emerging Ahiskan Turk ethnic identity in the United States. *International Journal of Human Sciences*, 11(1), 688–699.

Ziyanak, S., & Jordan, W. (2018). Global remedies: How a Turkish tycoon conveyed international culture to Oklahoma. In S. Ziyanak & B. Sert (Eds.) *Turkish immigrants in the mainstream of American life: Theories of international migration* (pp. 91–100). Rowman & Littlefield.

Ziyanak, S., & Sert, B. (2018). *Turkish immigrants in the mainstream of American life: Theories of international migration*. Rowman & Littlefield.

Index

Page references for figures are italicized.

About the Authors

Dr. Steven Aicinena received his bachelor's degree in physical education from the University of California Davis, a master's degree in physical education from Idaho State University, and a doctorate in education from the University of Northern Colorado where he was awarded the Graduate Dean's Award for Excellence. He joined the faculty of The University of Texas Permian Basin in the fall of 1988 and served as a professor of kinesiology until June of 2021. He is now retired. Dr. Aicinena's research interests are varied. He has peer-reviewed publications in the areas of sport sociology, sport pedagogy, youth sport, religion in sport, and athletic administration. Most recently, he has published three peer-reviewed articles focusing upon the Native American contest powwow. Excerpts from Aicinena's book *Through the Eyes of Parents, Children and a Coach: A Fourteen-Year Participant-Observer Investigation of Youth Soccer* has been used by U.S. Youth Soccer in its training materials for coaches and parents throughout the United States. Dr. Aicinena started the athletic program at the University of Texas Permian Basin and served as Athletic Director from 1993 through June of 2017. At the time he returned to the Faculty full-time, the program had grown to include sixteen NCAA Division II intercollegiate sports. In addition to his teaching and administrative duties at The University of Texas Permian Basin, Dr. Aicinena also served as the head volleyball coach from fall of 1993 through the spring of 2014. His teams won three conference championships and he received two conference coach of the year awards. Aicinena accumulated 325 wins as a collegiate coach. Before earning his Doctorate, Aicinena was a high school teacher/coach at Crownpoint High School, located on the Navajo Indian Reservation in Northwest New Mexico. He taught physical education, earth science, and biology. He was the recipient of numerous Coach of the Year Awards in basketball and volleyball while at Crownpoint.

Dr. Aicinena is also a professional photographer. He enjoys photographing wildlife, sports, and landscapes.

Dr. Sebahattin Ziyanak is associate professor in sociology at The University of Texas Permian Basin. Dr. Ziyanak holds a PhD in sociology from the University of North Texas. He received his MA in sociology from the University of Houston. He is the recipient of the President's Research Award in 2020, La Mancha Society Golden Windmill Research Award in 2018 and the Outstanding Excellence in Teaching with the National Society of Leadership and Success in 2018, Outstanding Instructor Recognition in Teaching with Thank A Teacher program for Commitment to UNT Student Success in 2012 and 2013. He contributed the following books: *Political Sociology* (2020), *Sociological Studies of Environmental Conflict* (2019), *Introduction to Sociology* (2019), *Turkish Immigrants in the Mainstream of American Life: Theories of International Migration* (2018), *Analyzing Delinquency among Kurdish Adolescents: A Test of Hirschi's Social Bonding Theory* (2015), and *Crossroad: A Grassroots Organization for the Homeless in Houston* (2008). He also contributed book chapters and articles to a variety of publications. He is a member of the Advisory Board of the Odessa Links for Odessa Homeless Coalition since 2016. He was the president of Peace Academy of West Texas between 2018 and 2019. His fields of research are in the subjects of delinquency, deviance, social organization, social movement, sociology of education, environmental studies, and race and ethnicity.